Ivan Tyrrell lives on
practises as marketing
and European compar
and design group. He
Research. As Informa
Advisory Group (Nu
civil defence experts and has become involved in a variety of related research projects. Currently NuPAG is assisting organisations, including emergency war committees of local councils, prepare to protect as many people as possible from the effects of nuclear war.

IVAN TYRRELL

The Survival Option

A Guide to Living Through Nuclear War

PANTHER
Granada Publishing

Panther Books
Granada Publishing Ltd
8 Grafton Street, London W1X 3LA

Published by Panther Books 1983

First published in Great Britain by
Jonathan Cape Ltd 1982

ISBN 0-586-06047-2

Printed and bound in Great Britain by
Cox & Wyman Ltd, Reading
Set in Times

The author and publishers would like to thank Sidgwick and Jackson Ltd for permission to quote the extracts on pages 20–21 from *The Third World War* by General Sir John Hackett.

To lead a people to war unprepared
is to throw them away.

Chinese saying, 600 BC

Contents

I would like to thank Peter Brent, Cresson H. Kearny, Malcolm Walker and members of the Nuclear Protection Advisory Group for help in the preparation of this book.

1982 IVAN TYRRELL

Reactions to the Threat

Nuclear War Survival as a Taboo Subject

Imagine yourself just before a nuclear war. In a few hours or days the United Kingdom is to be heavily bombed because, per head of population, it is one of the most densely targeted countries in the world. Your instincts scream self-preservation. You quickly realise that, if you wish to contribute to any possible future, your only hope will be to get underground with family and friends. You also realise that those who have made the most advanced preparations stand the best chance of surviving. The Government, the aristocracy and the military have shelters, paid for out of taxes, but you don't. And, in your desperate haste to find or build a makeshift shelter, you will hardly have time to ask why. Why did successive British governments not prepare public protection against the effects of nuclear weapons?

In answer to this question the State's usual sophistry is to say that we are protected – by our armed forces. There is no need to worry. Deterrence, so the theory goes, is our defence. It is all the defence we need and the stronger we become the less likely we are to be attacked. But this is a hollow argument, for two main reasons. First, the presumed enemy doesn't believe in the theory. The USSR has always thought it could survive a nuclear war and has planned accordingly. (Mutual Assured Destruction – MAD – was an idea peculiar to the West alone.) The second reason is that the only defence against nuclear weapons is shelters. Any enemy can see we have no civil defence. They therefore know we are bluffing, that our ultimate threats are empty.

Part of the bluff, as in poker, is to up the stakes, which is what President Reagan did after coming to office, when he announced massive increases in military spending. But the reality is that, if the bluff is called and we are attacked, our 'strength' would be irrelevant because all the armed forces in the world could not protect an unsheltered population.

At the last minute, if the country were threatened with nuclear attack, the Government would almost certainly attempt to capitulate to save the population. But that kind of brinkmanship is risky. Supposing there were not enough time to capitulate? Supposing the enemy did not believe us and were to attack anyway? Supposing an enemy, by the logic of war, still needed to destroy American bases on our soil? Our capitulation might be ignored.

Total reliance on deterrence, therefore, ignores a basic rule of war which is that the armed forces must protect the people and means of subsistence. If the military cannot give this protection then suitable alternatives must be added to defensive strategy. This rule is something our opponents have not forgotten. The USSR has an extensive civil defence programme under the control of the military.

The first duty of the State is to protect its citizens. That above all else. And, since the most effective defence against nuclear weapons (and chemical ones for that matter) is shelters, it follows that, as no shelters are provided, the State is failing in its most fundamental duty. Such a failure is a symptom of degenerate government. In this situation forward-looking individuals are forced to organise their own protection as best they can, just as communities, where there is no rule of law, resort to forming their own vigilante patrols.

As part of NATO we maintain a costly aggressive stance but, at the same time, are ridiculously vulnerable. It is as if we were threatening our enemies by saying, 'If you don't do what we want we'll jump off this cliff' – an empty threat, perhaps, but one that is endlessly repeated with every new step in the arms race. And repetition dulls the senses, hypnotises. Almost without realising it, we could make the final jump, commit mass suicide, forgetting that the threat was meant only as bluff.

For the State to pin all its hopes on the deterrence theory is dangerous. It is an 'all or nothing' policy. A gamble with our lives. It is not even true, as supporters of the theory keep saying, that deterrence has kept the peace for the last thirty years; that is an opinion not a fact. No one can say with certainty why nuclear war has not occurred. One reason may be deterrence, but another could be that, during that time, the two major power blocs enjoyed a period of great prosperity and influence relative to their respective pasts. They also had the recent experience of the horrors of the Second World War, and the effort needed to recover from it, to intimidate them. A new major war would seem unlikely in those circumstances anyway, though since 1945, the power blocs have fought through intermediaries.

Now, however, we are in a period of greater instability. The world population continues to grow at an alarming rate and unemployment is increasing in most countries. Starvation may return to parts of the USSR and Eastern Europe. Perhaps Western democracies will become less secure. We are already witnessing the proliferation of nuclear weapon technology and an arms race running faster than ever.

Proponents of the theory that deterrence is sufficient defence assume that the human race is essentially sane and reliable which, most of the time, it is not. Just how much out of control events are can be seen continually around the world. The British war with Argentina, for example, took governments and people completely by surprise. It was a war that nobody wanted but that, once started, nobody could stop. The principal characters in the drama were swept along in a wild and irrational current that they could only react to or try to exploit. Both sides felt they were fighting for justice and truth, exactly as do the various sides in the interminable Middle Eastern conflicts. The coercive agencies in human behaviour are not yet widely understood and so reactions are determined by beliefs and conditioning.

The deterrence theory also assumes that the USSR is as vulnerable to attack as NATO countries, whereas it has a massive civil defence programme and could conceivably come through a nuclear war in much better shape than the West. Another common Western assumption is that the

USSR would start the next war. It may not. (What usually happens is that smaller countries start wars and then drag bigger ones into them.) War can even start by accident.

The prospect is grim. The risk of war is not decreasing and members of the State establishment know this. Shelters have been organised for Government personnel, indicating that they do not have the same blind faith in deterrence that they expect from the rest of us. Vast sums of public money are spent on building nuclear shelters in this country. One project alone, for a deep, 12-acre (5-hectare) military shelter in the Chiltern Hills, is budgeted at £300 million. None of these shelters is for the public and yet if, as the Government claims, there is no risk of war, nobody needs protection. Why the contradiction? If one section of the community needs shelters, so do the others.

The Government says it supports civil defence, but does nothing to provide it. In effect, by its actions, it supports those in the peace movement who oppose civil defence. 'Civil defence is a confidence trick,' they say, and, 'Disarmament is the only true civil defence.' The slightest investigation shows these statements to be absurd. The humanitarian principle of civil defence cannot be called a 'confidence trick' because, as disaster research shows, it is well worth taking action in advance to deal with the effects of disasters. The costs of doing so are inconsequential when measured against the losses incurred when no such preparations are made. (Exaggerated claims for the effectiveness of present official arrangements could be seen as an attempt to deceive, but no Emergency Planning Officer would tell an enquirer that present arrangements would make much difference in a nuclear war.) Likewise, 'disarmament' cannot be 'civil defence' as claimed in the second slogan. The terms describe different concepts. One is concerned with saving lives in the event of disaster and the other with the process of demilitarisation.

That these simple slogans have an appeal is due to the ease with which it is possible to frighten people when discussing nuclear warfare. CND has become expert at raising anxiety levels. It has rediscovered the ancient technique for making converts by frightening people. Members of the public are encouraged to feel despair and helplessness in the face of the current overwhelming potential for destruction. They are then instilled with the idea that the only way out of this terrifying prospect is to join the CND campaign. And many of them do.

The horrors of nuclear war are real enough, and we should not be ignorant of them, but there has always been a price to pay when fear is used as a conversion technique. For example, those doing the converting are tempted to exaggerate and distort facts to speed up the process. They sacrifice truth to expediency. CND is frequently guilty of this. More seriously, converts to any belief or cause tend to stop thinking for themselves. They become passive receivers of dogma. They replace thought with slogans, lose touch with reality and fall prey to anyone wishing to dominate them.

There are, however, signs that some disarmament campaigners are looking beyond the slogans and realising that the civil defence issue should be taken seriously. In a letter to the *Sunday Times* (January 31st, 1982) one wrote:

> Without civil defence an estimated 40 million people would die in this country. With proper protection, that figure could be reduced to 15 million. Are the supporters of CND (of which I am one) so certain that disarmament will come before an outbreak of war that they are prepared to risk 25 million lives? In my view, only a madman would consider the possibility of 15 million deaths with anything but abhorrence but on the same grounds, I cannot understand how the prospect of a further 25 million unnecessary deaths can be acceptable.

As for the rest of the population, it tries to avoid anxiety by suppressing all thought on the subject. Even the slightest mention, to some people, is enough to produce a strong protest, as if, in some magical way, talking about surviving nuclear war brings war closer. This primitive response is one of the reasons why nuclear war survival is a taboo subject in some company.

But the taboo must be broken. We need effective civil defence because, however hard we work for peace, we could fail. The world is unlikely to rid itself of nuclear weapons in the next ten or twenty years. It may never do so. And, while these weapons exist, so does the possibility that they will be used. As the enterprising Dr B.D. Clayton has pointed out in his book *Life after Doomsday* (Paladin, 1980), though the probability of peace in any one year is 98 per cent over a period of, say, fifty years, this drops to only 35 per cent. There are four chances out of five that there will be a war within an average lifetime. He says: 'Several independent war prediction methods seem to point to a major war in the early 1980s. These methods are based on cyclic developments which precede important wars and are taken from political, literary and economic history.' The near future may show, therefore, that the lack of civil defence in many Western countries is the costliest military/political blunder, in terms of human lives, in the history of the human race to date. (Apart, of course, from that of having nuclear weapons in the first place.)

The only way to begin extricating ourselves from this predicament is by collecting and absorbing accurate information and thinking objectively about it. It is difficult, of course, to remain unemotional about protecting people against the effects of a nuclear war, but if we are to change our situation in a positive and useful way, we must do so. This is because emotion, all too often, blinds us from appreciating the significance of information. And information is the key to change.

The purpose of this book, therefore, is to provide information. First, information about the size of the problem before, during and after nuclear attack and about what is being done, or not, about it. And, second, information essential to maximise your chances of survival. By using this book you have a much improved chance of preserving yourself and your family. Amongst much else, it contains clear instructions for building, or having contractors build, various types of shelter. And you don't necessarily need the budget of a Rockefeller. Some structures can be made by hard work alone. Though small and uncomfortable, they could save millions of lives.

This book is written for people not stuck in our society's

prevailing pessimistic mode. It is for those who recognise that there is no future in giving up. No future as individuals, families, nations, or as a species. The human race will survive whatever occurs. Will your descendants?

Superstitions and Facts

The fatalism that equates nuclear war with the complete destruction of the world feeds, and is fed by, the superstitious terror in which atomic fission and fusion are commonly held. Often discussion of the subject and attempts to discover, or pass on, what knowledge exists about it, elicits only fear. It is as though to speak about it were to evoke it. In ancient days the gods received similar ambivalent reverence, awe mingled with fear. This refusal to look directly at the real risks and dangers surrounding a nuclear attack means that much of what is popularly believed is only partly true, or not true at all.

Since the Hiroshima and Nagasaki explosions (12½KT and 22KT respectively) the West has exaggerated reports of the destruction and misery caused by nuclear weapons in order to strike fear into its enemies. This has been done in pursuit of the deterrence policy. But the trouble with fear is that it is multidirectional. We have believed our own propaganda and this has inhibited our capacity to be objective. Nearly forty years later numerous erroneous beliefs about the effects of these early explosions are still with us, firmly entrenched. There are even people who believe that Hiroshima and Nagasaki are still uninhabitable, whereas, of course, they are thriving cities and people started moving back into them within days after the explosions.

Here is a cluster of facts about Hiroshima, Nagasaki and the survivors. (In detailing and refuting some of the common myths surrounding nuclear weapon effects I do not intend in any way to diminish the awful suffering nuclear weapons have already caused, or the terrible potential for future suffering embodied in them.)

More than 50 per cent of the population of Hiroshima,

situated inside the blast area at the time of the explosion, survived. There was a similar proportion of survivors at Nagasaki. Although these were relatively small bombs, it is the blast area that is significant, and similar or better survival rates could be expected from within the blast areas of larger air-burst weapons, if people had some warning.

Since 1945 over 109,000 Japanese survivors from the initial radiation from both bombs have been under constant study. Between December 1950 and 1977, seventy-seven contracted leukaemia and 130 died from other radiation-induced causes. Two thousand seven hundred and ninety-three died of cancer from various causes, not all attributable to radiation – exactly in line with the incidence of cancer throughout Japan (see the authoritative study by the USA National Academy of Sciences, *A Thirty Year Study of the Survivors of Hiroshima and Nagasaki,* 1977).

At Hiroshima, one day after the blast, the bridges were open to traffic, two days later trains began to run, three days after that some street cars were in action, within nine days telephones were operating and at the edge of the explosion area water, sewage and gas services were all uninterrupted.

In Nagasaki; some people survived uninjured in conventional air-raid shelters as close as one-third of a mile (half a kilometre) from the point directly beneath the explosion; even though their shelters lacked blast doors and were deep inside the zone of destruction of all buildings and the bomb was more powerful than the one at Hiroshima. Many simple earth-covered family shelters were essentially undamaged in areas where blast destroyed all buildings.

Common myths about nuclear war hazards can be listed as follows:

MYTH: Many people believe that the radiation resulting from a nuclear explosion, or from the multiplied explosions of a nuclear war, would poison the atmosphere and the entire physical environment. Nothing would be safe to eat, the air itself would be dangerous to breathe and life would cease to exist.

FACT: All life would not be destroyed by a major nuclear war, even if hundreds of millions died because they were not protected from the heat, blast and radiation. Neither would our developed technological civilisation be destroyed. There are approximately 4,500 million people on the planet and our technological civilisation has spread almost everywhere. Even the death of say 1,000 million as a result of such a war would not eliminate modern technology. The planet, and the human race, would recover.

Fallout is not an exterminating miasma that somehow fatally infects everyone and everything that comes in contact with it. It is a dust and, as such, can be screened out of the air by efficient filters; most of it will, in any case, settle within a few hours in any area where it is falling. Once settled, it can be washed off objects and, if they are wearing protective clothing, people. In a properly constructed and equipped fallout shelter, the occupants are likely to receive a radiation dosage well within the limits of what might be expected during a normal lifetime.

There is one possible long-term threat to all life and that is if a nuclear war were to cause considerable thinning of the ozone layer. This is theoretically possible because nuclear fireballs, by burning nitrogen, create oxides of nitrogen that float up into the stratosphere and react with the ozone, depleting it. Since the ozone layer protects us from ultra-violet radiation and ultra-violet radiation in excess is harmful to life, the depletion of the ozone layer would be dangerous. But such a consequence is not likely. The planet's eco-system is large and miraculously robust. Serious ozone depletion is only a possibility if tens of thousands of nuclear explosions occur, far more than are needed to crush the main protagonists in a nuclear war several times over.

MYTH: Because some modern bombs are more than fifty times as powerful as those that destroyed Hiroshima and Nagasaki the range of damage would be fifty times as great.

FACT: A 1MT bomb is approximately fifty times greater in explosive power than the Hiroshima and Nagasaki weapons but, because of the Cube-Root Law for Explosions, the range of damage is not fifty times greater. Some equivalent comparative ranges for overpressure (blast) are as follows:

20KT at 5psi overpressure	=	1 mi (1·6km) from ground zero
1MT at 5psi overpressure	=	3·8 mi (5·3km) from ground zero
10MT at 5psi overpressure	=	8·2 mi (13·2km) from ground zero*

MYTH: A nuclear war would result in overkill because the two major powers have enough bombs to kill the entire human race several times over.

FACT: This could happen only if the world's population were gathered together in dense circular crowds, unprotected, and a bomb let off over each crowd. All available missiles are unlikely to be launched in any war because the first side to run out of 'ammunition' would be the loser.

MYTH: A heavy nuclear attack would set practically everything on fire, causing 'firestorms'. All shelter occupants would be killed by the intense heat of the firestorms.

FACT: A heavy 200MT attack on targets throughout the UK would result in approximately 20–30 per cent of the land mass being affected by heat and blast. The great majority of occupants in properly sited and constructed shelters even in the dangerous areas would have little to fear from the heat. Firestorms can occur only when the concentration of combustible materials is very high, more than is present in most modern cities. People sheltering in rural or suburban areas need not fear this intensity of fire.

MYTH: Fallout radiation from a nuclear war would poison the air and all parts of the environment, killing everyone.

*KT = Kiloton
MT = Megaton
psi = pounds per square inch
See page 76 for detailed definitions.

FACT: Air remains unchanged by radioactive particles carried in it. Once particles have settled down, or been filtered out, the air is breathable again. At any place where fallout particles descend, deposition of all but the finest dust is completed in a few hours. The very fine dust carried into the upper atmosphere can stay up for months, even years, and by the time it comes down it will be widely dispersed and have lost its potential for harm. The air in properly designed fallout shelters is free of radioactive particles and is safe to breathe.

People can recover from radiation sickness provided the dose has not been so high as to destroy their body's ability to replace damaged cells.

MYTH: Radiation remains intense for years after nuclear explosions.

FACT: Radiation from fallout is very intense for two or three days. It decays rapidly, however, so that, even after a week, people could emerge from shelters for short periods (taking care to monitor the radiation dose they receive). In a matter of weeks or months, depending on the number of weapons exploded and the amount of fallout generated, organised life may begin again and people should be able to live twenty-four hours a day out of their shelters. By that time levels of radiation would be so slight as to present only statistically, minor long-term radiation derived problems; no less grim for the individual sufferer but not a problem for everyone.

MYTH: Fallout radiation penetrates everything; there is no escaping its deadly effects.

FACT: Three feet (1 metre) of earth stops virtually all radiation from fallout, as do lesser thicknesses of denser materials.

MYTH: So much food and water would be poisoned that people would starve and die in fallout areas.

FACT: If fallout particles were not mixed with the food eaten, no harm could be done. Food and water kept in dust-tight containers cannot be contaminated by fallout radiation. There must be contact with the isotopes in the fallout before dangerous irradiation can take place. Most vegetables would be fit to eat once they had been thoroughly washed, and so would most meats. The substance to be most careful of is milk. Water from most sources would not be contaminated, and if it were, would be easily filtered

MYTH: People exposed to radiation 'give' it to you. It is contagious.

FACT: 'People exposed to fallout radiation do not become radioactive and thereby dangerous to other people. Radiation sickness is not contagious or infectious, and one person cannot "catch it" from another person.' (USA Federal Emergency Management Agency, *In Time of Emergency*, 1979, p.7.)

MYTH: All unborn children will be genetically malformed.

FACT: At worst the chances of this happening after a nuclear explosion are slightly increased. The main risk is to the children of women who are pregnant when bombarded with radiation. Many would have to expect deformed still-births and other abnormalities. Most children conceived later will not be affected. It may be that none will be – these dangers, although theoretically present, have not been scientifically confirmed. On the contrary, the study by the National Academy of Sciences, *A Thirty Year Study of the Survivors of Hiroshima and Nagasaki* (op. cit.) shows that the offspring of women who conceived after being exposed to radiation suffered no more abnormalities than the offspring of Japanese parents who were unexposed. 'No genetic defects that can unequivocally be ascribed to radiation have ever been found in man' (P.A.H. Saunders, Environmental and Medical Sciences Division, Atomic Energy Research Establishment, Harwell, April 29th 1980).

It must be admitted, however, that there have been criticisms of the Hiroshima and Nagasaki findings, most notably that, by ignoring those who died in the first few years after the war, an unrepresentative population was studied, and that blood diseases other than those designated as cancers were not included, although they supply evidence of bone-marrow damage. Nevertheless, the kind of continuing genetic holocaust which many people imagine was the consequence of the atomic explosions in Japan has clearly not occurred.

MYTH: Neither of the major powers would start a nuclear war because each knows they would both be wiped out if it did.

FACT: The major powers know no such thing. Various Russian, and American, estimates of Russian casualties from a major nuclear exchange put, in certain circumstances, the probable Soviet death toll at no more than that country suffered in the Second World War. This is to say, in the low tens of millions. American casualties, because America has no effective civil defence, are normally expected to be in excess of 50 per cent of the population. (UK percentages would be greater still because of the higher concentration of targets on a smaller, densely populated land mass.) Whether these figures prove, in the event, to be accurate is beside the point. It is what is believed by strategists on either side now that matters. Whatever happens, it is clear that neither side would be completely wiped out and that there is now a major imbalance in survival potential between the major powers, owing to differing civil defence programmes.

Facts of this kind, set against the more common apocalyptic superstitions, lay the groundwork for action, both collective and individual. The calculations involved are statistical, showing that survival is possible. That being so, a larger part of a prepared population will survive than of one that is unprepared. In either event, of course, millions of people are likely to die. What is more, no one can guarantee that given precautions will protect given people – a direct hit by a megaton warhead can falsify the most confident forecast. The only way to make certain that no one will die is not to fight the war at all and outlaw nuclear weapons totally and for ever. But all the pressures are against this happening.

One such pressure shows itself in the increasingly desperate scramble for control over dwindling natural resources. The material world is finite and every industrial nation is driven to compete for what is left of what is useful in it. Nations lacking sufficient raw materials to feed and supply their growing populations are at risk. That means just about every one. In this economic war, as in any war, the moment will come when one side or the other sees defeat ahead of it. Beyond defeat lie poverty, social collapse, starvation: a return to the sickness and destitution of earlier ages. Without the means to produce the surpluses upon which contemporary prosperity is founded, our profligate way of life cannot be sustained.

Idries Shah in *Reflections* (Octagon Press, 1969) relates a modern fable of the possibilities of collapse built into overpopulation and over-consumption:

> Once upon a time there was a cheese. A number of cheese-mites took up residence in it. As time passed, they bored more and more holes in the cheese, and, of course, they multiplied.
>
> Then, one day, there were so many holes in the cheese that it collapsed into a powder, leaving the mites scrambling in the ruins of their homes.
>
> 'What traitor is responsible for this?' screamed the mites. They formed parties, each opposed to the other, whose objectives were to restore the former ideal situation.
>
> Some mites, it is true, found another cheese. But as for the majority – they are fairly rapidly consuming the remaining cheese-powder.

If this is intended – as seems certain – as an allegory of the human condition among peoples of the developed nations, there does not seem to be much time to 'find another cheese' for the majority of the 'mites'.

Both the Communist and capitalist worlds are vulnerable to collapse under the pressures of military spending, economic depletion, unemployment, social unrest and the like. If either economy were to collapse the attached ideology could hardly survive. Neither is mature enough.

The threatened leadership would be left with the temptation of risking nuclear retaliation by trying to annex the desperately needed sources of raw materials. And, faced with such provocation, would the other side not retaliate? In a crisis of this sort, sooner or later, the weapons would be used.

Only a remarkable development in human affairs can bring about the necessary world-wide co-operation needed to reduce the danger. There seems little chance of that. Human greed and insecurity will not be overcome in time. The ideological differences that divide the world have drawn us into the ring and now we are squaring up to fight. We have been primed for it.

> The United States of America not only maintains an enormous army itself, but also forces its allies in the aggressive bloc to spend a large portion of their budgets in preparing for a new world war. The capitalist world has set up a warlike network of aggression – NATO, CENTO and SEATO – designed to subject the people of these allied countries to U.S. influence and use them in the interests of aggression, especially against the Soviet Union and other socialist countries . . . The deepening crisis of capitalism, the accentuation of its contradictions, has strengthened imperialist adventurism . . . The imperialist predators are achieving militarisation of the economy on a gigantic scale and are preparing for thermonuclear war via the armaments race. On the basis of a profound Marxist analysis of contemporary international conditions, the Communist Party of the Soviet Union has concluded that the danger of attack by imperialists on the USSR and other socialist countries is currently increasing, and the countries of the socialist bloc must play a basic role in defending the peace.

Thus runs part of the introduction to the Russian handbook *Grazhdanskaya Oborona* (*Civil Defence* – 1970). It seems unlikely that these views will change.

> But the gravest potential threat is posed by the military forces of the Soviet Union and other Warsaw Pact

> states, which could be used directly in a military confrontation with NATO or indirectly to challenge the broader political and economic interests of the West worldwide. The size and reach of these forces makes them a potent political weapon. If not counter-balanced, they could be exploited to bring unwelcome influence to bear on the domestic and foreign policies of countries which cannot match the military power of the Soviet Union and its allies . . . Our allies, facing the same threats, share much the same perception.

Another introduction, this time to *Defence in the 1980s,* the British Government's defence estimates for the first year of that decade.

> To gain predominant influence in the world, imperialism and socialist-imperialism are going all out to develop atomic, chemical and biological weapons in order to carry out aggressive warfare on a large scale. Therefore we must actively respond to Chairman Mao's important call to 'Dig tunnels deep, store grain everywhere, and never seek hegemony', and be vigilant, strengthen our war preparations and make a success of the work of protection against atomic, chemical and biological weapons.

The quotation identifies the source – it is the Chinese view of civil defence, first published in 1974. Its general attitude of 'a plague on both your houses!' has not been deeply modified by the post-Nixon rapprochement between China and the West.

The tone of these quotes is familiar, the phrases stale. Similar blinkered proclamations stare at us from the newspapers every day. This is the ritual rhetoric foretelling disaster.

The probable nature of this disaster is well understood. Only its scope may vary according to the different scenarios.

The Lethal Area

In an article entitled 'The prompt and delayed effects of nuclear war', published in the *Scientific American* in July 1979, K.N. Lewis, of the Arms Control Project at the Massachusetts Institute of Technology, forecast the effects a nuclear attack would have on the city of Boston. He supposed that 10 1MT weapons would strike the area, instantly creating a blast pressure of almost 20 psi – 'an overpressure of 5 psi' – affecting some 500 square miles (1,295 square kilometres). (Overpressure means the degree to which the pressure from blast exceeds normal pressure.)

> More than 1·3 million people would be killed by the prompt blast and thermal effects . . . and more than 80 per cent of the area's industrial capacity would be destroyed. It is likely that the secondary effects of the explosion, particularly fires and fallout, would increase these totals. If conditions were favorable to the attack, the most devastating effect might be incendiary. Under certain weather conditions each one-megaton burst could ignite fires as much as 10 miles away . . . Flash-induced fires would be joined by blast-triggered fires from toppled furnaces, stoves and boilers. Scattered debris and ruptured tanks and pipelines would add fuel to the fires . . . water mains would be shattered and firefighting crews would be destroyed or disabled.

The result would be either a firestorm – 'driven by a strong vertical updraught of heated air, which is replaced by cool air sucked in from the periphery' – or a conflagration – 'driven in addition by a strong ground wind'. The fires that followed the dropping on Hiroshima of a 12·5KT bomb lasted for 6 hours and utterly destroyed just under 4·5 square miles (11·5 square kilometres). The greater fire-resistance of American buildings would be countered by the vast stores of oil and petrol normally held in a Western city. And the released force of the expected 10 million tons of TNT-equivalent would set up reactions much greater than the 12·5 thousand tons dropped on the Japanese city.

In Sir John Hackett's *The Third World War,* (Sidgwick and Jackson, 1978) the English city of Birmingham is destroyed when a SS-17 missile detonates a 200KT warhead 9,600 feet (3,500 metres) above Winson Green prison.

> The incredibly brilliant flash which accompanied the detonation was visible in London . . . Lightly clad yachtsmen on the Chasewater about nineteen kilometres from Winson Green felt their skin begin to burn as the lasting pulse of the heat from the fireball hit them . . . The varnish on their boats bubbled, nylon sails melted and newspapers lying in the boats burst into flames . . . Fires were started inside and outside buildings to an increasing extent as the epicentre was approached, with apparently almost total conflagration occurring within three to four kilometres of Winson Green.

Almost at once the blast-wave descends upon the city.

> Within three kilometres of Winson Green nothing survived, every building and structure being reduced to rubble and strewn across the roads so that the entire area looked like a gigantic rubbish heap. The effects of the blast-wave began to decline as it travelled outwards, so that between three and six kilometres from the centre a few of the smaller and more strongly constructed buildings remained standing, some at crazy angles and missing many portions of softer construction around reinforced concrete or steel skeletons . . . Within three or four kilometres of Winson Green very few people survived the immediate effects of the detonation. Outside this range, and up to about seven or eight kilometres away, the collapse and destruction of most buildings trapped people in hundreds under fallen masonry . . . The air was full of flying objects, picked up by winds moving outwards from Winson Green at speeds which, even at ranges of four or five kilometres, approached 500 kilometres per hour . . . People caught in the open were picked up, flung

through the air and dashed against any solid object in their path.

At Birmingham Airport, nine miles (twelve kilometres) from Winson Green, the winds still blew at some 100 miles (160 kilometres) per hour, overturning aircraft or tearing off their wings and tailplanes. 'Even at this point the roar of the explosion was stupendous, lasting for ten or fifteen seconds. The same roar was to be heard in London, approximately eight minutes later, as a rumbling, roaring noise . . . ' Fires were breaking out in 'towns as far away as Wolverhampton, Stourbridge, Halesowen, Solihull, Sutton Coldfield, Walsall and Brownhills', while, 'within twenty minutes of the original detonation, an area of approximately thirty square kilometres in the centre of Birmingham was totally engulfed in a fire-storm. The flames and smoke rose hundreds of metres into the sky as the in-rush of air fed and fanned the fires.' In a total population of some 2 millions, 300,000 people (nearly one in seven) had been killed in the first few minutes, or would die shortly thereafter because the destruction of half the hospitals and most of the road system had made it impossible to aid them.

The contemplation of possible nuclear disasters has produced a formula for predicting the probable numbers of dead and injured. This is the formula of the lethal area, by which the area within the overpressure of the blast wave reaching 5 psi is calculated – in the case of a 200KT weapon, a circle of roughly 6½ miles' (4 kilometres') radius. The formula is, quite simply, that the number of survivors from the explosion within that circle will equal the number of those killed outside it, given an even overall density of population. Since the percentage of people likely to be killed in a given area of overpressure is known, a simple calculation will determine what the survival rate might be in a particular case. It is a handy rule of thumb; though in reality the succession of variables that must be fed into the computation – the state of the weather, the intensity of the fireball, the precise ingredients of the explosive device, the nature of the shelters provided, the location of ground zero (the nearest ground to the point of explosion) – inevitably make any such predictions imprecise.

Using the lethal area formula shows us how, for example, an unprepared Britain, suddenly struck by an aggregate of 200MT, might lose three-quarters of its population: a death-roll 40 million names long. Warned and prepared, that number could be reduced: 'only' 15 million might die. Five per cent of the country's land area would see everything on it destroyed; at least another 15 per cent would show very severe damage. Sixty per cent of the United Kingdom would have at least some scars to show. Four 1MT weapons exploded over London would leave 3½ million dead – each one death a separate disaster of pain and loss. A 1MT explosion over Bristol would halve that city's half million population; only a quarter of Glasgow's million occupants would survive the strike needed to destroy a city of that size. A 1MT strike would leave 240,000 dead in the motor-manufacturing city of Coventry, no stranger to indiscriminate destruction by aerial bombardment.

Like Britain, the United States is inadequately prepared and deeply vulnerable to nuclear attack. Professor S.P. Huntingdon, the director of Harvard's Center for International Affairs, predicted in 1979, 'If an all-out nuclear exchange were to occur now, the bulk of US industry and urban structures would be destroyed and a high proportion of US leadership and probably over 100,000,000 citizens would be immediate fatalities.' He considered that in the end the number might be over 130 million – in other words, about half the population would die either instantly or within a few days.

What of the United States' expected enemy, the USSR? The estimates of the CIA are that, in the best circumstances, with a nuclear strike occurring after a week or more of crisis and, therefore, of warning, no more than 'a few tens of millions' would be killed. If there were only a few hours' warning, an American attack, even if not specifically aimed at the main centres of population, might leave as many as 100 million dead in Russia, too. Given two or three days to prepare, that figure might be halved. Fifty million Soviet dead is also Professor Huntingdon's prediction.

Nevertheless, even in the worst of situations, the overall statistics of survival can be improved, and prudence surely suggests that this would be the desirable course. As Kenneth E.F. Watt, of the University of California at Davis, states in his book *The Titanic Effect*, 'The magnitude of disasters decreases to the extent that people believe that they are possible and plan to prevent them, or to minimise their effects.' Acting upon conclusions of this kind, governments around the world have made preparations to defend their civilian populations. Their efforts, unfortunately, have not always been vigorous or potentially effective. Among the feeblest have been those ordered by the governments of the great Anglo-Saxon democracies, the United States of America and the United Kingdom.

Civil Defence: the Soviet Union

Several assumptions have persuaded the Soviet Union to pursue a relatively thorough civil defence programme. One relates to their own strategic intentions, which seem to lean towards the application of what they call 'counterforce'. This means that their primary targets in a nuclear offensive are the missile systems and command centres of the Western alliance, and areas of obvious economic or governmental importance. If such an assault were mounted, it would cause immense loss of life and damage on a disastrous scale. Yet it would be, especially with today's accurate weapons, an assault very different from that envisaged in a 'counter-city' policy. This policy, which has many American advocates, sees nuclear war as a constantly increasing interchange of civilian deaths, a coldly brutal process in which the obliteration of a city on one side is matched by the obliteration of a similar one on the other. Megadeath is balanced against megadeath until the swift bleeding-away of its population persuades one side or the other into surrender. If the Russian preference for a 'counterforce' war, as expressed in their comprehensive 1962 manual, *Military Strategy,* is as firm as it seems, then the conflict the Russians envisage will have an important place for civil defence. The annihilation of entire cities, and clusters of cities, that would result from the alternative strategy, allows rather less room for manoeuvre.

Russia's experiences during the Second World War have also added vigour to their civil defence effort. Millions of Soviet civilians died in the course of that war – perhaps as many as 25 million. In any future conflict, many more are likely to die. Russia learned the hard way that 'absorbing a surprise enemy attack was not the best way to fight a war'. The Russian leadership knows very well the appalling effects of large-scale losses. It has experienced the difficulty of regaining ascendancy from such a devastated position.

The head of the Soviet civil defence effort is a Deputy Minister of Defence. Even in its administrative structure, it is clear that the protection of the Soviet public is part of a wider military and political strategy. At the same time, there is hardly a separate civil defence organisation – existing groups simply have wartime obligations grafted on to their normal peacetime activities. Thus a department of the local government in each of the Soviet Union's fifteen republics has specific civil defence responsibilities, the people in day-to-day charge being the directors of factories, colleges, stores and other establishments. They become the civil defence chiefs of the units for which they are responsible.

Each service or department is in charge of its own area of expertise. For example, the Construction Department, Communal Housing Department and Building Guild will control, between them, the construction of shelters before an attack and the housing of the homeless after it. Those protecting an establishment in time of peace would be responsible for maintaining public order in it when war or disaster struck. The established medical services would switch immediately to an emergency role. Meanwhile, in industry, groups already organised on the basis of workshops, shifts or other working units, would become the nucleus of a civil defence army. In many cases, these groups would simply extend their normal duties – welfare workers and janitors, for example, would become the decontamination specialists, using the plant laundry or showers. Plant cafeteria staff would run mobile feeding stations and carry uncontaminated water to where it would be needed. Mine rescue teams are also trained to burrow beneath the rubble of a stricken land. Those in the transport department would instantly take on the duties of maintaining road communications where possible. The activities of these and many similar groups are, of course, planned to cover ground much wider than that of the plant or establishment where they normally work. They would fan out into those areas where their specialist help would be needed. They would examine and report on damage and casualties, monitor radioactivity and decontaminate where possible and necessary, and provide emergency teams of high technical ability.

In addition there are an estimated 100,000 full-time civil defence workers – administrators, instructors, co-ordinators and experts of various kinds. Between them, they appear to give the Soviet civil defence force great strength and mobility, as well as a wide and highly-developed range of skills.

Above the clamour of the holocaust it is planned that officials of the Communist Party will continue to exercise ideological control, specifying the priorities of Marxism-Leninism. Slightly absurd though this may seem to us, it will help to give coherence to whatever rehabilitative effort becomes possible.

The extent of the Soviet preparations was described by Lord Chalfont, the president of Britain's Association of Civil Defence and Emergency Planning Officers, at a meeting held in 1978. There had been a systematic reorganisation of the Russian civil defence system during the 1970s, he pointed out, with the result that 98 per cent of the population now had some protection. Everybody in the active working population was receiving at least a measure of training in civil defence techniques. It is clear that Lord Chalfont, like the Russians themselves, saw all this as inseparable from the wider intentions of Soviet diplomatic and military strategy.

It certainly seems to be the case that every group in Russian society is intended to take part in the national training programme. One suspects that, as with many other plans that look comprehensive on paper, the reality is somewhat sketchier; nevertheless, whatever the gaps, the effects are likely to be quite discernible. Schools are supposed to offer at least fifteen hours of civil defence instruction every year, and in the summer camps of the Pioneers, the Soviet equivalent of the West's Boy Scout and Girl Guide movements, children are taught, in the words of the civil defence manual, 'how to use individual and collective means of defence, how to respond to civil defence signals, and how to help themselves and others when there are injuries'. Meanwhile, 'workers, employees, collective farm workers and the unemployed' are given basic training at their places of work (potential rather than actual, one presumes, for the unemployed), which includes listening to lectures and using the available equipment during their off-duty hours. Annual refresher courses keep them up to date once they have understood their general obligations and skills. Older schoolchildren and students are put through programmes 'designed for them on the basis of their major curriculum'.

Even those who work at home, or are retired or disabled, are not exempt; area civil defence supervisors or local councils are supposed to make sure that they know what the effects of nuclear and other weapons might be, that they understand what might be done to combat these, are able to follow the code of signals through which civil defence will be co-ordinated and have some skill in rescue and first-aid work. At the same time, those who will take responsibility for running the programme in the event of some disaster are given their own special training.

Shelter is also to be provided for every Russian. Until the 1970s this did not seem a practical programme. Shelters were incorporated into public buildings and installed in industrial plants, but, other than that, no effort was made to build them. In the 1970s, however, a much more comprehensive effort was begun. General A.T. Altunin, the chief of civil defence, announced in 1974 that there must be a continuous readiness 'to shelter the entire population in protective structures', a readiness that would be additional to the extensive evacuation plans already in existence. The basis of this new intention is a recently increased fear of a pre-emptive strike by the West 'forestalling nuclear attack' (as Russian military writers phrased it in 1975).

The General Secretary of the Civil Defence Organisation of Finland, Colonel Gunnar Öhman, writing in a 1982 study on civil defence around the world, states that shelter places now exist for about 70 per cent of the Russian population. And, he says, 5 per cent of their defence expenditure goes on civil defence.

Rural fallout shelters are constructed in any location that can provide some structural basis for them. Vegetable storage cellars and mine shafts, as well as ordinary cellars and basements, have been adapted, as have caves and abandoned tunnels. The basement shelters in cities are designed to take the collapsed weight of the building above them, not negligible when one realises that modern apartment blocks in Russia are usually eight or nine storeys high. These shelters, and those which have been put up as separate buildings, are largely constructed from the grades of concrete able to survive even such high levels of compression as 6,000 or 7,000 psi.

The shelter roofs may be as much as 20 inches (50 centimetres) thick, sometimes with a layer of sand between two concrete plates making a sandwich designed to muffle the most potent blast. Every 20 feet (6 metres) a concrete pillar gives additional support, while above a detached shelter there may be 3 feet (1 metre) or more of earth. There is no definite information in the West about what pressures such shelters are designed to withstand, although it certainly seems to be an overpressure of about 7 to 40 psi. The lower range should protect people about 2 miles (3 kilometres) from ground zero of a 1MT bomb; the upper range, those who have taken cover at half that distance from the burst.

Shelters at industrial plants are generally large enough to take all the workers on a shift, and those in basements can be of a size to protect some 300 people, but those which have been purpose-built sometimes have accommodation for up to 1,000. In addition, there are shelters designed to maintain production and these have room for machinery and technical facilities. To prevent all this space being wasted, the authorities encourage the peacetime use of these vast, reinforced rooms – as garages, storehouses, rifle ranges, cinemas, or overflow classrooms. They are, on occasion, rented out to organisations that have need of space, but those taking them over must maintain the emergency equipment and guarantee that their own can be removed within two hours.

The doors to these shelters are of metal, and heavy rubber edging ensures a hermetic seal. Usually these will be double doors, creating a sort of airlock between them, the second set at right angles to the first. Often they are cylindrical and either concave or convex, with mechanical locking devices to make the seals effective. The doors will not give under blast pressure and create near-impermeable barriers against fallout.

The main protection against radioactive dust, however, must necessarily lie in the ventilation system. The most effective used by the Russians involves no intake from the outside world at all: it is bottled compressed oxygen. Shelters with this high degree of protection tend to be reserved for those whose skills or socio-political standing render them indispensable. Somewhat more complicated and less foolproof is the pure-air system, which draws at least part of its oxygen from outside. This is passed through a thorough cleaning process and augmented with bottled oxygen. Such careful precautions are unnecessary for fallout dust, relatively coarse as it is. They are designed for chemical and bacterial defence. The most common Soviet system is filter-ventilation. An electric blower forces air into the ventilation duct, where it passes a blast valve and then goes through a dust filter and an absorption filter. The first consists of an assembly of fine screens impregnated with machine oil. Airborne dust – that is, in these circumstances, fallout particles – adhere to the oil, leaving the cleaned air to carry on. These filters are screened from the people inside the shelter, since they might become a source of dangerous radioactivity. Absorption filters contain a layer of carbon absorbent and an additional cardboard filter. Air goes in through openings at the top and bottom, and comes out through a third opening in the side. When it emerges, having passed through a battery of filters, it has been cleaned of all harmful bacteria or toxic chemicals. Sometimes, in areas where fire might be expected to create dangerous carbon monoxide fumes, another filter is added. Similar screens are used in industry for the same purpose, linking the carbon monoxide through the action of a catalyst with oxygen from the air to produce carbon dioxide. This is not a substance calculated to make breathing easy, but at least the gas is not actively poisonous and can be expelled by the ventilation system. Outlets for the depleted air are ducts governed by exhaust valves. These can be installed in lavatories or may even pierce the airtight doors. At the surface wooden deflector casings give them some protection against blast.

The ventilation system, in a shelter holding up to 75 people, can be driven by a bicycle-driven fan. A cycle is mounted rigidly on a wooden platform, with its rear wheel suspended from low trestles that fit under the axle. The friction of the back tyre against the drive shaft of the fan provides the energy. The fan itself is mounted in a small box fixed to the side of the platform, with an air-intake tube to one side and a vent at the top.

The Russian manual *Civil Defence* points out that it is quite possible to install an air-regenerating plant, which can absorb carbon dioxide and give off oxygen through the use of sodium or potassium peroxide compounds. Such a plant needs no power, since convection currents move the air. The filter ventilation system produces 2·6 cubic yards (2 cubic metres) of breathable air per person every hour, an amount likely to create difficulties if people have to bear several days of voluntary entombment; air regeneration would ease their circumstances considerably.

Since fallout may take several days to clear, many Soviet shelters have their own water supply – some even have their own wells. These can be used if normal supplies cease. It is calculated by Soviet experts that each person will need between 6 and 7 pints (3 and 4 litres) in every twenty-four hours for drinking and the most rudimentary washing. Then there is the operation of a sewage system, which uses between 3½ and 4½ gallons (16 and 20 litres) per person over the same period. The Russian conclusion is that a shelter holding 300 people needs a daily supply of 9 cubic yards (7 cubic metres) of water – 85 per cent being used for sewage. The sewage is pumped out into the normal sewage system; once this is damaged, Soviet Russia provides for the comfort of its citizens little more than, to quote the civil defence manual again, 'vessels for collecting sewage (temporary waste holdup containers)'. To purify the water there should be a supply of chlorinated lime, 0·35 ounces (8 or 10 grammes) of which are added to every cubic yard (metre).

In many cases the tunnel-like ducts of the ventilation system also act as emergency exits. These are essential, since the fall of débris or distortions caused by blast pressure could make the main doors unusable. The mouth of each such tunnel is protected by a circular or box-like concrete structure, with an opening on one side covered with wooden louvres. It is these that often give the most obvious indication of a shelter's existence. If the shelter is under some assembly hall, municipal office, factory or apartment block these fortified outlets are designed to be far enough away to avoid being buried should the structure collapse – a distance that is taken to be 9 feet (3 metres) more than half the height of the building.

In case even this turns out not to be long enough, every shelter is required to have in readiness picks, shovels and buckets so that those inside can dig themselves out, as well as fire extinguishers, flashlights, candles, a telephone and at least one radio. There are also monitoring instruments for radiation levels. The procedures for maintenance are laid down (for the guidance of seven-men teams led by the shelter commandant, all from the Blast and Fallout Shelter Service), as is the order in which those seeking cover are to be allowed in (children and old people first, people with children into a separate area). Inside the shelter, domestic animals and pets, inflammable materials, noisy behaviour, smoking and all naked flames are forbidden – and with very good reason.

China

In China, civil defence – like so much else – has been placed in the hands of the population. Local governments may administer the programme, but practical responsibility lies with street committees, which co-ordinate the efforts of their own localities. Public order in wartime would be maintained by the People's Militia, rather than by the heavier hand of the army. Most public energy has been expended on providing shelters, many of them in great tunnel-systems hollowed out in the course of countless volunteer man-hours. (These have been seen by many Western experts.) However, as Dr Frank Barnaby, director of the Stockholm International Peace Research Institute, pointed out in an article published in spring 1979, it is not only their complex tunnels, but also the great size of their country, that has convinced the Chinese that a nuclear attack on China does not pose the threat of a decisive blow, as it does elsewhere. They feel that enough of their number would always survive to face any invader with a monumental and prohibitively difficult task. The determination of the Chinese to plan and execute a widespread programme to preserve the civilian population comes from their conviction that a global war is inevitable; though they are far from convinced, or so they claim, that when it comes it will involve the use of nuclear armaments. Dr Barnaby reports:

> De La Street near the centre of Peking, may have at any one time as many as 10,000 people in the 270 metre long street. When my guide pressed a button on the wall, part of the floor slid over to expose a large entrance to a system of tunnels capable of sheltering up to 10,000 people . . . the civil defence chief assured me that the 10,000 or so people are now so drilled that they can get underground in about five – yes five – minutes. This is no record. The bulk of Peking's people can, I was told, get underground within about five minutes of a warning signal. ('Dig Tunnels Deep' by Dr Frank Barnaby in the Canadian *Emergency Planning Digest*, April-June 1979, p.17.)

Dr Ishwar Ojha of Boston University has also described the Chinese shelters:

> . . . they took us to the busiest marketing section of Peking and into a large department store. And on one counter they pressed a button: the counter rolled away, and we saw steps leading down. We went down about eight metres, about 28 feet, and found tunnels, all right – well-built brick and concrete tunnels, miles and miles of them. The entire city of Peking, they told us, has tunnels under it, with an entrance from every department store, every apartment building, every residence. Inside the tunnels we saw kitchens, running water, sanitary facilities, food storage, medical facilities, all ready for use. In the event of a nuclear attack, they said, Peking's 7 million people can be safe in the tunnels in seven minutes, and can walk through them to 20 miles outside of the city. And they told us that, since 1968, every major city in China has had similar tunnels built. So whenever we went to another city, we asked to see the tunnels – and they were there.

The Chinese are not playing about.

Switzerland

The Swiss response to the possible dangers of nuclear war has been vigorous and comprehensive. A referendum held in 1962 showed that a clear majority of the nation wanted a civil defence programme, and one was therefore put in train. Its cost is just under half of 1 per cent of the country's gross national product, 8 per cent of the total defence budget. Its goal is, quite simply, the protection of every person and every thing of value. Every new public building is required to have a communal shelter, or to include an area which can be instantly adapted for the purpose. Go skating in Berne's new ice-rink: far beneath the white trace left by your skates lies the area's civil defence command post, a 400-bed hospital, accommodation for the firemen and engineers of the rescue service and shelter space for 2,000 people. The hospital, one of 600 such spread throughout the country, is permanently equipped. Should a nuclear emergency catch you near the same city's neat new railway station, make for its ticket hall: the steel doors at one end will open to reveal your sanctuary, a fully-equipped shelter, proof against blast and radiation, large enough to take in 4,000 people.

The Swiss claim that they can now find room in their shelters for all but 10 per cent of their 7 million people: they have available over 6 million shelter places in structures all over the country – in tunnels of mountain roads and at the lowest levels, newly dug in the substantial bulk of ancient buildings. Nearly 2 million of these, however, are in structures built before the mid-1960s and so lack the latest equipment – most critically, the new air filters. These filters are able to screen out the effects of atomic, biological and chemical assaults (hence their coding, ABC filters) and can be incorporated in the air conditioning systems of the larger shelters, as well as in the more straightforward ventilation systems of family-sized reinforced basements.

One of the most effective pieces of equipment in Swiss shelters is designed to deal with the problem of blast which renders so many shelters vulnerable. It is an explosion protection valve, the first component through which air must pass, and it is mounted in a steel frame over the intake duct. Within the frame there is an assembly of fine and sensitive leaf springs. Instantly affected by the shock waves of an explosion, these springs will close within one millisecond.

Power for the shelters is supplied by diesel-driven alternators. These are placed behind concrete, in a sealed room. The fumes and exhaust from the machine, and air coming in for the cooling system, both have outlets and intakes with protection valves. Thus these underground refuges are almost entirely self-contained.

Swiss shelters, in addition to a power generating plant and a protected air conditioning system, often have a hospital attached to them, a well-equipped canteen or kitchen, an adequate water supply and, with it, adequate toilet and bathroom facilities. So complete are these underground environments that there has been some discussion about whether permanent populations might exist in them without insuperable difficulties. The studies that resulted from these speculations showed that a controlled climate would have to have variations built into it: in a steady temperature, people lose their ability to resist the normal alternations between heat and cold. Night and day, too, produce different conditions and a failure to simulate these leads to a faltering of an individual's 'biological clock'. With these basic rhythms disturbed, the ordinary twenty-four hour cycle begins to break up and people's inner sense of time establishes itself differently on a quite arbitrary basis. The consequences to the sheltering community, and the inhabitants' psychological state, could be harmful.

The official level of preparedness is matched by every city in Switzerland, by every town, by almost every village. Every individual household is required to construct a shelter of its own, an ordinance which makes the communal precautions, elaborate though they are, only an additional defence for the population.

Meanwhile, energy equal to that deployed in defence of the population is beginning to be spent on protecting industry and culture. Essential administrative documents and priceless ancient manuscripts are all preserved on microfilm. Should the originals perish, they will not disappear unrecorded. Buildings of historic or aesthetic importance have been carefully photographed: should they be destroyed, peace may permit their reconstruction. Communication systems command their own methods of protection, particularly the railways, the telephone and telegraph networks and the broadcasting stations.

Parallel to all this, there run the measures of military defence, including underground hangars, cliff-face gun emplacements and deeply concealed radio installations and computer centres. Switzerland, far from adopting an all-or-nothing attitude of helpless fatalism, is vigorously intent on survival, whatever happens.

A visit to the headquarters of the Swiss civil defence authorities during the research for this book provided some light relief in addition to a dauntingly comprehensive briefing by the hospitable Swiss specialists.

As the premier Western exponents of public protection,

the Swiss suffer, with fair fatalism, the constant – sometimes hysterical – applications from individuals, firms and governments for information, training, co-operation . . . anything. Their impression of the British and French, and especially their proliferating 'cowboy' shelter peddlers, was something less than favourable. They made no secret, either, of their feeling that the British administrators were of poor quality and badly informed, though quite unaware of this. Being professionals of twenty years' standing, the Swiss do not find it easy to deal with people of lower standards. Their civil defence organisation has its full share of well-trained and high-calibre people. That they could not find their equivalent in the representatives of certain countries who sought their help caused an obvious degree of frustration.

'Surprising ineptitude' was one of the phrases used in describing the booklet *Protect and Survive*, which has been trumpeted as excellent (and laughed out of court as absurd) in Britain, its country of origin.

'Get rid of the eccentrics and recruit a new generation of non-bureaucratic administrators, and we can begin to talk' is an example of the attitude in Berne, and elsewhere, among some of the well-disposed but perplexed Swiss.

Sweden

In Sweden it is the law that every citizen must play some part in the military or civilian defence of the country. There will be, therefore, no shortage of personnel for the protection of the population. In each of the country's 24 provinces there is a civil defence director, with some twenty specialists and an administrative staff to help him. The provincial directors appoint area controllers who will take charge of their districts should war make this necessary. Such controllers will have the task of co-ordinating the various emergency services in their areas: the medical teams, which in Sweden are well-equipped and heavily motorised, the rescue services, the fire-fighting forces, teams able to make some response to the radiological and biological hazards of a nuclear conflict, and the armed civilian detachments responsible for public order. Directly answerable to each controller will be the control service, which provides his administrative staff, operational executives and manpower for the district's warning system.

Sweden is the fourth largest country in Europe, but its population is only some 8 millions. Thus evacuation of the cities when emergencies threaten is an attractive option. The present plans are for nearly 4 million people, half the total, to be moved from urban into rural locations. Some 700,000 would be moved from Stockholm alone, leaving the capital with only 100,000 people to run its services and undertake the work of rescue and relief. Since the shelter programme, both public and private, now provides accommodation for well over 4 million people – a figure that was for a while increasing at the rate of a quarter of a million places every year – it is not surprising that Sweden claims that it has provided every one of its citizens with at least some measure of protection.

Finland

Shelter places exist for over 60 per cent of Finland's population. In target areas this rises to 75 per cent and in the capital, Helsinki, to 85 per cent. Most of the shelters are built in hard rock and are designed to withstand conventional as well as nuclear attack. In designing the sheltering programme it was, for economic reasons, decided to give as many shelters as possible a peacetime role. Thus they serve as road or pedestrian tunnels, laboratories, broadcasting stations, sports centres, warehouses and entertainment complexes. And the new Helsinki Metro is also a series of massive public shelters. Each dual purpose shelter can be brought to readiness for an emergency in a few hours by highly trained personnel.

Norway

Almost half of Norway's 4 million people can find protection in the country's purpose-built shelters – which double in peacetime as libraries, bars or swimming pools. Because, with less than one-tenth of the population, it has a land area greater than that of France, Norway has also decided that for many of those living in the cities evacuation is a suitable option. Detailed plans for evacuation have been laid, area by area. These are not, as in some countries, held in secrecy by the relevant bureaucracy, but are published in what must be one of the most widely distributed and convenient of media: the telephone directories.

The Federal Republic of Germany

In West Germany, the provincial governments, the *Länder,* provide the fire-fighting, fire-protection and medical services that form the major part of the civil defence system. This allows the Federal government to spend its funds on equipping and training a force of some half million full-time and part-time specialists. At the same time, the country has begun a vigorous attempt to provide shelter for large numbers of its people. Already 10 per cent of the population of some major cities such as Frankfurt are protected. New shelters have been built and old ones, surviving from the Second World War, refurbished. Ordinary homes, as well as many public buildings, are in future to have blast-proof shelters as an integral part of their construction, while financial inducements are intended to persuade owners of older houses to equip them, too, with shelters. By the end of the 1980s, a third of the Federal Republic's population at least will have protection from nuclear war. In the public sector, the Technical Aid Service, busy in peacetime with shelter maintenance and various training programmes, would in a time of emergency take over certain welfare obligations for those seeking communal protection.

Middle East

Iraq, Syria and Israel are well advanced in civil defence and are building nuclear shelters for the public. Israel is the most advanced and is not far behind Switzerland in its thoroughness. The Israeli civil defence organisation makes up about 35 per cent of the entire defence force. Libya, Tunisia, Algeria, Morocco and Egypt all have active civil defence organisations and Saudi Arabia and the Gulf States are also making progress.

Shelter technology in these regions is being copied or imported directly from Switzerland, Sweden and other European countries. Major British companies are involved in designing and building massive public shelters in the Middle East.

France

Civil defence in France is understood to mean all defensive activities that are not, in the most literal sense, military. Measures to ensure the safety or relief of the population come under a different heading: civil protection. This is under the direction of the Minister of the Interior and bases its operations on the seven defence zones into which the country is divided. Each zone has a permanent 'zone defence committee' which, although largely civilian, includes some military members. Its work is co-ordinated by a secretary-general, who has close contacts with the civil protection directors of the Departments in his zone, and with the region's military commander. Thus the skeleton of an administrative structure, largely autonomous in each zone, already exists.

If a war should break out, certain civil protection units would mobilise. Among the most interesting are the 'lodging units', which are intended to aid the homeless and displaced, perhaps a consequence of France's experience with refugees at the time of the German invasion in 1940. There would also be 'civil protection centres', each deploying between 100 and 200 people, which would oversee firefighting, rescue, the clearing of roads and making safe of damaged buildings, the decontamination of radioactive areas where that is possible, and the bringing of aid to victims. These centres are run at a departmental level. There are several hundred of them scattered throughout the country and two mobile assistance forces in each zone ready to reinforce them.

As in many other Western countries, however, French civil defence plans are more advanced on paper than they are in reality. For example, there has been little dissemination of hard information or of instructions on behaviour in the event of nuclear war. The Ministry of the Interior, which has prepared a detailed booklet and was planning to publish it in an edition of 20 million, has been as reluctant as the British Home Office has been to release theirs. The reason, critics assume, is that politicians are afraid of popular reaction. The dangers, officially spelled out, may, among other things, create another wave of anti-nuclear revulsion.

The absence of any vigorous shelter policy has also been attacked. The booklet issued by the Service National de la Protection Civile, *Savoir pour vivre,* declares, 'Because of their [public shelters'] high price they can only be built in small numbers and will protect only a tiny part of the population.' A government survey into potential shelters in private homes has been started but its budget allowance is little more than £500,000 and the entire project is in the hands of just three civil servants. It can hardly help that the information it relies on must be disentangled from the general public's tax returns.

Should the existing shelters ever be needed, users would be warned by the howls of sirens. These, however, are centrally controlled from a telecommunications installation at the prefecture of each of the country's 42 Departments: the network is the ordinary public one administered by the postal authorities. It is therefore dangerously vulnerable to a pre-emptive strike; certainly, by the time a second nuclear assault struck the country, communications would be so disrupted that many millions of Frenchmen might never receive that essential warning. The warning system as a whole is, in any case, the responsibility of a small, mainly volunteer body, the efficiency of which, in the stresses of an emergency, may not be wholly adequate. It is points like these, raised by journalists and opposition politicians, which have come to the surface in public debate. As one might expect, they have given rise to widespread unease.

As a sidelight on French civil preparedness, we may mention that when a respectable, educated Frenchman, seeking straightforward information from the Paris civil defence authorities, went to their headquarters recently, he was treated with disdain and even suspicion: whatever was he doing asking about civil protection? He was, in fact, collecting material for this book, but all his questions were those of an ordinary French citizen anxious to know how he might protect his family in time of nuclear threat . . .

The United States

The Americans do not think a world war inevitable, but believe that if it does break out it is bound to include a nuclear exchange. Indeed, the use of nuclear weapons may now be their means of defining a major war. All non-nuclear conflicts, in other words, may be regarded as local and limited brushfire affairs. Despite this opinion, the United States normally spends only one-tenth of 1 per cent of its defence budget on protecting its civilians. By contrast, the Soviet Union now spends 5 per cent of its defence budget on similar precautions. President Carter tried to boost civil defence spending and asked Congress for an increase in the money allocated to it. The response of Congress was to cut the programme's finances even further. By 1980, the rate of expenditure was running at only a little over 40 million dollars a year. Thus, during the 1970s, the United States spent just under a billion dollars on civil defence – less than 2 per cent of Russian expenditure, which in the same period has been estimated at over 50 billion dollars.

The not unexpected result of this is that in the first strike of an all-out nuclear exchange, over a third of the entire population of the United States could be killed. Most of the country's administrative centres and the bulk of its industrial installations would be destroyed. Its pulverised leadership and devastated communications would leave the nation paralysed. Its sad condition would probably be matched by that of its allies. The Western powers, it seems, see war as a form of national suicide: the bee stings its enemy, then dies.

The implications are disturbing. The deterrent effects of the nuclear arsenal are a powerful factor in today's diplomacy and anything diminishing belief in its potency, by one side or the other, has instant repercussions. As the director of Harvard University's Center for International Affairs, Professor S.P. Huntingdon, recently pointed out to a Senate committee,

> The most stable situation in a crisis would be one in which neither side had a meaningful civil defense. The least stable situation, on the other hand, is one in which there are marked asymmetries in civil defense capability . . . If the United States does not undertake an expanded civil defence program, the least stable situation will exist in a future crisis.

The Federal Emergency Management Agency, and proponents and organisers of civil defence at state and city level, do what they can. Many individuals, too, have made their own arrangements to protect themselves and their families, sometimes taking self-help to the point of arming themselves against their neighbours – a foretaste of the anarchy that might threaten some areas in the post-nuclear world. But whatever individuals manage to do, a total civil defence expenditure of about a dollar a head per year is not enough to protect the mass of the people. Many European civil defence expenditures are higher than those of the United States when reckoned in dollars per head. Both Switzerland and Norway spend ten times as much as do the Americans; West Gemany, Denmark and Finland about four times as much, Holland just over double. It is as if America, so swift in ideological belligerence and eager to accept the role of leadership of a great world power, has not realised that its citizens will be placed, in any future war, where they have not been before – in the front line.

Plans for public sheltering seem inadequate. On the whole shelters are intended to be of value only against fallout; they do not have the extra protection against blast envisaged by Soviet civil defence planners. They have been set in the basements of public buildings, in subways, mines and other suitable locations, and are marked with a black and yellow sign familiar to all who know American cities. In some places, people are assigned to particular shelters, in others they are asked in an emergency to make their way to the nearest one.

These shelters, however, come under frequent criticism from experts, perhaps none more eloquent than Messrs Calvin C. Zehring and William O. Brownell:

> The problem is that almost none of these [American] structures is a shelter. A shelter to be valid shelter against the technology of modern Soviet warfare, must have a hand-operated air pump. These do not. A good shelter needs an air filter that excludes most particles. These have no filters at all. A good shelter must have good nutritional food in freeze-dried or dehydrated form, which can be stored for a long time. These do not. A good shelter should have radiation meters that are checked frequently and that function. And dosimeters that have rechargers. And decontamination equipment and suits. And medicine. These shelters have nothing of the kind, and they cannot be termed 'shelters' since they will not give shelter to anyone. (*Protect & Survive Monthly,* March 1981.)

The lack of American foresight, compared to that of the Russians, is astonishing. The ventilation systems in most of these public shelters, for example, are run on electricity supplied by municipal power sources. These are unlikely to survive intact in a nuclear attack; they are in any case vulnerable to the same electromagnetic pulse (EMP) which may distort and suspend communications. The fans of the ventilation systems are not protected against blast so that an overpressure of just 1 psi can destroy most of them. This is the blast pressure experienced 10 miles (16 kilometres) from the epicentre of a 1MT burst. So, without a powered ventilation system in shelters crammed with over 1,000 people, the air will not be able to circulate properly, neither will radioactive dust be filtered from it. Thus it is likely that within seconds of a nuclear explosion, most of the shelters, in an area some 18 miles (30 kilometres) across, would be rendered useless.

> The problem would not be so great, frankly, if Americans had ever realised that survival through a nuclear war does not require *shelters* but rather *shelter systems*. The shell of a shelter is no more complete than, say, the shell of a Concorde. It may be splendid, it may be substansive, but it is quite incomplete in itself – a concept lost on most Americans. (Zehring and Brownell, op. cit.)

In America, as in the United Kingdom, the only decent shelters are built by rich individuals and private groups or by the authorities for military and Government personnel. As for the public, 'We have no civil defense program, merely the apparatus to start one.' This was said by the civil defence chief of America, Bardyl Tirana, in 1978. 'When you look at civil defense in America,' he said, 'you find that the emperor has no clothes.' He should know.

The United Kingdom

The uncertainties and irrelevancies of the civil defence programmes in the United States and France are echoed in Britain. In a leading article on January 19th, 1980 *The Times* of London went beyond criticism to accusation:

> If war were to occur . . . the lack of adequate civil defence would be seen as a terrible dereliction of duty of Government. It is not alarmist to make reasonable preparation. Civil defence does not imply war any more than fire insurance implies arson. The present lack of preparation is a lethal failure of duty.

The Government strategy has a strong administrative bias. That is, the first priority seems to be to prepare for a continuity of government, no matter how few of the governed may survive to benefit from it. The country has been divided into twelve Home Defence regions. If an attack seems imminent, a minister of Cabinet rank will be despatched to each of these to take up the duties of regional commissioner. Provided with quasi-dictatorial powers, he or she will guarantee the continuity of authority during the emergency.

The nine English regions and Wales will each be divided into two sub-regions, while Scotland, taken to be a region of its own, will be administered in three zones. The sub-regional commissioners will not generally be politicians, but senior civil servants. Appointed by royal warrant, however, and with authority corresponding to the regional commissioners', it is they who will bear most of the day-to-day responsibility. Thus the country will, during a nuclear emergency, find itself largely in the hands of a small body of men whose powers and position have never been directly endorsed by the electorate. Answering to them will be the 211 county and metropolitan county authorities, who will, within their narrower geographic limits, have similar powers. This administrative freedom at every level is considered to counter the possible disappearance of one or other of the tiers of command and the consequent breakdown of authority and public order.

From the beginning, the closest connections that the commissioners will forge are those between themselves, the police and the Army. Indeed, so close will these connections be, it is widely believed that the regional commissioners – about whose whereabouts in an emergency very little has been officially revealed – will be accommodated in the headquarters of the army zone that approximates to their region. In time of war, therefore, it is the regional armed forces headquarters which will become the centres of administration. Executive power will lie with the sub-regions, but the sub-regional commissioners will not only be answerable to commissioners deeply embedded in the military system, they will themselves have close contacts with military commanders of their own equivalent level and have military members on their advisory committees. Thus in any given region a question may well arise as to who is actually in charge – the elected minister of the Crown, who is the commissioner, or the general in charge of the corresponding army district, who is the regional military commander. Since the regional police commander would probably see eye to eye with his colleague from the army, it is feared by some that it would be a strong politician who, in those circumstances, would be able to place a civilian restraint upon their actions.

Warning

The best prepared of Britain's defences is that section designed to give us warning of our fate. It includes, of course, the great domes and dishes of Fylingdale which, as part of the Ballistic Missiles Early Warning System, are linked to the computers – at times so distressingly temperamental – deep inside the mountains near Colorado Springs. But any signals of approaching danger they may flash out are also instantly received in Whitehall, and in such strategic headquarters as that of RAF Strike Command in High Wycombe, in Buckinghamshire. At High Wycombe there is a Home Defence officer on permanent duty. Given a confirmed alert, he will set in motion a process that seconds later will send the unnerving howl of 7,000 sirens bawling across the land. Following them one by one the hand-operated sirens that cover the distant sections of the countryside will sound out, 11,000 of them feverishly operated by local policemen, council employees or volunteers. Radio and television programmes will fall silent and, in their place, tapes, long prepared, will pass on their pre-recorded messages. (That is, if the whole communications system is not totally disabled by EMP, electromagnetic pulse, a likely opening gambit designed to cause maximum confusion.)

Much of this will be the responsibility of UKWMO – the United Kingdom Warning and Monitoring Organisation – with which is linked the Royal Observer Corps, whose allowances were increased in 1980. The latter, tried and tested in the Second World War, is almost the only section of the old civil defence structure left intact. It is through the five sector headquarters of the Observer Corps, manned by volunteers, that the signal to broadcast the warning will be sent to regional centres of the BBC. Thus if London has already been demolished, or the link with London has been cut – or even the link with High Wycombe and the south – the rest of the country, in theory, will still be warned.

And what are the terms of that warning? In the main, snippets of advice that, if followed, will make life simpler for the authorities. The message will claim that no one place in the United Kingdom will be safer than any other. It is fallout that will shortly be the danger, and it makes clear precisely what is meant by this: 'Fallout can kill,' the tape tells us firmly. The safest place, it goes on to assure us, is the one we know best – our own home: 'So stay where you are!' The last thing that a government at war wants is to have the roads crowded with panic-stricken people. Having therefore persuaded us not to flee, it goes on to give us a little basic advice about blast and fallout protection and ends by warning us, 'Keep in touch. Use your radio!' A swift downward sequence of bell-like, vaguely electronic bleeps, managing to combine urgency with reassurance, make up the signal which accompanies these exhortations. It is the herald of a new order in broadcasting, the voice of Armageddon; the tinklings of both the BBC and the Independent Broadcasting Authority will be replaced by the tones of the Wartime Broadcasting Service (WBS). It is through this that our leaders hope to speak to us.

The Dispersed Government

The BBC has an alternative network of protected headquarters for radio and television broadcasts, just as it has special emergency studios inside each of the sub-regional headquarters. The continuity of output of the new WBS information is thus assured, at least over the major part of the country. In these first moments of the emergency, switches will be flicked and red lights will shine out as the little studios go into action.

Each of the sub-regional headquarters is like a small, heavily protected office block, sunk into the earth and rendered inconspicuous by having some mundane building at its entrance or by being placed under an ordinary government office. Behind the blast-proof and radiation-deterring steel doors are the essential facilities for monitoring and, where possible, countering conditions of extreme social upheaval. As well as the broadcasting studio, there is a comprehensive telecommunications centre. There is equipment to measure radiation levels. There is a canteen. There is a conference room where the sub-regional commissioner can meet the 'cabinet'. There is a sick-bay. There is a dormitory with rows of three-tiered bunks for the personnel who will operate these installations.

Two hundred people will move into this sophisticated bunker. None will carry much in the way of luggage. Most of them will be burdened by a private terror – that while they work in safety, their families, husbands or wives, brothers, sisters, friends, neighbours, may one by one or at a single sweep be incinerated or slowly destroyed by radiation.

The existence of anxiety, coupled with the problems arising naturally when 200 people, mostly strangers, are incarcerated for many tension-packed days, raises questions about the level of morale within the SRHQS. If it were to sink very low consequent behaviour – ill-considered actions, precipitate decisions, fatalistic procrastination and so on – might reinforce the dangers the population already faced. It is as well, perhaps, that each of the senior people will have his or her own office accommodation, with a fold-away bed: privacy should help to ease the strain on them.

The national government will hurriedly move out of central London. Just north of the city, close to Harrow, the Central Communications Establishment, run by the Home Office, will be brought into use. The headquarters of United Kingdom Land Forces, probably near that traditional military proving ground, Salisbury Plain, will see an influx into its reinforced underground bunkers of a number of civilians – representatives of the Prime Minister and the Government, of the various agencies charged with maintaining services and of the police. High-ranking liaison officers from the Navy and the RAF will take their places on the various emergency committees. In every practical sense, the ultimate responsibility for running the country will lie here.

The essential core of the administration is also likely to move westward from London, its destination unknown, but areas combining rock, remoteness, good communications and, frequently, existing government installations, have all been suggested. It may be that there will be an official scattering, a great flight of bureaucrats, with thousands of the functionaries of state going to ground in suitable locations in various parts of the country.

Information Networks

Communications will be vital. The telephone and telex networks are the natural first resort. Given that the Regional Seats of Government, each with its presiding Minister (regional commissioner) as the Prime Minister's representative, will all be housed in military headquarters, it is likely that the Army's excellent radio network will also be brought into use. The Post Office's microwave system, however, may become the most important means of linking the scattered elements of government; the chain of heavily reinforced towers that will relay beamed messages has aptly been codenamed Backbone.

The main threat to communications might well turn out to be, not direct physical damage, but the deliberate or accidental explosion of a nuclear device at a high altitude, say, 100 miles (160 kilometres) up. This would create an electromagnetic pulse (EMP) of such power that, in an area over a 1,000 miles (1,600 kilometres) across, radio aerials, power mains and telephone equipment would be severely damaged. Because the pulse is much faster than lightning it causes its damage before most lightning arresters can prevent it. The EMP then blows any weakness in a circuit over the entire area that its energy can reach, that is to say, to the far horizon, in all directions, from the point of the explosion.

EMP is attracted to any features on the earth's surface likely to conduct electricity – overhead cables, steel radio towers and any tall antennae. When it strikes, it produces a surge of power in the system that bursts into any instrument hooked up to it. Most modern electronic equipment cannot withstand this and would be put out of action unless protected. This is a great worry to those men and women who are being trained to use the information network in times of war. Even police communications are not protected against EMP.

The immediate effects on radio communication are likely to be least damaging in the high-frequency ranges – UHF, VHF – but the long-wave transmitter at Droitwich near Worcester, through which in normal conditions the entire nation can be reached, would be rendered useless. An explosion in the megaton range would be even more disruptive, creating disturbances in the ionosphere that would drastically reduce the efficiency of radar as well as radio. It is possible that the two Army networks, one relying on tropospheric scatter and thus dependent on upper-atmosphere conditions, the other using the Very Long Wave band, might, for a period, experience the most unsettling difficulties.

Across the country, meanwhile, the Royal Observer Corps would as swiftly as possible be manning its 873 monitoring posts. Three volunteers are assigned to each of these, clambering 20 feet (6 metres) underground into their concrete bunker. Inside are the dials and gauges of the devices which enable them to measure the direction of nearby bomb-bursts, the weight of blast and the intensity of radiation and fallout. When a bomb or missile lands, one of the team will race to the surface to take ground-level readings of radiation counts before the fallout can take effect; otherwise, the team, protected against radiation even at very intense levels, is equipped to sit out the emergency.

Information on the position of explosions, and on the effects both immediate and prolonged, is passed to the military, to the Home Defence controllers of the Home Office and to those making policy decisions at high governmental level. The Corps is thoroughly trained and holds frequent exercises.

The warning and monitoring service, UKWMO, can independently set in motion a nationwide alert from its new headquarters in Oxford. Its sector controllers, like the RAF Strike Command, can break directly into a Post Office network linking it to some 18,000 warning points, the majority of which will be local police stations. Once that has been done, the process is irrevocably under way: a policeman somewhere will press a button and, in his area, all the sirens will scream out their warnings. The prepared tapes will start to unroll in Army headquarters, hospitals, fire stations and other emergency centres; linked-in alarms will give their eleventh-hour message. Thus, if we ignore the Achilles heel of the lack of protection against EMP effects, our warning system has reassuring flexibility.

Target Island

So Britain faces its attackers. Whatever the reason, the island has become a target. The warheads are in flight. Ten thousand members of the Observer Corps await their impact.

Deep under earth and concrete, embedded in rock, far below the darkest cellar, those who have helped bring the nation to this destiny crouch, wait, and, as far as their cramped policies permit, plan for the future. Authority, widely dispersed, suffers its particular fear – the fear of how a fearful population will react.

Indeed, every politician and bureaucrat that, prior to the war, had prevented the development of adequate sheltering and other defensive measures against nuclear weapon effects, will know he or she is liable to be held responsible for causing *more* British deaths than the enemy. (This is because, instead of losing, say, 15 million if we were sheltered, unsheltered we can expect deaths to exceed 35 million.) The surviving population might justly regard the assumption of power by the criminally negligent remnants of pre-war authority as intolerable.

And what of that population? Left largely to its own devices, only a few weeks earlier indifferent to the disaster it faced, with provision for neither evacuation nor public shelters, what is the population to do?

Take Cover!

During the Second World War, Britain developed civil protection skills that were probably closer to absolute efficiency than anywhere else on earth. From the Battle of Britain in 1940 to the 'doodlebugs' or 'buzz-bombs' (ancestors of the cruise missile) and the supersonic V-2s of 1944, the organisations dealing with the effects of air attack worked at full stretch. The expertise painfully acquired in those years remained a part of the country's official heritage until, in 1968, James Callaghan as Home Secretary wound up the Civil Defence Corps. It was in this volunteer body that much of the wartime wisdom had been enshrined, a wisdom entirely directed to the preservation of civilian life.

In February 1980, the revival of the Civil Defence Corps, suggested by the new drift towards a dangerous state of East-West tension, was stopped by a Cabinet decision. Home Defence, where it was not to be administered by and, to a large extent, for the bureaucracy, was to remain fragmented and in the hands of a number of separate voluntary agencies. The Women's Royal Voluntary Service, the WRVS, with the Red Cross, the St John Ambulance Brigade and perhaps the private charity, Civil Aid, would become the spearhead of whatever welfare effort was possible after a nuclear strike. Medical services, where they survived, would be totally inadequate and there exist no plans, like those already carried out in Switzerland, for example, to prepare hospitals that could survive attack.

Even the term Home Defence has rendered the effort to counter aerial bombardment (which is not, after all, guaranteed to be nuclear; lesser weapons still exist in enormous quantities) unfamiliar to many who might otherwise take part in it. As Civil Aid recently told the Home Defence Review body, set up in politic haste by the government as both crisis and criticism grew intense, 'Although Home Defence is now used by authorities, we consider that the words "Civil Defence" will have to be used if the Government require a full response.' Fortunately the authorities took heed and the term 'Civil Defence' is back in use, as shown by recent official publications.

The last repository of civil defence expertise lay with the Regional Scientific Advisers who were dismissed in 1977, because, it is said, they had become too critical of the Government's lack of concern over the fate of the population at large. Civil Aid, in its recommendations to the review body, pointed out how much might be done. There was no reason, it said, why new buildings, and especially new hospitals, should not be required to include in their plans shelters that are proof against blast and radiation. There was no reason, either, why people building their own shelters should not be publicly assisted, or at least not penalised by being charged Value Added Tax. Neither was it really necessary to make a few extra thousands for the Government by auctioning off surplus equipment, when a pool of trucks, cars, blankets, waterproof clothing, even hatchets, might make a critical difference in an emergency. Above all, however, there should be some form of national organisation to weld together the efforts of local Emergency Planning Officers and Emergency Liaison Groups, and to co-ordinate the training of those volunteers who would take up essential duties if nuclear disaster were to strike.

Meanwhile, a few of these locally responsible authorities are facing up to their obligations very seriously. Some a long way from the probable centres of attack, for example Devon, are making plans for dealing with an influx of refugees. The county is to build up its emergency volunteer force to some 4,500 members from the 1,000 that it numbered at the beginning of 1980. The dangers of fallout and even of direct attack on ports and naval installations make this kind of foresight directly relevant even to so rural and apparently peaceful an area. Other parts of Britain are taking an equally thoughtful and practical attitude, but the picture overall is one of hesitancy, dilatoriness and indifference. Some areas are actually cutting back on what little emergency planning there is, thus condemning even more to die if we are attacked.

Such national planning as exists relies very heavily upon the dubious conviction that there will be a period of severe tension and finally of direct warning during which the Government will have time enough to get everything right. The problem with this approach is that it presumes no difficulties over timing. Yet clearly there may be a long time, perhaps a period of weeks, during which the authorities' call to mobilise the civil defence legions would itself seem like a provocative act. Defence and attack are indivisible, and activating the first may appear to the enemy as a prelude to the second. The temptation in Government circles will be to hold back from embarking on civilian protection in order to prevent making a bad situation worse. The end result of that could be the sacrifice of 20 million people who might have been saved had the effort to do so been made earlier.

Absurdly, it is only at the time of a near-certain nuclear attack that the Government proposes to inform the people of what they should do. To tell them what they need to know before this may, the official attitude seems to imply, alarm them unduly, and indeed if more people understood the costs in life, injury, disease and property that might one day be demanded of them some might well become vociferous in their dismay. In any case, for whatever reason, *Protect and Survive* became, in 1979–80, one of the most famous publications never to have been properly issued: it is the booklet that gives precise instructions about what precautions we might take in the event of nuclear attack. It was grudgingly put on sale in May 1980, and the Government has assured us that every household in the land will be given one free when the situation becomes grave enough to warrant it – a gift that will certainly seem like the knell of doom to many of its recipients. One can hardly imagine a surer recipe for spreading panic.

Somewhat patchily available when at last in print, the booklet was not produced in sufficient numbers to meet the ultimate emergency. (It sold 85,000 copies in the first year.) The plan is to print enough copies for everyone when war threatens. That may be too late – especially if, as many believe, the build-up will take not weeks but days, or may even not occur at all: a pre-emptive strike, on the model of Pearl Harbor or the Israeli air attack on Egyptian installations in 1967, is at least as probable as the old-fashioned diplomatic huffing and puffing envisaged by the Home Office. In the few hours that are the most that would then be available to them, the administrators might have enough time to scramble for their bolt-holes. Anything they would be able to arrange from their spartan caverns in the way of civil protection might well be swiftly overtaken by the devastation and carnage occurring on the surface. To leave until the final crisis almost all the crucial precautions that are to be taken seems curiously extreme – though it is hard to be sure whether the extremes are of optimism or pessimism.

The twenty-six-page booklet itself bases all its advice upon the assumption that people will remain in their own homes. They are instructed to:

> *Whitewash their windows* against heat-flash (a precaution which excites much ridicule, but which is actually effective – should there be time enough to take it).
>
> *Fill their baths* with drinking water and *protect it* from fallout, perhaps with a polythene sheet.
>
> *Gather food* enough to last at least two weeks. (The nationwide panic-buying that would ensue would be unthinkable, if people were to begin acquiring this only during the last stages of a crisis.)
>
> *Retire* to a point in the house *as far as possible from the walls and the roof* – preferably a cellar or basement.
>
> *Reinforce this place of safety by making an interior shelter,* using the materials to hand – planks, table tops or doors taken off their hinges to make a lean-to against one wall, this strengthened by sandbags, bales of clothing, piles of books. A solid table could provide the basis of a shelter. The outside room should be strengthened by adding sandbags to stairs and walls.
>
> Make what *sanitary arrangements* are practicable.
>
> *Keep* in the fallout refuge *cutlery, crockery, a tin-opener and a bottle-opener, and clothes* warm enough for the worst possibilities of the season.
>
> Have available *a portable radio with spare batteries* to maintain contact with the authorities, who will be disseminating instructions and information.

Much of this information is also more graphically given in a film already prepared by the Central Office of Information entitled *Choosing a Fallout Room.* It is one of a series which will be shown on television during those tense prewar weeks envisaged by the Government. Again, the emphasis will be on persuading people to remain in the places where they live, however likely these are to become prime targets. The argument is that, with fallout drifting unpredictably and the island both small and overpopulated, nowhere in Britain will be safer than anywhere else.*

It is hard not to feel that the Government has, up to now, shirked its prime duty, that of protecting the people, and loaded all the responsibility for personal survival upon the private individual, opting to concentrate its efforts on keeping the administration intact and the roads clear. It is a policy that is consonant with the message of the booklet, films and radio tapes. Put at its most brutal, it may be expressed as, 'No evacuation. No public shelters.'

Peter Laurie in *Beneath the City Streets* (Panther, 1979) points out that if a conservative estimate of shelter costs comes out at £200 a place, then to protect the people of metropolitan London from the effects of a 5MT burst would cost £1,600 million. (One must remember, though, that Britain's *annual* defence budget is £13,500 million, an expenditure that will not save any lives if we are attacked.) Two hundred pounds a life may not seem very much but, in the context of peacetime taxes, it is probably prohibitive.

In the latter part of 1980, responding to public pressure, and a growing questioning from the media, the British Government announced in Parliament that something – though very little – would be done by Whitehall in the direction of civil defence. The Home Secretary, Mr William Whitelaw, promised that the national nuclear warning and monitoring organisation – a remnant of the old British wartime air defence – would be modernised. The public would be advised as to which shelters would be their 'best buys'. Great emphasis was placed upon voluntary effort, which would be co-ordinated by 'a person of high standing'.

*The film shows fallout apparently emitting a sharp crackle, which even Government scientists claim will mislead the uninstructed public to imagine that this killer makes a noise!

Air-Marshal Sir Leslie Mavor was appointed to carry out this task.

The amount of money allocated would rise from the tiny sum of £27 million to £45 million – an increase of something over 60 per cent: in other words, an increase from 49p per person per year to 81p per person per year; an increase that Sir Leslie Mavor said in a speech at Brighton 'would make the Russians believe this country was serious about defending its population'. The Government also promised to make more information available, and to increase the training facilities at the single civil defence institution, the Home Defence College at Easingwold, in North Yorkshire.

The British Government, it was clear, had virtually written off the large urban populations of the country's great cities. Mr Whitelaw said that, in the face of an attack, 'dispersal is not a practical policy'. He added that, 'In any event no part of the country would be regarded as safe from both direct and indirect effects of nuclear weapons.' The Minister, of course, certainly knew that while this last statement was true so far as it went, it is also true that many parts of Britain are considerably safer than others. In obvious target areas, almost nobody would survive a nuclear attack because of intense prompt radiation and blast; in other areas, fallout, from which shielding is possible, would be the main problem. Less than three months before the Minister's statement, the Vice-Director of the Swiss Federal Office of Civil Protection had written to a British architect specialising in anti-nuclear structures: 'Provided that the shelter occupants act correctly, protection from the so-called secondary radiation [fallout] is almost total.'* At the time of writing, very few people in Britain know how to 'act correctly' in shelters.

There are deep shelters in London, which lie between 90 and 140 feet (30 and 45 metres) from the surface. They were built in 1941 (it was known in the Second World War that the Germans were working on an atomic bomb), and can be reached from certain Northern Line tube stations. The

*Letter Ref. 100. 8–116 Sg/Ah, to R. Burton, a London architect, dated May 16th, 1980.

shelters are 400 yards (427 metres) long and each consists of two tunnels, five yards (metres) in diameter. They are supplied by mains electricity, but in an emergency could be switched to London Transport's own supply. This, however, seems hardly less vulnerable than the ordinary metropolitan network. The shelters have no blast doors, no tanks to store water, and no fallout filters in the ventilation system. Even if they were properly prepared they could give cover to no more than 56,000 people – a number of small significance when compared to the millions who live and work in London, though doubtless important enough to those chosen for survival.

And this official irresponsibility extends to the nation's economic lifeblood. There is little civil defence planning for industry and the commercial world, though the means by which industry can be protected, to facilitate a speedy post-attack industrial recovery, are known. (By speedy, I mean a few years as opposed to generations.) Protecting objects is, after all, easier than protecting life. But there is little willingness to face up to the need for this in much of Western Europe.

The first glimmer of interest in shielding the countries' means of production came when the Nuclear Protection Advisory Group held a well-attended international seminar called 'Nuclear Attack – Protection for Industry' in London in 1981. The purpose of the seminar was to help people in industry think constructively about the problem and help them assess what their companies could do with regard to the possibility of nuclear war.

It was pointed out that protecting industry is as important as protecting people. This is because the commercial and industrial community is our most important human resource. Our society rests on it and, whatever of that is left, will depend on it again in the aftermath. Industry feeds and clothes us, provides our medicines, makes and distributes essential goods, builds roads, factories and houses. It would have to perform these same tasks under the enormously difficult conditions after a nuclear attack. Its ability to function then would depend on the amount of forethought and action taken now.

Millions of survivors would depend on essential industries operating again as soon as possible. In addition, special equipment and supplies appertaining to a pre-attack phase need to be produced (for example: radiation monitoring devices, protective clothing, shelters). Industry has to prepare itself so as not to let people down if this tragedy occurs. But such preparation has hardly begun and receives no official encouragement.

Here and there in Britain, however, there are signs of a dawning awareness that something must be done. The Government is reviewing its 'stay put' policy and making surveys of existing facilities which might be used as public shelters; though they have shown no enthusiasm for finding the money or arranging for the conversion of such premises. Again and again in the newspapers there are articles warning against the band-waggon entrepreneurs who, without appropriate technical expertise, are offering shelters without money-back guarantees.

The *Irish Times* reports that the Woolwich Building Society would 'rather lend money on a shelter than on a swimming pool'; at a time of financial stringency, when thousands of houses await a buyer, a man in Yorkshire finds that people clamour to buy his bungalow – because it has a nuclear shelter. *Time* magazine runs a piece on the growing survivalist industry in the United States, with redoubts and nuke-suits, special shelter diets and training for sharpshooters. Eric Willcock, Emergency Planning Officer for the West Midlands, is interviewed in his £43,000 ($80,000) bunker, in the hypothetical situation that he will have about a week's warning before he has to occupy it, together with his thirteen-man team and up to 200 local council employees. Life after the bomb will be completely different . . . different rules will apply . . . people worry about looters, 'But how do you distinguish between looting and scrounging . . . I would be inclined to pass a law making scrounging legal.' He is better off than most. Although his 'bunker' is only half underground, it does have twenty rooms . . .

The *New Scientist*, architectural magazines, and women's papers alike run articles on which are the best shelters to make or to buy. A magazine called *Protect & Survive Monthly* was launched in 1980 to cater for public interest in civil defence issues. The *Evening News* puts a family underground to see how they would face up to life in a shelter. A *Daily Mail* reporter exposes the boom in bogus shelters – while the same paper's gossip columnist features the 'immensely wealthy son of Lord Cowdray', who has had a shelter built in his new, £250,000 house. His neighbours 'wonder what Pearson knows that they don't'.

Rumours are rife that such-and-such members of the Royal Family, certain tycoons and show-business personalities, have their own nuclear insurance in the form of shelters.

The Home Office, the *Sunday Times* tells us, is inundated with letters from people panicking for advice. The same sort of thing is remembered, almost to precise details, by people who recall 1937–8 . . .

Evacuation

Although there are lonely and underpopulated areas of the British Isles, none of them is far enough from cities or other targets to be certain to avoid all the effects of nuclear war should there be an all-out attack. The density of population in the United Kingdom is more than 550 per square mile; the comparable figure for England alone is over half as much again, 850 per square mile.

The 2 million people, many of them children, who were evacuated in the first months of the Second World War, in a repeated exercise in some future conflict might be little safer at their destinations than their points of departure. The vagaries of fallout flung hither and yon by the wind, render no part of a small, vulnerable country secure.

Such are the arguments for staying put, and they are earnestly advanced by the authorities. It is true, certainly, that the nations which have at their command vast stretches of unoccupied territory are most advanced in their plans to evacuate people from the cities. The Swedes and Norwegians, with a mountainous or lake-bright, heavily wooded wilderness to choose from, have already selected the routes and destinations of their projected urban exodus. The Soviet Union has on average 25 people per square mile – plenty of room exists for the refugee from the city.

But millions of British people live near obvious targets, and they know it. Do they know that they, at least, are *not* safer at home? Moreover, do they know that if they were quickly evacuated a comparatively short distance, say 20 or 30 miles (30 to 50 kilometres), away from target areas and into waiting fallout shelters, their chances of survival would increase many hundreds of times?

The Russians, who remember the removal of entire industrial enterprises, with their staffs and equipment, from the war zones of the Second World War, begin by establishing the zone of possible destruction around a city. Those working in essential industries are to be removed beyond the limit of that zone, but close enough for them to be brought back to their places of work in a daily round trip of up to five hours. Thus factories and services installed in reinforced premises could be manned and operating within a relatively short time.

Those not connected with essential work, or those such as office staff or teachers and students, who have no fixed installations where they must perform their duties, can be sent farther away to places of even greater safety. Thus, at any given moment, there would be in the city only people working one of the two daily shifts at those plants that must be kept running, and just sufficient numbers of municipal employees to maintain the basic services. For a population of this small size, shelters can easily be provided, usually at or very close to their places of work. Russian civil defence planners believe that in an unprotected city where there has been no evacuation, as many as 90 per cent of the inhabitants would be killed in a nuclear attack. However, if there is 'a timely and complete dispersal and evacuation of the population, the losses may be reduced to a few per cent of the total population'.

The United States is also actively reconsidering its evacuation policy. What the Federal Emergency Management Agency's booklet, *In Time of Emergency,* calls the relocation option is the approach that seems, to American authorities, to be suitable for any city with more than 50,000 inhabitants. People will be asked to make their own way to holiday cabins, to boats or the houses of friends or relations in the (supposedly) safe areas. They will be encouraged to seek out mines, tunnels, caves and deserted basements or to use whatever materials come to hand to build expedient shelters. If no such options are available, they will report to whatever reception area Government officials designate. As in Russia, workers in essential industries might be asked to commute from the countryside to plants and factories where shelter will be provided for them in an emergency.

As in Britain, a wartime service, the Emergency Broadcasting System, will have, EMP permitting, a monopoly of the air. Everyone will be warned to keep one ear on a radio throughout the emergency. Above all, no one should court unnecessary danger by returning home until the radio has confirmed it is safe to do so.

As against the optimistic, self-help attitude of America, the French approach seems repressive and authoritarian. In *Savoir pour vivre,* the section on evacuation is headed by the stern injunction, 'Stay where you are'. There are, it points out, only two possibilities for the population at large – either to stay put and use the shelters, or to evacuate. At once, grim memories surface of how French civilians reacted to the German advance nearly half a century ago. 'Don't let yourself panic and rush off in a flight similar to the exodus of 1940,' the book instructs its readers. On the highways, people would be exposed to all the dangers of fallout. 'The Government alone, if it considers it necessary, will give the signal to leave selected towns . . . If evacuation does become necessary, precise instructions will be issued by one of the official services.'

British attitudes to evacuation seem curiously muddled. In the early 1960s, arrangements were made to evacuate the London area and 10 other great centres of population. People were to be sent to Wales, the West Country and the southern counties. It was thought that the operation would take a week, a lengthy time in the circumstances.

The timetables governing this dispersal still exist; the

same cannot be said for all the railway lines to which they refer. As things stand now, any unplanned spontaneous public evacuation would be by road. It is unlikely that the congestion this would cause would be welcomed by a Government and a general staff preparing for war. This is probably the principal reason for the Government's 'stay put' policy.

But rapid evacuation, even of a city the size of London, is certainly still possible by train. Graham M. Stathers, a cartographer and member of the Royal Institute for Defence Studies, has demonstrated, using standard train timetables, that, even if road transport were 'frozen', the population of London could be moved to safer areas in less than two days.

And sensible solutions exist to the problem of sheltering a quickly dispersed population. For example the distinguished architect, Richard Burton, in a paper delivered in 1981, to a conference called 'The Survival of the Nation' suggested a plan for 'expedient cities':

> In my view it is worth looking at a pre-attack 'limited evacuation' policy. By 'limited' evacuation I mean that those in the central areas of our most vulnerable cities, and those near obvious strategic targets, would be moved to the nearest area considered likely to be *relatively* free from blast and fire effects, leaving a proportion of city dwellers behind to administer the cities.
>
> Thus, I am speaking of large amounts of people being moved a short distance to safe areas and being protected from fallout and minor blast effects in expedient shelters. For instance, the limit of the evacuation for those in northern London might well be the green belt to the north. Those left behind, perhaps 10 per cent of the city population, would need protection to a high degree mainly in converted existing underground structures and in properly adapted basements of buildings made ready for such an eventuality.
>
> The great advantage of such a policy design is that it can respond to both scenarios; that of total city destruction, or, destruction only of strategic targets. It

also can be achieved in a relatively cost effective way.

I call the areas designated suitable for the reception of evacuees 'Expedient Cities'. Like any complex operation, if it is to succeed, an Expedient City programme requires detailed planning, training and much advance preparatory work, however it does not require vast expensive building works immediately. The organisation, logistics, stocks of materials and life support systems, however, would all have to be *pre-arranged* in-situ.

Clearly, evacuation needs careful planning and trained people to supervise it.

Devon – one of the recipient counties in the original government plan – certainly expects refugees from the cities and has designated reception centres where some kind of welfare and accommodation will be offered. Yet, as things stand now, these are most likely to be unofficial evacuees, people who, far from having been moved in an orderly fashion and under supervision, will have cluttered the roads in a panic-stricken rush, probably with no fixed destination in mind. Thus it appears that some segments of Britain's fragmented civil defence system are laying plans in the absence of any national planning.

But, despite its 'stay put' policy, the Government does have a plan for moving between 9 and 10 million priority cases some 18 miles (30 kilometres) from dangerous city centres and inner suburbs where they normally live. In this plan almost all of those involved will be mothers with babies or school-age children, though there are no special sheltering facilities envisaged. The evacuees will be billeted in ordinary homes. Neither is there any intention of creating a class of essential worker-commuters to maintain industrial production, as foreseen by both Americans and Russians. Nor is it clear what is to happen to the men who are left behind. Presumably they are intended to accept incineration sustained by the knowledge that their families are safe. It is just as likely, of course, that they will prefer to express their affection for wives and offspring by following them to the country. Unless the Government actually forbids civilian travel such personal decisions to leave target cities will have much to recommend them. But, whether one evacuates or not, *a fallout shelter and a radiation meter will become the essential adjuncts of survival.*

Planning Requirements for Public Shelters

In Switzerland, people will go to shelter as soon as a war situation appears critical. Swiss communal shelters that are both blast and fallout proof are therefore built very close to those needing protection. It is the people of cities – who are at most immediate risk – who need such communal shelters. And in cities, there will be stragglers seeking cover during that strange interval between explosion and fallout. In the vicinity of the explosions, initial fallout will start to come down after about thirty minutes. Depending on wind, natural features and so on, the farther away you are the longer it takes to reach you. The Swiss, realising this, have installed close-circuit television in their most recent shelters, so that those controlling the entrances can recognise latecomers and let them in.

The adventures of a minority in the city will be the norm for country dwellers. Such shelters as may be publicly provided in rural areas must take account of the fact that most of those likely to use them live too far away to reach them before the missiles have hit their targets. It is also true, of course, that in these areas there are likely to be few targets for enemy missiles (though the farmers and villagers of an East Anglia studded with British and American military installations might – like the wheat growers of the American mid-West and the people of Russian Central Asia – think themselves at some risk in a nuclear war). The main danger that most of those living far from cities will face is likely to be that from airborne, radioactive residues from explosions elsewhere. For them, therefore, especially where great peasant populations are scattered over vast distances, as in the USSR, protection will be mainly in the form of fallout, rather than blast/fallout, shelters, which are more expensive.

An early decision that planners in all countries must take is how big a communal shelter should be – that is, how much space there should be per person and how that space should be allocated. Yugoslav experts have defined the areas of a public shelter as:

a) Traffic rooms – entrances and exits, including those for emergencies, and their associated vestibules and airlocks.

b) Service rooms – lavatories, store rooms, and the ventilation room with its standby generator. filter units, etc.

c) Common rooms – sleeping, sitting and eating areas.

Once the calculations are made – and they must take account of everything including water tanks and whatever space is devoted to treating faecal matter – the Yugoslav conclusion is that there should be about 9 square feet (0·84 square metres) allocated per person. This figure seems to be confirmed by the results of eighty-two studies made on the subject in the United States. R.L. Garrett of the Defense Civil Preparedness Agency reported that many of the 7,000 people who spent thousands of man-hours in shelters, provided with only the barest necessities, were able to manage for two weeks and more in areas that allowed each of them on average between 8 and 10 square feet (about 1 square metre). To go below this minimum figure risks the creation of tensions, hostilities and psychological strain among shelter occupants, no very important matter perhaps if they must remain together for only a few hours, but of significance if they must, as is widely anticipated, stay under cover for two weeks or more.

The wide range of resources, in money, manpower and authority available to governments lays on them the responsibility for providing the larger communal shelters. The organisation necessary is formidable and the specifications are stringent and expensive to meet. Both are usually beyond the capacity of even a most co-operative group of individuals – though this certainly does not mean that people living or working on the same premises must resign themselves to the impossibility of collective action. There is a great deal that can be done by united effort other than through heavy financial expenditure. With the well-co-ordinated help of a shelter specialist, local self-built communal shelters are certainly feasible.

Peter Laurie in *Beneath the City Streets* (op. cit.) makes the cogent point that 'although the weapon that demolishes a house may vary enormously in size and range, the weight of a house remains the same', from which the conclusion may be drawn that when the collapse of buildings is the main danger, quite flimsy shelter can provide protection. In the aerial bombardments of the Second World War, there was a very wide difference between the damage done to a property and the numbers of civilians killed in that same property. Only when, as in Hamburg, incendiary bombs kindled a firestorm or, as in Dresden, a city was packed with refugees, did the casualty figures rise to distressing proportions. Even in the circumstances of a nuclear attack, *to take cover under the stairs may save your life* – certainly this is likely to be so at distances of 6 miles (4 kilometres) and more from ground zero, assuming a 1MT burst.

Hasty last-minute measures of this kind, however, are not the best. Forward planning and preparation will save more lives. For this, the individual must take responsibility, organising his or her home or garden in the knowledge that a corner of it might one day become a refuge.

The increase in international tension has seen shelter-building expand into a small industry. Some of those who have leaped on this commercial band-waggon have little more to offer than some information on basic building skills and a gift for public relations. The range of shelters on the market runs from the excellent to the ridiculous. The problem for the layman is the lack of reliable guidance for making his choice. There is hardly a nation that has an inspectorate capable of giving official approval to the designs and workmanship of these contractors. Yet such control is not difficult to organise; in Switzerland, where the law demands that everyone must have shelter, the experts of Protection Civile pass the design and layout of the models available. Without official supervision of this sort – and such an absence is the norm in the Western nuclear nations – entire families that think themselves secure may, in an emergency, discover that they are as vulnerable as their improvident neighbours. Others will learn only when they have spent some time in their shelters how essential are such factors as ventilation and sanitation: the structures may certainly protect them, but by themselves cannot supply conditions that are tolerable over periods of several weeks.

In Britain there are some glimmerings of hope for those who may seek authoritative advice on their individual needs. NuPAG (the Nuclear Protection Advisory Group) was set up by a number of distinguished scientists and scholars in early 1980. It researches the whole range of needs for shelters and other forms of protection in case of nuclear war and other disaster, even interesting itself in protection against bacteriological and chemical weapons. Completely independent, and hence subject to no official influence, the Group has assembled specialists in medical, engineering, electronics and social areas involved in planning and executing protection policies. Although all its immediate members are based in Britain, the Group has drawn on the expertise from all the major countries which have specialists in the field. Its members have attended civil defence programmes in Switzerland and elsewhere, amassed data on available instruments, commissioned research into the development of advanced radiation (and other) monitors, and surveyed various parts of the country to ascertain the possibilities of providing protective facilities. Such interest has been aroused in NuPAG's work worldwide that their advice has been sought by concerned people in more than a dozen countries.

The following sections of this book contain the essential information you and your family and friends need to increase your chances of survival dramatically in the event of this country's involvement in another major war. It is presented to fill the vacuum created by the same official negligence that prompted NuPAG into existence.

How You Can Survive the Third World War

HOW TO DECIDE ON A COURSE OF ACTION NOW

Work your way through the following questions until you reach the final selection of alternatives for protection

Ask yourself:

Do I and my dependants want to survive the Third World War?

Yes

No → Pass this book on but don't forget that, even with the worst human tragedies, plague, war, famine, earthquake, etc., t is no evidence that people give up when disaster strikes. However awful their circumstances people want to live. Whe the time actually comes you will too.

Do I want to prepare for survival now?

Yes → Act now. Nuclear war could come sooner rather than later.

No → Study this book carefully then keep it safe so that you can use it if circumstances make you change your mind.

Do I live near a target?

I don't know → Find out

Yes → Can I move away from the target area easily and do I want to?

No

No → Can I build a deep, blast and radiation shelter where I live?

Yes → Move to a target free area. Emigration to a country not likely to be involved in a nuclear exchange could be considered.

Can I build a deep, blast and radiation shelter where I live?

No → Select an evacuation plan

Yes → If you have £10–£20,000 and provided you are a mile away from a 1MT ground zero, or two miles or more away from a 10 MT you stand a chance. But this is risky. You might do better to consider an evacuation alternative and move to it in times of tension.

Select an evacuation plan

This is the best evacuation plan. Pre-arrange with relatives or friends living in a target free zone that you will share their accommodation/shelter if you have to evacuate. Make sure you know of alternative routes to your refuge. You are advised to assist in preparing the shelter and stocking it so you will not be a scrounger. Scroungers risk not being accepted during an emergency. At the very least send money in advance to pay your way.

Plan various evacuation routes in advance. You need more than one because roads may be jammed in times of panic or closed for some reason. Preselect an area that you know to be 'target free'. Be prepared to switch to an alternative 'target free area' in case something goes wrong with your first choice. Take as many provisions as you can. Find a site to make an improvised shelter, or somehow utilise an existing building or structure, and prepare the best protection against radiation possible under the circumstances.

PROTECT AND SURVIVE

To protect yourself, family and friends you must provide adequate shields against the energies released by nuclear weapons.

Ideal protection is provided by a properly constructed, well stocked, underground shelter. This would shield you against all eventualities, except a fireball going off directly overhead. Blast and heat is deflected or withstood and radiation is kept at bay and filtered from the air and water. As many people as possible should make this provision.

There are those for whom building a deep shelter is impossible, usually for reasons of money or space. For these people there are various alternative survival opportunities. If you wish to increase your chances make sure you know what the alternatives are.

Make as many advance preparations as is feasible.

→ Do I want to chance that a stray bomb will not explode near by?

Yes

Build a permanent shelter against radiation. The very nature of such an enterprise means that the shelter will give some protection against blast and heat too.

No → Build a blast and radiation proof shelter.

An ideal shelter, safe, comfortable and large enough for eighteen people, would cost say £1,000–£2,000 a person assuming you have the land to build it on. Call in a reliable contractor.

Are there cheaper alternatives that do not sacrifice safety?

Yes → If you have no land and little money you can start or join a community protection project. There are large economies to be made when more people are involved. For example, thirty people can go through a blast door just as easily as three.

→ You can obtain reasonable degrees of protection but at a considerable reduction in comfort by building a trench shelter. All this will need is tools, waterproof sheeting, etc. and a lot of hard work.

→ You can modify part of your existing property such as a cellar, basement or garage.

→ Get away from the target area and take advantage of improvised community shelters that local councils or other bodies might be organising. Plans for helping evacuees in the Third World War already exist in some counties. Find out about them through Citizens Advice Bureaux.

Information and Survival

The first thing to remember is that *it is possible to survive.* Millions of people will die needlessly, simply because they don't know this. There is no need for you to be one of them.

To survive a nuclear attack you need, in addition to a little luck, basic, accurate information. *Study this and the following sections carefully.* They are a life-saver. They tell you what to do and why. The more you know about what you are up against the better.

This section will help you decide the quality and quantity of advance precautions to take. It sets out the minimum you need to know about weapon effects and offers various courses of action. The choice is yours but the rule to follow is: *the more preparation you make in advance the less luck you and your dependants will need to survive.*

Nuclear Weapons

Any explosive weapon that depends for its power on the energy released by reactions involving atomic nuclei is a nuclear weapon. Atomic bombs and hydrogen bombs are nuclear weapons.

An atom bomb destroyed Hiroshima on August 6th, 1945. It generated a temperature as hot as the sun. There is a limit to the size of atom bombs because of certain physical restrictions arising out of the nature of the fissile material used in them. But there is theoretically no limit to the size of a hydrogen bomb. Hydrogen bombs are triggered by atom bombs. These are the weapons we are principally concerned with. They produce the effects of an atom bomb many times magnified and are the human race's most cost-effective method of wreaking physical destruction.

A neutron bomb is designed primarily for battlefield use. It emits intense initial radiation that can penetrate tank weapons and kill or incapacitate instantly without damaging the tanks. Compared to other nuclear weapons it is a small, 'clean' bomb. Neutron bombs or warheads are not powerful by nuclear standards; severe blast damage is limited to a few hundred yards. There is virtually no secondary radiation.

Nuclear Weapon Effects

The problem, once a nuclear weapon is exploded, is to survive the enormous amount of energy it releases. The energy is divided into four main forms:

1. Initial radiation – prompt radiation from the fireball of the explosion
2. Heat radiation
3. Blast
4. Residual radiation – from radioactive fallout.

Heat radiation 35 per cent Blast 45 per cent

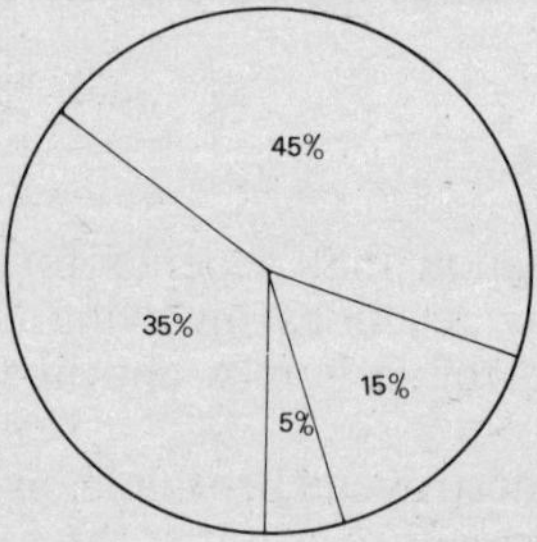

Initial radiation 5 per cent Residual radiation 15 per cent

Figure 1. The approximate distribution of energy from a typical 'air-burst' nuclear explosion.

Light

When a bomb explodes there is a brilliant flash of light. If you are unlucky enough to be looking in that direction at the time of the explosion you will be temporarily blinded for minutes, hours or days. It can affect you even 100 miles (160 kilometres) away. Explosions are, therefore, more dangerous at night when the eyes' pupils are wide open.

Initial Radiation

Immediate radiation is lethal. But it kills inadequately shielded persons only within a limited radius of the source of the explosion. For large nuclear explosions this radius is within the circular area of intense heat and blast. Deep shelters are designed with enough mass above them to absorb initial radiation.

Figure 2. Showing how far initial radiation penetrates through the atmosphere from differing bomb yields measured in Roentgens (a milliroentgen is one-thousandth of a Roentgen).

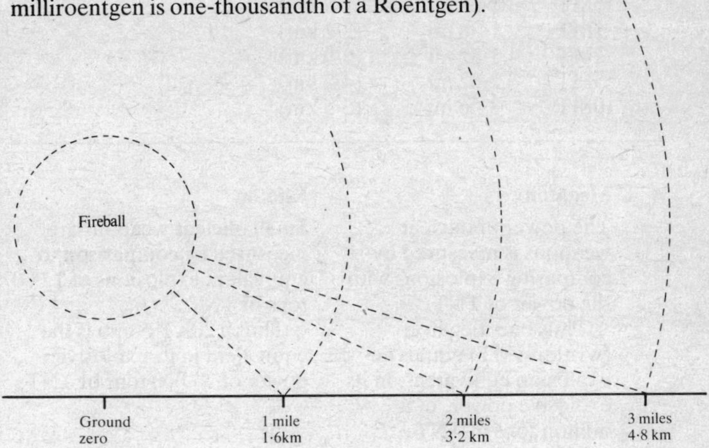

	Ground zero	1 mile 1·6km	2 miles 3·2 km	3 miles 4·8 km
20 KT		160 r	200 mr	0·6 mr
500 KT		8,000 r	10 r	30·0 mr
1 MT		16,800 r	21 r	63·0 mr
10 MT		400,000 r	500 r	1·5 r

The Fireball

Exploding a nuclear weapon instantly creates a fireball. Only persons in excellent blast shelters near the outside radius of the fireball can survive. For a few seconds the centre of the fireball is as hot as the centre of the sun. It rapidly expands, vaporising everything in its path, creating a wave of very hot, highly compressed air. This rapidly expanding 'wall' of hot, pressurised air is the blast wave. It takes 10 seconds for a 1MT fireball to reach its maximum diameter of approximately 1·4 miles (2·24km). The fireball rises at an initial speed of more than 250 mph (400 kph).

The point on the ground nearest the fireball is known as *ground zero.* If the fireball touches the ground it pulverises and sweeps up vast quantities of dirt, rock, and débris, forming the famous mushroom cloud.

Table I: showing the diameter of air-burst fireballs from different bomb yields.

½MT	1·04 mi	(1·6 km)
1MT	1·38 mi	(2·2 km)
2MT	1·82 mi	(2·9 km)
5MT	2·62 mi	(4·2 km)
10MT	3·46 mi	(5·5 km)

■ **Megaton**

The power of nuclear weapons is measured by comparing explosions with the power of TNT.

Thus one megaton (written 1MT) equals an explosion equivalent, in its explosive power, of a million tons of TNT.

5MT = 5 million tons of TNT

½MT = 500,000 tons of TNT

Kiloton

Small nuclear weapons are measured by comparison to equivalent explosions of 1,000 tons of TNT.

Thus a 20KT bomb is the equivalent in its explosive power of 20,000 tons of TNT.

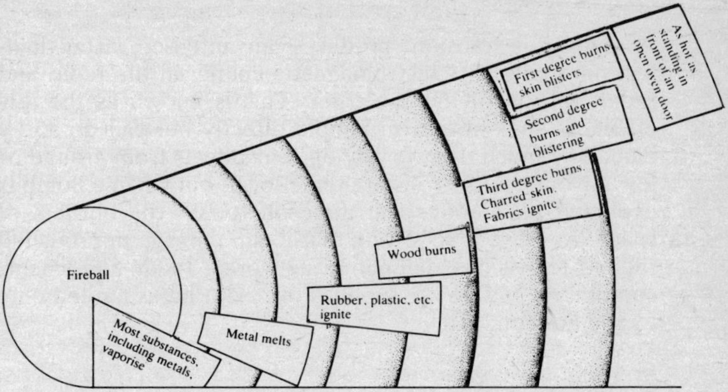

20 KT*	1,107 ft 337 m	1,566 ft 477 m	2,215 ft 675 m	3,132 ft 954 m	4,430 ft 1·3 km	1·2 mi 1·9 km	1·7 mi 2·7 km	2·2 mi 3·5 km	3·8 mi 6·1 km
500 KT	1 mi 1·6 km	1·4 mi 2·2 km	2 mi 3·2 km	2·8 mi 4·5 km	3·9 mi 6·2 km	5·5 mi 8·8 km	8·5 mi 13·6 km	10·5 mi 16·8 km	18·5 mi 29·7 km
1 MT	1·5 mi 2·4 km	2 mi 3·2 km	2·8 mi 4·5 km	3·9 mi 6·2 km	5·9 mi 9·4 km	8·3 mi 13·3 km	10·7 mi 17·2 km	15 mi 24·1 km	25 mi 40·2 km
10 MT	4·3 mi 6·9 km	6 mi 9·6 km	8·5 mi 13·6 km	11·9 mi 19·1 km	16 mi 25·7 km	24·5 mi 39·4 km	33 mi 53 km	46 mi 74 km	80 mi 128·7 km

*The Nagasaki bomb used 20 KT.

Figure 3. Approximate effects of heat at different distances from the fireball.

Heat Radiation

Tremendous heat travels at almost the speed of light, in a direct line away from the fireball. Readily ignitable materials that are exposed and in its direct path will flare up or be charred, out to distances somewhat greater than those of serious blast damage. Exposed skin is also burnt. Because the heat is delivered in a short pulse *it is survivable if you are not too close to the source and if you are shielded.*

Figure 3 above shows the approximate effect of the heat at different distances from the fireball, depending on the size of the bomb.

Electromagnetic Pulse

A nuclear explosion produces an intense, faster-than-lightning pulse of electromagnetic energy in the radio and radar portion of the spectrum. This is known as the EMP effect. It does not harm people directly but can do so by damaging much that we rely on. EMP effects from ground or low air-burst explosions are quite local, but when a bomb is exploded high above the atmosphere, on the borders of space, its pulse is so strong that it can damage unprotected radios, televisions, telephone networks, radar equipment, computers, and power supplies over vast areas limited only by the horizon.

Radiation

A nuclear explosion instantly creates large quantities of nuclear radiation. This radiation comes in various forms but abnormal amounts of any radiation break the electrical connections between the molecules in living cells. This damages the cells or stops them from functioning. Fortunately most cells can in time recover from this damage, if the radiation has not been too severe. If you receive more radiation than a critical number of your cells can recover from, however, you will die. It is not possible to detect radiation by means of the human senses.

■ The Measurement of Radiation

The original measure of radiation was the Roentgen (R), named after the discoverer of X-rays, and was based on the absorption of X-ray energy in the air. It offered only indirect guidance on the more important question of how much radiation entered into, and was absorbed by, living tissue and so a new measure, the *radiation absorbed dose* or RAD was established. However, the simple absorption of radiation in biological tissue was found to be insufficiently discriminating as a measure of potential damage, since differing forms of radiation have differing effects. The RAD was therefore multiplied by a 'quality factor' which was a direct reflection of each such variation. The result was that the virulence of alpha rays, for example, which cause ten times as much biological damage as do the less malevolent gamma rays (though both are short-lasting), now became an integral part of the new measure. This, to localise it, was termed *Roentgen equivalent mammal,* or REM. There are minor refinements to give this even greater precision, but the REM is the most accurate widely used unit for measuring the amounts of dangerous radiation that a person may have received or been exposed to. Nevertheless, all three kinds of calibration remain in use and, for practical, general calculations, any may be employed.

Initial Radiation

If you are exposed close enough to receive a lethal dose of the intense initial radiation you may be killed instantaneously by the combined effects of the explosion. But the range of initial radiation is limited (see Figure 2). If the bomb is 'small', Hiroshima-sized, for example, you might survive the heat and blast but still receive serious or fatal doses of initial radiation. Most radiation victims of the Japanese bombs suffered from initial radiation – not fallout radiation. There are large numbers of such small weapons in the arsenals of nuclear powers today. Initial radiation is also a hazard to people in shelters close to ground zero because the blizzard of neutron and gamma radiation can penetrate deep into soil. People in very good shelters about a mile from ground zero of a large bomb may survive all the other bomb effects only to succumb to this invisible one.

The long-term problem caused by initial radiation is that nuclear explosions, on or near the surface, shoot neutrons some depth into the soil around ground zero, inducing long-lasting radioactivity. After a nuclear war such areas would need to be marked out and avoided until the level of radiation declined to an acceptable amount.

Residual Radiation (known as radioactive fallout)

This is the radioactive mixture formed by the vaporised and pulverised dust and débris that is swept up with the rising, radiation-emitting, fireball. As the deadly mixture cools it solidifies into large grains, small grains, and powders. Snowflake-like particles are also formed from surface bursts on rocks such as limestone. Unvaporised particles of many

Figure 4.

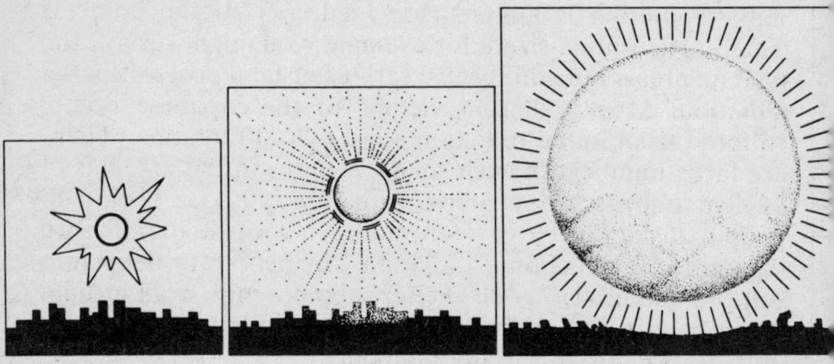

(i) Light (ii) Initial radiation (iii) The fireball

sizes are contaminated by the radioactive elements produced by the explosion. All this becomes the fallout.

The winds that rush in and up, following the vacuum caused by the fireball, transport these particles and form the famous 'mushroom' cloud. The clouds of radiated particles are then affected by the prevailing winds which disperse the fallout. If there is a heavy cloud layer at the time of the explosion, or the fireball sucks up a quantity of water, fallout will descend with the rain. The danger comes as the radioactive dust and débris reach the ground.

Radioactive fallout is deadly for the first few days after an explosion. If it is swallowed, inhaled or absorbed through open wounds the radioactive beta and alpha particles

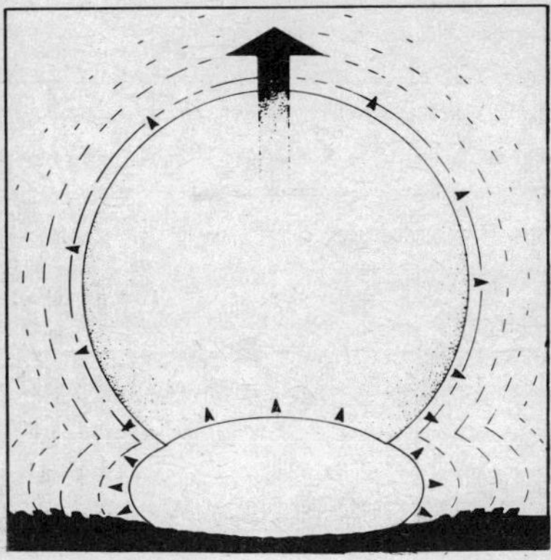

(iv) The blast

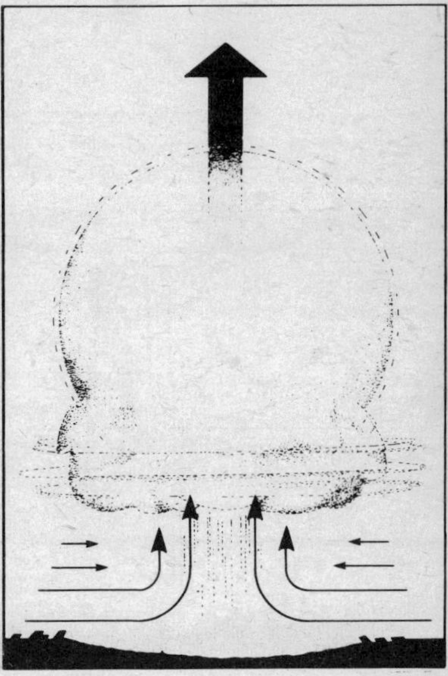

(v) Fireball rises. Winds rush in to fill the vacuum.

interact with living cells inside the body, doing enormous damage. But each form of radiation has different characteristics. Alpha radiation, for example, does little damage from the outside, being unable even to penetrate skin; but once alpha-emitting particles are inside the body, alpha radiation is very destructive. Beta radiation is harmful to the inside and outside of the body, where it causes severe beta burns if left on or close to the skin. Gamma radiation can penetrate some distance through substances and travel right through humans, leaving a trail of malfunctioning and dying cells.

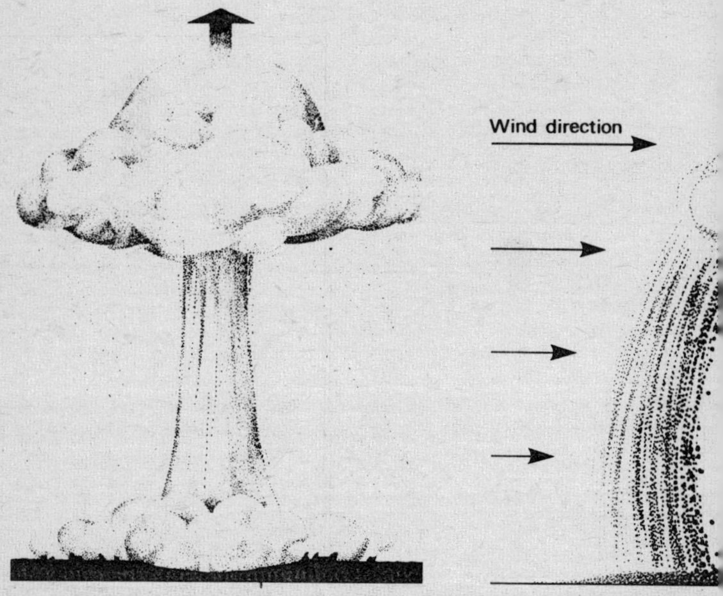

(vi) Mushroom cloud forming.
Fireball diminishes.

Radiation decays quite rapidly, however, and within a week or two reaches levels that humans can tolerate, at least for short periods, while outdoors (see pages 180–91).

Blast

Travelling at about the speed of sound, much more slowly than the heat radiation, is a shock wave. This, and the following blast winds, do enormous damage. The larger the

(vii) Radioactive fallout affected by wind.

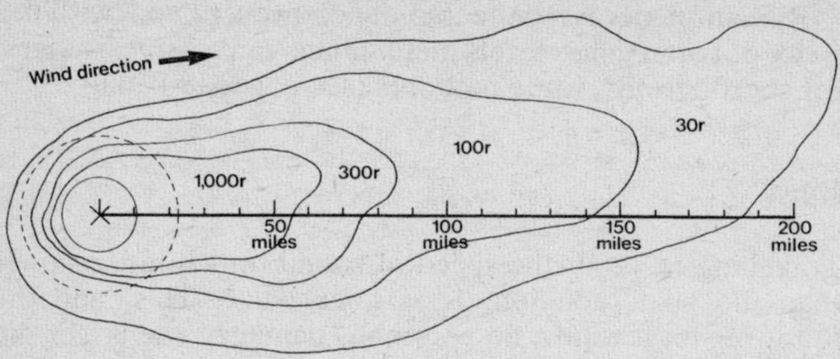

Figure 5. Diagram comparing typical spread of the various weapon effects from a 1MT ground burst. The cross marks ground zero. The inner circle defines the spread of blast damage. The dotted circle shows the range of serious heat effects. The contours show the total accumulated radiation dose on unprotected people in the first eighteen hours after the explosion.

explosion the more damage, not because the pressure at any one point is greater, but because the blast winds last much longer.

The shock wave is created by the pressure front of an expanding wall of highly compressed hot air radiating from the enormous energies unleashed by the detonation. When a shock wave from an air burst warhead or bomb hits the earth it is reflected back up into other parts of itself. This results in its progression being not so even as the emission of heat from the explosion. The tangled forces it unleashes are equivalent to a major earthquake, but are damaging over a smaller area.

Near the explosion the blast winds blow at velocities that initially peak at thousands of miles per hour. At distances from the explosion where the peak blast wind velocities are about 1,000 mph (1,600 kph), good blast shelters are undamaged by the combined blast effects. Where the blast winds peak at hurricane velocities, 75 to 150 mph (120 to 240 kph), homes are badly damaged or destroyed by the shock wave and blast winds.

The blast wave from a 1MT bomb takes about 15 seconds to extend 4 miles (6 kilometres) from the source of the

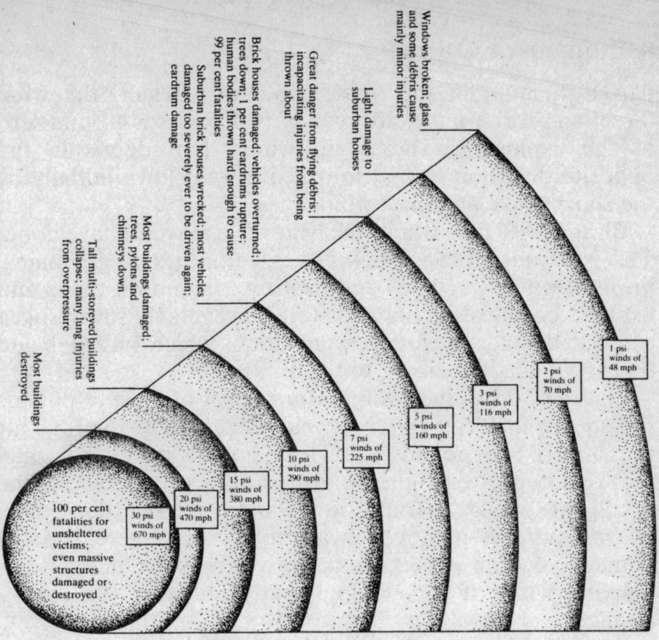

Size of bomb	Distance of blast effects from air burst bombs in miles and kilometres								
20 KT*	2098 ft 639 m	2533 ft 772 m	2894 ft 882 m	3619 ft 1·1 km	4523 ft 1·3 km	1 mi 1·6 km	1·3 mi 2 km	1·6 mi 2·5 km	2·7 mi 4·3 km
500 KT	1·1 mi 1·7 km	1·4 mi 2·2 km	1·6 mi 2·5 km	2 mi 3·2 km	2·5 mi 4 km	3 mi 4·8 km	3·8 mi 6·1 km	4·7 mi 7·5 km	8 mi 12·8 km
1 MT	1·4 mi 2·2 km	1·8 mi 2·8 km	2 mi 3·2 km	2·5 mi 4 km	3·1 mi 4·9 km	3·8 mi 6·1 km	4·8 mi 7·7 km	5·9 mi 9·4 km	10 mi 16 km
10 MT	3·1 mi 4·9 km	3·8 mi 6·1 km	4·3 mi 6·9 km	5·4 mi 8·6 km	6·8 mi 10·9 km	8·2 mi 13·1 km	10·3 mi 16·5 km	12·8 mi 20·5 km	21·7 mi 34·9 km

*The Nagasaki bomb was 20 KT

Figure 6. The effect of overpressure blast over normal air pressure.

explosion; 4 miles (6 kilometres) from ground zero of a surface burst houses will be badly damaged and possibly ignited but occupants of a properly constructed earth shelter would not be injured. For a 10MT bomb to travel 4 miles (6 kilometres) it takes slightly less than fifteen seconds. The blast wave from a 1MT takes one minute to travel 14 miles (22 kilometres) and from a 10MT bomb extends 15 miles (24 kilometres) in one minute.

The fireball rises and draws air up behind it, creating a

partial vacuum in the blast area. As a result, the wind direction reverses: the 'afterwinds' rush towards ground zero of the explosion. These 'afterwinds' hurl débris in the opposite direction to that in which it was blown initially by the shock wave and blast wind.

Blast causes fires where the heat wave may not have done. This is because it can wreck stoves, furnaces and gas mains, bring down power lines and destroy gas and oil tanks and explode chemical plants and stores. Extremely severe blast can also damage nuclear power stations which may then add their own deadly poisons to the atmosphere.

Figure 6 shows the overpressure effect of blast in pounds per square inch (psi) over normal air pressure. (Normal air pressure is 14½ pounds psi. Three pounds psi over normal air pressure, for example, is written 3 psi.) It also shows the speed of winds in mph in relation to the decreasing overpressure as it moves away from ground zero and the damage you can expect from the overpressure and accompanying winds if the bomb is exploded near the earth's surface.

Blast shock waves from test nuclear explosions had the disconcerting tendency of passing into the upper atmosphere, whence they were refracted and refocused earthwards. Several minutes later, 200 or 300 miles (320 to 480 kilometres) away, the shock wave reappeared and was strong enough to break windows.

This additional hazard means that you might be hit by minor blast effects during a nuclear war wherever you are, and no one can predict the tumult that large numbers of explosions would cause as blast waves collide, rebound from the upper atmosphere and return to earth.

Ground Burst

A ground burst is a nuclear explosion sufficiently near the ground for its fireball to touch the ground and the heated air to rise and lift up pulverised earth and débris. If a bomb goes off on the ground, or just above, the fireball gouges out a crater. When this happens the sides of the crater deflect the blast and heat upwards. This reduces the blast damage done, but even more material is lifted up to be contaminated and thus to become fallout. This is a 'dirty' bomb. Maximum combined blast and fallout damage is done by a bomb that explodes low enough to lift up considerable amounts of surface material but not so low as to form a crater with sides steep enough to deflect the blast energy upwards.

Air Burst

An air burst is a detonation that occurs too high for the fireball to touch the ground and lift up material from the surface. Consequently there is virtually no dangerous local (twenty-four hour) fallout problem with an air burst – unless rain brings down the small quantities of intensely radioactive atoms produced by the nuclear explosion and of contaminated, radiated powder, which is all that remains of the missile and its warhead, or of the bomb. However, blast from an air burst can cause damage on the earth's surface over approximately twice as large an area as from a ground burst of equal power.

Water Burst

When the fireball touches or explodes in water it carries up into the atmosphere vaporised water and, perhaps, mud and sand; this condenses and falls as radioactive rain. This rain tends not to travel as far as 'dry' radioactive fallout, so the pattern of fallout is denser and therefore more intense and dangerous. Wet fallout is harder to remove than dry because it can soak into the earth, and any nook and cranny, just as ordinary rain does.

■ Firestorm

A firestorm is a huge stationary fire that occurs in built-up urban areas where the heat of the conflagration causes a strong and steady inrush of winds from all sides, feeding it with oxygen. The oxygen maintains the fire's intensity for a long period.

There is a myth that a nuclear attack would set practically everything on fire, causing firestorms. It is claimed that the occupants of shelters would all be killed by the intense heat. The fact is that firestorms occur only where there is a high concentration of combustible structures. Such areas are rare in modern towns. At rural and suburban densities most people in earth-covered shelters would have nothing to fear from fire. The answer to the firestorm problem is to not build a shelter in an area likely to suffer.

Long-lasting smouldering fires in ruined buildings above basement or cellar shelters are a more serious hazard because of the carbon monoxide produced by the fire. If shelter occupants are unlucky enough to have a fire start above them while fallout radiation outside prevents them from leaving, they should close all ventilation openings and wait. Open them again when the level of carbon dioxide from the occupants' breathing in the shelter is high enough to put a match out (usually between four and seven hours). In most cases the fire should no longer be dangerous.

Possible Nuclear Targets in Britain

Important: The map is shown to give some idea of the extent of the target problem, and to demonstrate that there are areas of the United Kingdom relatively free of targets. Each individual must attempt to determine his or her nearest targets. But do not rely on this map. It does *not* necessarily show all targets. Some may be out of date. There may be others, not shown, which are unknown to civilians although known to an enemy.

The black dots represent possible targets. These are mainly military and governmental centres. If you are very close to any of these targets, and it is bombed accurately, you will not survive. And in the vicinity you risk being killed

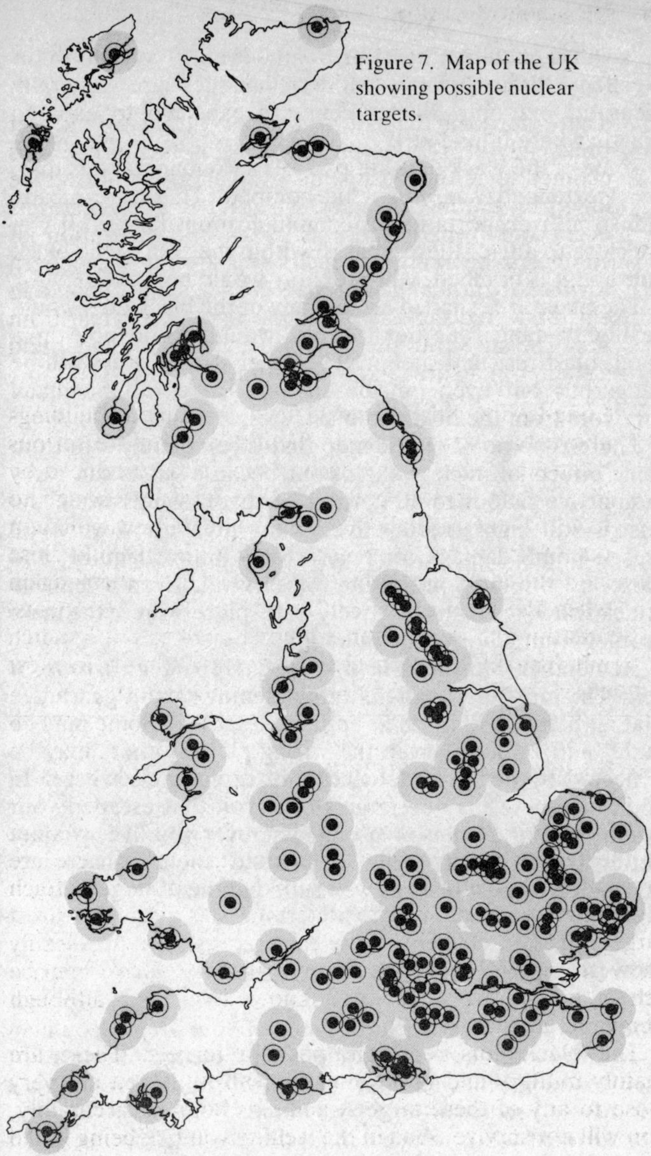

Figure 7. Map of the UK showing possible nuclear targets.

by an inaccurate warhead or bomb, even if you are in an excellent blast shelter. (Modern missiles are generally accurate, but only 70 per cent are expected to explode exactly where intended.)

Some of the black dots are possible secondary targets that, in an extended war, might be bombed. These are mostly industrial, transportation or communications targets. If you are close to any of these, that is, within the area of the black dot, and it is bombed, you probably would not survive.

The inner area shaded around any of the black dots would be highly dangerous but survival would be possible in a good, blast-resistant shelter. The outer shaded areas will be dangerous but even outside shelters there will be many survivors from the heat and blast.

There is no point on the map that is completely safe from some effects of nuclear explosions because winds can carry radioactive fallout to all corners of these islands while the dust is still highly radioactive. Many areas, however, will escape bomb damage, or receive only minor damage, and these are the most promising for survival. Even a massive attack will leave many relatively 'safe' places where the main problem, initially, will be radiation.

Remember Murphy's law: *if anything can go wrong, it will.* The most thorough military planning cannot guarantee that all bombs will hit their appointed targets. Some may be faulty and come down in the wrong place. Others may be deflected by our own defences and explode elsewhere. In addition, there may be targets near you that escaped your attention. For all these reasons, wherever you live, you are better off in a properly constructed shelter that gives protection against blast as well as radiation.

How to Locate Targets in Your Area

You need an Ordnance Survey map of your area. (You may need two or three if your home is on the edge of one.) Pin this up and spin circles of 10 and 20 miles' (16 and 32 kilometres') radius around your home.

Your next job is to mark in all the possible targets. Each

time you identify a target stick a little red circle on it. Principal targets are military establishments, especially American (of which there are over 100), naval dockyards, military and civilian airfields, central and regional government headquarters and industrial centres. Some targets are obvious; others are not well publicised or are secret.

Fill in the 10-mile (16-kilometre) circle first. If you have any targets in that circle, you should consider (1) moving (2) evacuation plans for times of tension (3) preparing a deep, blast and radiation proof shelter. The first of these choices is the best and the last is the most risky, especially if there are several targets in the area.

If you are satisfied that there are no targets within 10 miles (16 kilometres), start on the larger circle. If you locate a target here, especially at the outer limits of the circle, you still face the above three options but you would be safe in a good shelter if the bombs were on target.

Sources of Information About Targets

Approach local libraries, local newspaper offices, maps, estate agents, your town hall – ask about their plans for the eventuality of war; the planning department may have information on local government building activity, etc. (military building is exempt from planning regulations so may not be included). The CND produce very good target maps.

Talk to policemen, government officials, Emergency Planning Officers. Above all, use your eyes. Look for strange buildings with blast barriers round them, such as banks of earth or solid concrete walls. Unusual aerials sometimes denote underground communications systems. Unidentified top security areas are suspect.

When you locate a target, measure just how far it is, in a straight line, from your home. Study Figures 3 and 6 on pages 77 and 85 showing the area of damage caused by heat and blast to assess the effects you are likely to suffer from 1MT and 10MT bombs. Then decide on one of the courses of action listed on pages 70–1.

Evacuation

Obviously evacuation is risky: if you are exposed when bombing starts survival chances will be minimal. Nevertheless, if you live near a target, you are best advised to evacuate to a less vulnerable part of the country. At the time of writing it is not Government policy to encourage evacuation though, in the face of sustained expert criticism, the official 'stay-put' policy is being reviewed. If Government evacuation plans are not ready or practicable you must make yourself responsible for your family's or community's evacuation.

The best alternative is to arrange shelter in advance with friends or relatives who live in a target-free zone. This assures you of a welcome when you arrive.

Plan a route to your chosen refuge area. This must avoid those roads the Government plans to close in the build-up period to an attack. (The *New Statesman* publishes a map showing the roads to be closed.)

If you don't have a pre-arranged shelter to go to, buy large-scale maps of target-free zones now. Study them and keep them handy. Plan in advance a course of action. Familiarise yourself with the area where you intend to seek refuge because, if the day comes, that is where you must find, or construct, a radiation shelter of your own. Ideally it should be at least 20 miles (32 kilometres) away from the nearest target.

What to Pack

Prepare a list now of what you should take if you are forced to evacuate.

In times of international tension, check that you have those items in your home ready to gather quickly together.

Break the list into categories. It is much easier to keep a clear head when you have to move fast if you compartmentalise what you have to do. You can also allocate the packing of different categories to different people to speed up the process. Remember, you may not have much time. Before a crisis occurs you should decide which of the desirable items in each category you will need most and will be able to take with you.

Category One : Information

Maps, shelter-building plans, survival books including this and *Nuclear War Survival Skills* by Cresson H. Kearny (National Technical Information Service, Oakridge Laboratories, USA, 1979). One battery-powered radio or more, and spare batteries (the best type of radio for withstanding EMP effects is a small battery-powered radio that can be operated without an external antenna – wrap it thoroughly in layers of foil and keep it in a metal box); a dosimeter per person and a survey meter for reading radiation dose-rate levels (see pages 180–5 for details of these).

Category Two : Tools

Tools that would be most useful for digging and building the type of shelter you plan; include tough working gloves to protect hands not used to physical labour. Don't forget nails, screws, wire, string and rope.

Category Three : Materials

Take any materials that you may not find easily at your destination: plastic sheets, large plastic bags for filling with earth, a ventilation pump (homemade if necessary, see page 150), etc.

Category Four : Water

Containers, buckets, plastic bags, plastic bottles, water purifying chemicals and a spoon for measuring them, a hosepipe and clean funnel.

Category Five : Valuables

Documents, deeds, passports, cheque book, etc.

Category Six : Light

Flashlights, candles, materials for improvising lamps: plastic containers, string for wick, cooking oil for lamp fuel; matches in waterproof containers, firelighters.

Category Seven : Clothing

Including rainwear, boots, overshoes, spare socks, jerseys – remembering that clothes for seasons not yet arrived may be unobtainable after the emergency is over. Take plenty of work clothes and those clothes that are difficult to make.

Category Eight : Bedding

Sleeping bags, blankets and sheets (sheets have many uses).

Category Nine : Food

Take as many 'compact' foods as you can pack. Also powdered milk for babies, cooking oil, sugar, salt, vitamin pills; tin openers, cutlery, bowls, plates, cups, cooking pots and pans, foil. Take stoves and the means for making stoves (see pages 161–3 for details of these).

Figure 8. Categories of equipment to gather in event of evacuation.

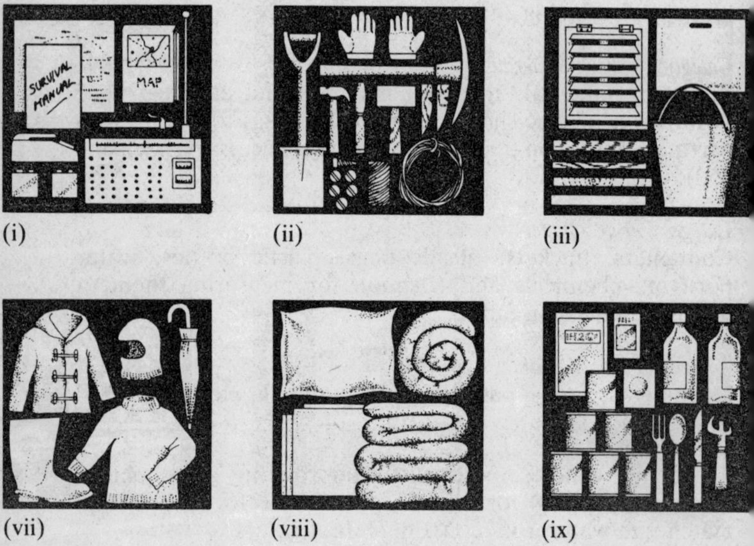

Category Ten : Sanitation
Bucket for urine, plastic bags for excrement, personal hygiene items, towels, flannels, soap, toilet paper, detergents.

Category Eleven : Medicine Chest
First aid kit, aspirin, antibiotics, disinfectants, insect repellent. Take stocks of potassium iodide, which protects against radioactive iodine. Include useful books such as *How To Be Your Own Doctor* (*Sometimes*) by K.W. Sehnert (Grosset & Dunlop, USA) or *The Emergency Medical Guide* by Dr. J. Henderson (McGraw-Hill).

Category Twelve : Miscellaneous
Things that are important to you; books, games, etc.

(iv)

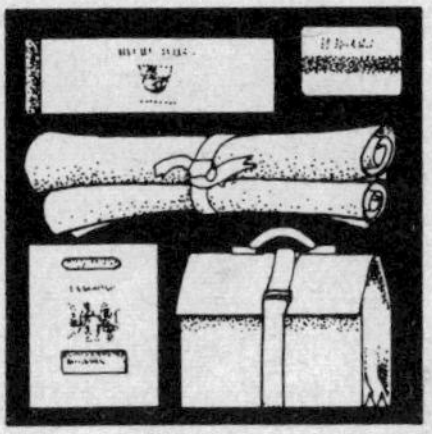
(v)

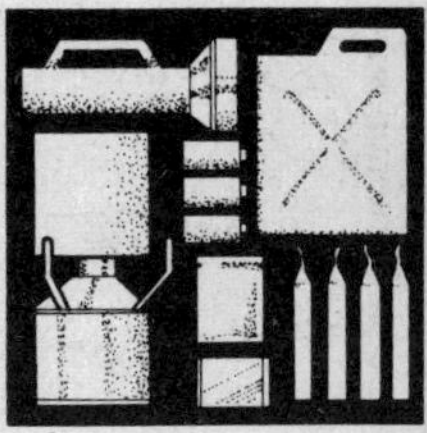
(vi)

(x)

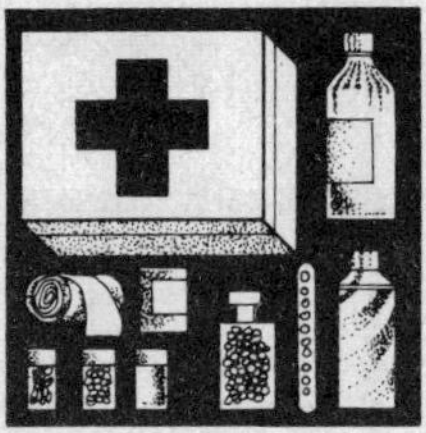
(xi)

(xii)

Departure

Before leaving, make your home secure. Lock doors and windows, hide any remaining valuables. Turn off water, gas and electricity. With luck you may be able to return. If time allows, whitewash windows to deflect heat and remove curtains that a thermal pulse coming through the glass may ignite.

Travel

If there is a family or group of you, you will need more than one vehicle to carry essential items. Move in a convoy for protection. What you have gathered together will, with luck, save your lives. Don't let anyone take it from you. Keep on the move until you arrive at your chosen destination.

Listen to car radios at all times. You may hear vital information about bombings that would necessitate a change of route. Many roads may be jammed. You may see signs of panic. Keep calm and use your maps. There is always more than one route to any place. Seek out alternatives.

Arrival

Don't head into wild country, thinking you will be safest there. Building a shelter and finding food, water and materials will be that much harder in the open countryside. Taking to the wilds should be your last resort.

If no pre-arranged shelter is waiting for you, try to obtain permission to construct a shelter in part of an existing building. Small towns and villages offer buildings, or parts of buildings, that can be upgraded to provide shelter from radiation much more easily than starting from scratch in a field. Consider building a trench shelter (see page 108), which gives excellent protection but is cramped, if in your judgment you have enough time to complete it.

Do everything to be friendly towards the population you descend upon and, with luck, they will help you. You may be able to advise them in return. For example, if they have no fallout meter and don't know how to combat the fallout hazard, you could help them with yours and show them how to upgrade buildings to shield them from radiaton.

Don't take people's willingness to accept you for granted. They will be under stress too. If you force yourself on a reluctant resident you could become the focus of his anger when things get worse. Anger can turn into violence in times of crisis.

This is why it is sensible to make yourself known, in your chosen evacuation area, to the local residents long before the need to evacuate arises. Familiar faces are more likely to be tolerated than strange ones.

If you have banded together with a group of families it is advisable to elect a leader, or, if the group is large, a responsible committee. This will produce an inner cohesion and sense of purpose. Leadership should also provide a channel of communication to those local officials whose advice and guidance in the aftermath may prove invaluable. After the outbreak of war many of the essential services will have disappeared, or will shortly cease, so take early steps to improvise or maintain such services. Create the necessary working parties, each with a particular task to perform. These should include:

- Food gathering
- Cooking, feeding and washing dishes
- Providing and maintaining a water supply
- Seeing that order and calm prevail
- Ensuring that there is quiet during sleeping hours
- Keeping the refuge clean
- Providing whatever medical care is possible wherever it is needed
- Assisting the handicapped or injured
- Organising some central support for mothers with small children
- Maintaining a fire and radiation watch
- Guard duty

Once you have found your refuge, don't rest.
Everything possible must be done to keep radiation out.

Shelter

Fallout Shelters

A fallout shelter can be *any space* that provides thick walls and ceilings to absorb the dangerous rays given off by fallout particles. You can pile earth, sand, furniture, almost anything up against or on walls and ceilings to increase protection. Be sure to strengthen roofs or ceilings (by putting in extra columns) if you plan to support 1 foot (30 centimetres) or more of earth. If you are below ground you have only to worry about radiation from above. The longer the route that air has to travel to reach you, the less chance there is of radioactive fallout (which is heavy) reaching you.

Protection Factor

The protection factor (PF) of any shelter is the estimated amount of protection the shelter gives against gamma (fallout type) radiation. For example: a shelter with a PF of 50 means you receive 50 times less radiation than you would if you were unprotected and outside. This means that if, outside the shelter, an accumulated dose of 1,000R built up in a week, inside you would receive a harmless dose of 20R in that time. In areas suffering heavy fallout, a total outside accumulated dose rate of 15,000R, or more, in the few weeks after the explosions would require a PF of at least 100 to keep the shelter's dose down to 150R. And 150R is the highest dose most people can take without suffering radiation sickness.

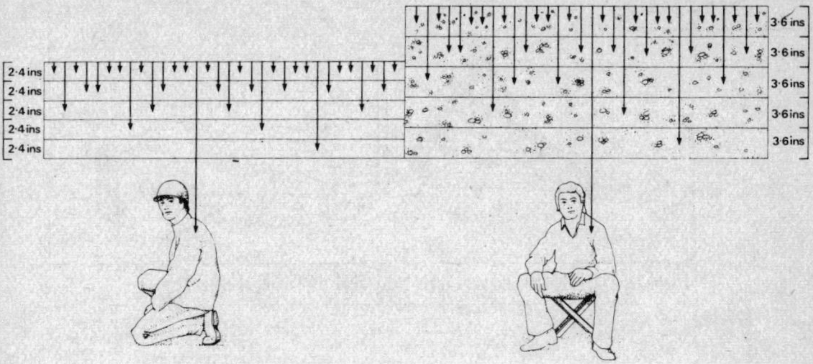

Figure 9. Showing the half-value thicknesses of earth and concrete. Every 3½ inches (9 centimetres) of earth halves the amount of radiation going through it; as does every 2¼ inches (5¾ centimetres) of concrete.

Table II. Approximate PFs of typical British housing in fallout areas undamaged by blast or fire.*

■ Types of Housing	PF
bungalow	5–10
detached two-storey	15
semi-detached two-storey (11-in cavity walls)	25–30
semi-detached two-storey (13½-in brick walls)	40
terraced two-storey	45
terraced back-to-back	60
blocks of flats and offices: lower floors	50–500
second floor and above (decreasing)	50–20

The above figures are for ground floor refuge rooms with timber upper floors and with windows and external doors blocked. An internal shelter which is built in a refuge room and surrounded with dense matter such as earth increases the PF.

*Source: Home Office, *Nuclear Weapons*, Her Majesty's Stationery Office, London, 1974, page 55.

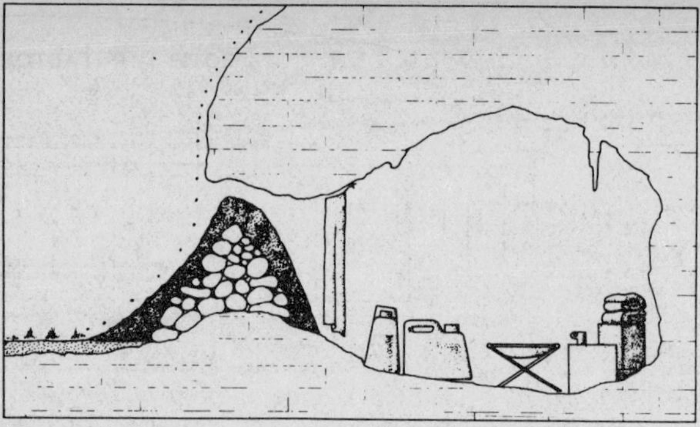

Figure 10. Some caves can be used as fallout shelters.

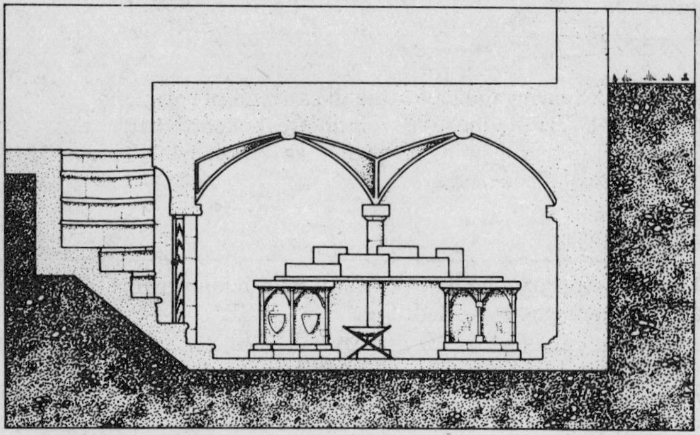

Figure 11. Crypts will need careful ventilation if they are to house people for any length of time.

Figure 12. If possible, seal gaps where radioactive dust may blow in.

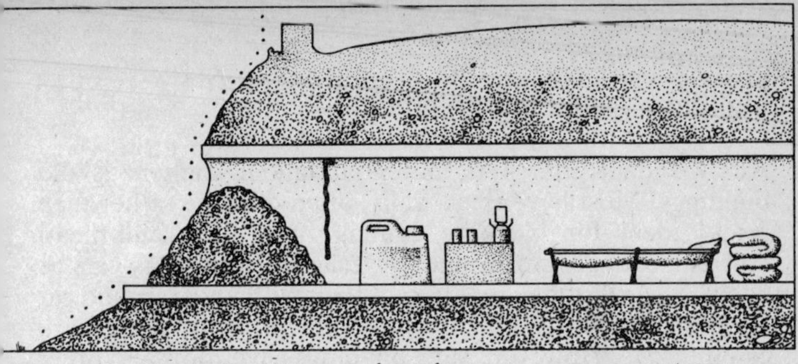

Figure 13. Use pedestrian tunnels under motorways; even storm sewers in good weather. Pile up earth at the entrance, for added protection.

igure 14. Underground car parks away from rgets could make useful shelters, but block the ntrances at ground level.

Figure 15. Manhole covers usually hide underground rooms or tunnels.

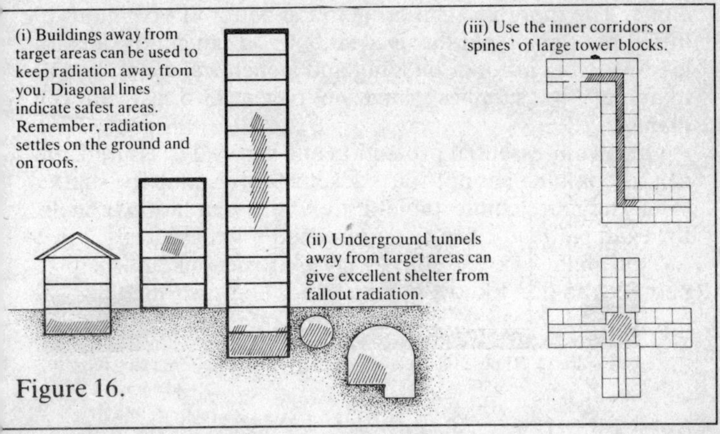

Figure 16.

Making a Shelter in a Building

An abundant source of potential fallout shelters is old buildings. Most have thick walls, often of stone rather than brick, ideal for blocking gamma rays, blast and heat. Ancient cottages, farm and ecclesiastical buildings can be adapted. And some modern buildings with underground car parks may offer rudimentary protection which hard work can improve. However, most buildings have roofs and other parts that may be ignited by heat rays from a nuclear explosion about 10 miles (16 kilometres) away, so only a few give as good protection against fire as do purpose-built shelters.

If possible, construct barriers inside the building you have chosen to give greater protection against radiation. Block points where radiation might enter. Build a small room, taking care to position it to gain maximum radiation protection on as many sides as possible. If your room is open to one side, or has no thick roof, build a strong wall or roof at least 3 feet (1 metre) thick with planks, stone, earth and sandbags.

Split your party into three and divide the following tasks among you: 1) seal the room except for ventilation holes and install a means of air flow if possible (see Kearny Air Pump, page 150) 2) bring drinking water into your room in plastic containers, clean dustbins, gallon bottles, etc. You need a minimum of 2 pints (1 litre) per person per day for drinking alone. The more you can bring in the better. Two gallons (9 litres) per person per day is ideal but you can get by on a lot less. 3) Bring in food, bedding and a chemical toilet, and as many of the supplies listed on pages 93–5 as you can manage.

Once your essential protection and survival is assured you can, if bombing has not started, set about making the shelter safer and more comfortable. Extend the ventilation tunnels, for example, and construct a screened toilet area.

You might also be able to give instructions and help to people who don't know how to build their own shelters.

Boats as Shelters

Just as it is not sensible to seek shelter from a storm by taking to a small boat or light aircraft, so is it unwise to try and survive the violent effects of nearby nuclear explosions in one. There are some circumstances, however, when a small boat with a cabin can be useful as a shelter against *radiation only* (not blast).

If you are at least 50 miles (80 kilometres) from the nearest explosions and radioactive particles are drifting your way, a small boat can give a good degree of protection from fallout. This is because fallout sinks in water and so the occupants of a boat have only to worry about fallout that lands on the boat itself; this can be periodically swept or rinsed into the water. You should ideally moor at least 200 feet (60 metres) from the shore, in water that is at least 6 feet (2 metres) deeper than the draught of the boat, to give effective shielding from the dangerous particles that will gradually collect on the sea, lake or river bed.

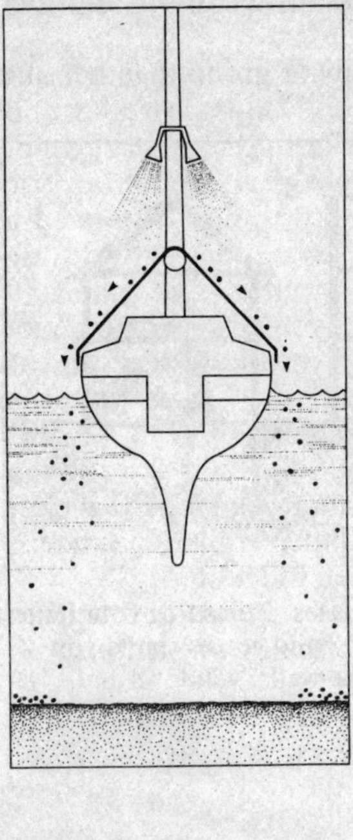

An awning should be fixed across the cabin to protect against radiation (see Figure 17), and a shower arrangement may be fitted, operated by a pump. This allows the occupants to rinse the awning of dust as often as necessary without leaving the safety of the cabin, thereby reducing exposure risks.

If you own a boat that is moored some distance from a target area purchase, or make yourself, the awning and shower arrangement now. Keep boxes of emergency stores (see pages 93–5) ready to take on board your floating shelter at short notice.

Figure 17. A boat equipped as a shelter.

Improvising a Radiation Shelter at Home

Assuming you decide not to evacuate, your main priority must be to select a site for a fallout shelter that is protected against heat, blast and radiation by surrounding features such as walls, rock or earth. You may prove to be outside the region of severe blast damage, in which case you have only radiation to deal with. Do not scorn this effort. It will save the lives of many who make it.

Not many modern houses have a suitable area for converting into a good shelter. And sheltering in houses near obvious targets is unwise. In blast areas most brick houses will be blown away or severely damaged, and many will burn. In addition, under some circumstances, they will be subject to fire risks beyond the farthest reach of blast effects. If you must make a refuge in your home, use whatever seems the safest area in it (Figure 18). If you can, use a basement or cellar and build a separate escape exit, in case the house collapses or burns above you. For the same reason keep picks, crowbars and other tools in your basement to dig your way out.

Work rapidly to gather your family or group together and

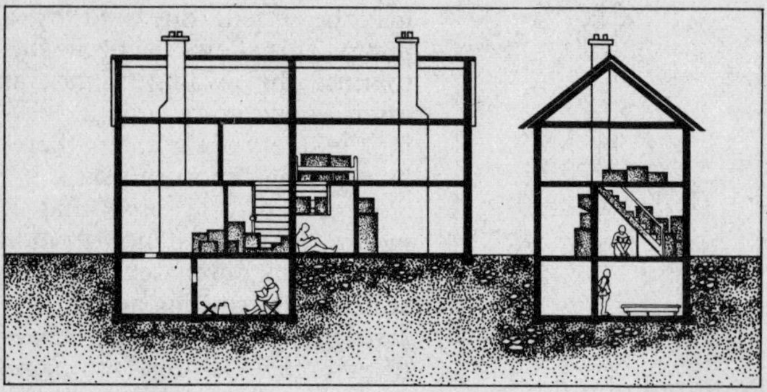

Figure 18. The safest areas in typical houses. Reinforce your inner shelter and pile dense matter over and around you to shield you further from radiation that penetrates the walls, windows and roof.

build a makeshift fallout shelter. You must aim to keep as much distance and mass as practical between you and the radiation particles. Fallout radiation cannot penetrate far through earth, concrete or water and all solid materials impede its progress (Figure 9).

You must also make it as hard as possible for fallout particles to blow, drift or fall into your living area. The biggest difficulty is that you still have to breathe and, in warm or hot weather, avoid becoming dangerously overheated. Therefore, spend as much time as possible on a ventilation system.

Instructions for installing an improvised system are given on pages 150–4. If you do not have time to do this, remember that any air that has to travel a route that includes moving upwards at low velocity before it reaches your refuge is going to lose almost all dangerous fallout particles. The danger of fallout particles reaching you can thus be practically eliminated by placing a 'wall' of any material in the air supply passage way, to force the incoming air to flow upwards for a distance, leaving the particles behind.

These particles are *heavy*. They gravitate downwards and are swept about only by wind. The first hours and days after an attack are the deadliest. In the vicinity of an explosion,

Figure 19. Fallout settles and drifts like snow.

initial fallout will start to come down after about thirty minutes. The farther you are away the longer it will take to reach you. Fortunately the particles rapidly lose their radioactive potency. Within two or three weeks you will probably be able to move about again. If you have a dependable fallout meter, you may be able to go outside your shelter for short periods starting a few days after the attack without serious risk of radiation injury.

If you have a basement or cellar, a strong table or a workbench can provide the structure for a small shelter; simply pile as much shielding material as you can collect on the top and around the sides, slide inside with your family or companions, then block the point of entry. Alternatively, you can build the basic structure out of large pieces of furniture or the heavier domestic appliances, roof this with doors taken off their hinges and then, as before, reinforce the whole with shielding material.

If your house has no cellar or basement, constructing a

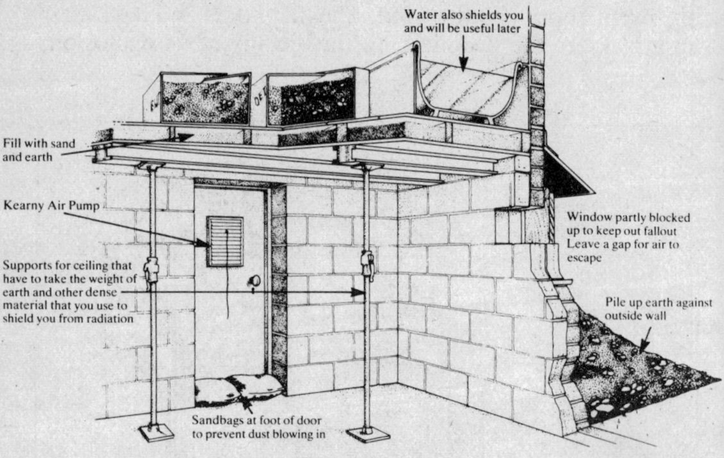

Figure 20. Ground-floor room reinforced with an inner wall and 'ACROW' supports.

lean-to shelter may be your best solution. Dig a shallow ditch, about 5 inches (15 centimetres) deep and about as wide, parallel to and some 1·2 yards (metres) out from an outside wall of your house. Take your heaviest doors off their hinges – you will need two for each occupant – bring them out, lean them against the wall and anchor them in place by fitting their bottom edges into the ditch you have dug. Make sure they are firmly in place then pile shielding material all over the shelter to a depth of 3 feet (1 metre), and on the wall inside the house: it may seem solid, but radiation will penetrate it if you don't reinforce it. Dig channels along the edge of the lean-to roof to carry off any rainwater. If you have time, add to your comfort by excavating the interior of the shelter a little; a few inches more of headroom and of solid earth walls around you may prove of benefit.

Consider, if at all possible, a garden shelter. There are several good ready-made shelters on the market that you

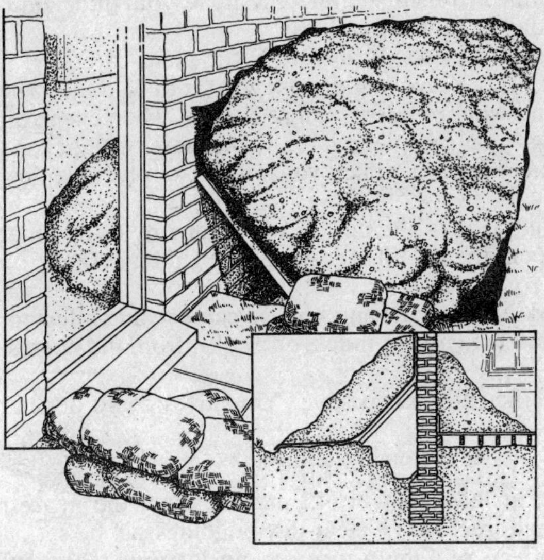

Figure 21. A lean-to shelter. The inset is a typical cross-section.

could install, finances permitting, but an expensive purpose-built shelter is not the only solution. A covered trench shelter can be dug at fairly short notice and provides much better protection against blast and fallout than an improvised shelter in, or alongside, your house. Two fit adults with the right tools can build a basic shelter of this type in thirty hours. This time could be considerably bettered with more hands making less work. Older children, for example, can fill sandbags, fetch and carry and gather supplies.

Building a Covered-Trench Shelter Suitable for Garden or Field

Do not attempt to build this shelter if bombs have already started to fall on our country. You will not have enough time to finish before heavy radiation reaches you unless you are very lucky with the winds constantly keeping the fallout away. Attempt a trench shelter only if, in your judgment, you have a day or more.

Read all the instructions and study the plans carefully. It will help if all those involved discuss what is to be done, who is to do it and what problems might be met. Then check off each step as you complete it to make sure you haven't omitted something vital which you will waste precious time correcting.

Make sure too that you do not waste time by using blunt tools. Sharpen them – if necessary by rubbing them on concrete or rough stone.

Wear work gloves: cuts and blisters can become infected, a serious matter if you are miles, or weeks, from the nearest antibiotics.

Work as efficiently as possible. Your lives could depend on it.

The ideal site for a trench shelter is:

In the open, at least 50 feet (15 metres) from the nearest building or tall trees. On a clear day buildings can be set on fire by the effects of a multi-megaton nuclear burst 20 or 30 miles (30 to 50 kilometres) away. In dry weather, too, conifers might be set alight by the thermal pulse. There is also the danger from trees blowing down: besides, digging through a root-system doesn't make the shelter-builder's life any easier.

Where the earth is firm and will not cave in on unsupported walls. Dig a little hole 18 inches (45 centimetres) deep: if you can push your thumb more than 1 inch (2·5 centimetres) into the soil at the bottom, the location is not safe. Try again elsewhere. If nowhere available is suitable, be sure to shore up all shelter walls that are below ground level, or build an above-ground shelter.

Where there is a deep enough layer of earth above either impermeable rock or the water table. Test for both hazards: dig an exploratory 4½ foot (1·3 metre) hole before excavating the entire shelter, and see if water seeps in. Test for rock by hammering down a sharpened pipe or metal rod to the depth you intend to dig.

Where there is no danger of some other catastrophe rendering the shelter uninhabitable – flooding after heavy rains, for example, or a rock or mud slide, or a rush of water should a dam at a higher level be destroyed by a bomb.

On flat or gently sloping ground if at all possible. If the shelter really has to be built on an incline, place it *across* the slope, at right angles to it.

■ List of Materials and Tools

1) Shovels (preferably 2)
2) Mattock
3) Trowel
4) String
5) Pegs
6) Waterproofing: whatever you can gather – plastic sheets, tents, tarpaulins, etc. Even light plastic film, if used to make an earth-covered 'buried roof', will withstand severe thermal pulse and blast

effects and, if the roof is gently sloped, will shed water.

7) Strong household doors: not hollow hardboard-faced doors; they are too weak. No glass either. Allow 6 doors for a 4-man shelter, and add at least one per person in addition.
8) Planks, sheets of plywood, etc.
9) A new, clean 3½ cubic foot (¼ cubic metre) dustbin with lid, or a plastic rain barrel for water storage
10) Chemical toilet and supply of chemicals
11) Plastic bags and pillow cases to make sandbags
12) A rule and sticks of known lengths for use while digging, to keep the width and depth even
13) Canopies (or material to make canopies)
14) Spare canopies

---

1) Clear the area of vegetation and other obstacles and mark out your shelter with pegs and string. The entrance and ventilation trench will be half the width of the main trench. Make these as long as you have space for. The longer they are the more protection you will have from radiation (Figure 23(ii)).

2) Start digging methodically from the entrance. Wear working gloves. It is important to avoid cuts and blisters. If two people are digging, start at opposite ends. Once you can get down in the hole it will be easier. When using a mattock, break off chunks right across the width of the trench, moving forward, and shovel out the loose earth. Shovel the earth at least 3 feet (1 metre) away from the edge of the trench: if you pile it up on the edge it will impede progress by falling back in. Besides, you will have to move it away before laying the roof. Arrange for someone else to keep the edge clear if possible because throwing shovel loads is tiring (iii).

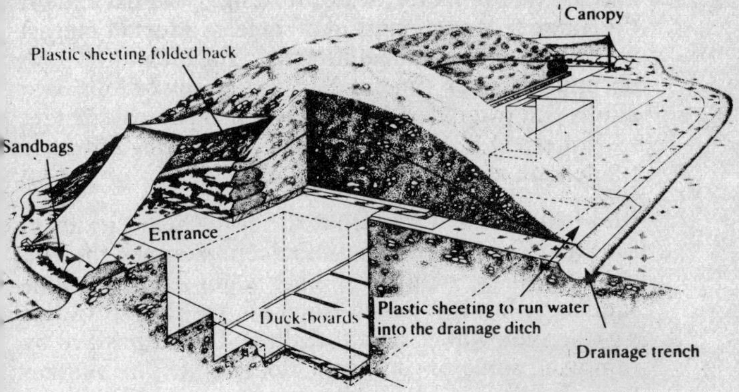

Figure 22. Cut-away drawing of a trench shelter.

Figure 23. Building a covered-trench shelter. (i)

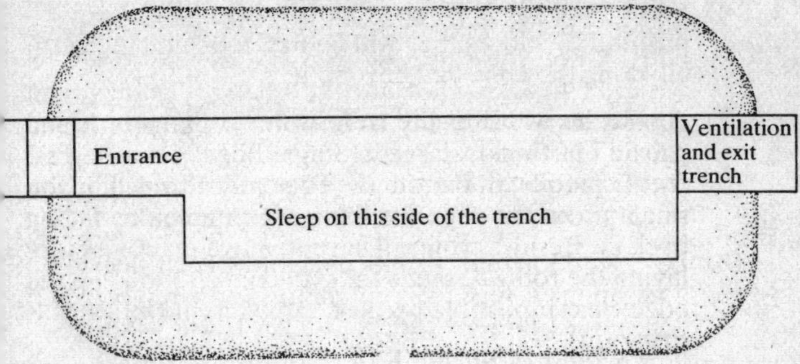

Be sure you don't undermine the side walls as this weakens the trench and it could cave in (iv).

The main trench will be 4½ feet (1·3 metres) deep and 3½ feet (1 metre) wide. Its length will depend on the number of occupants. Add at least 3 feet (1 metre) for every junior or adult (two small children will occupy 3 feet, or 1 metre). Thus a family of four, two adults and two older children, will need at least 12 feet (3·7 metres). To this must be added an entrance tunnel and ventilation trench.

3) Make the ventilation trench at least 3 feet (1 metre) long and 2½ feet (0·9 metres) deep. You will then be able to fill it with food and water containers or sandbags, leaving only a small air passage. In warm weather you will be able to enlarge the air passage by removing some of the items blocking it. The ventilation trench can be used as an escape exit if your entrance becomes blocked or accumulates too much radioactive dust and débris.

4) Line the insides of the finished trench with plastic sheeting, or similar waterproof material. Let the sheeting hang to within 2 inches (5 centimetres) of the bottom to stop people pulling it down by treading on it (v).

5) If you can lay a floor of hardboard or planks to hold down the dirt and damp, so much the better.

6) Flatten the earth around the trench so that when you position the doors they will lie flat, touching the earth all along the edge and beyond it.

7) At this stage place any large water containers (clean plastic dustbins), large storage boxes, mattresses, chemical toilet in the trench. The entrances will be too small to do this when the shelter is completed.

8) Lay the doors and planks over the trench, leaving a hole about 2 feet (65 centimetres) square (bigger if you have a large occupant to fit in). The ventilation hole should be smaller (vi).

(ii)

(iii)

(iv)

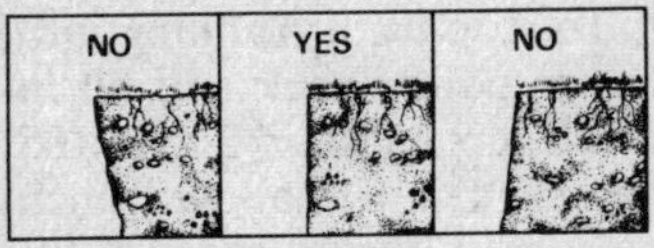

(vi)

(v)

(viii)

(vii)

9) Cover the cracks with cloth or plastic to stop earth falling through (vii). Use sandbags to form barriers around the entrance and ventilation holes to stop earth falling in and those fallout particles that get blown along the ground from blowing in.

10) Pile earth over the trench roof to a depth of about 1 foot (30 centimetres) over the centre line in a low mound. Pat the mound smooth and remove any sharp bits that might tear your waterproof material (viii).

11) To make the shelter waterproof, lay plastic sheeting or any waterproof material (tarpaulin, tent material, etc.) over the smoothed earth. The mound shape will ensure water will run off. To stop water running into the entrance, fold the waterproofing back and fill in (see cross section, (ix)). Pile up another 2 feet (65 centimetres) or more of earth. Dig a shallow trench round the mound and away to lower ground for drainage.

NOTE: if soil and general conditions are wet, your roof must slope so that water can drain off it. This is an easy step. Along one edge of the trench, lay an earth roll (see pages 128–9). Place each door so that one end

(ix)

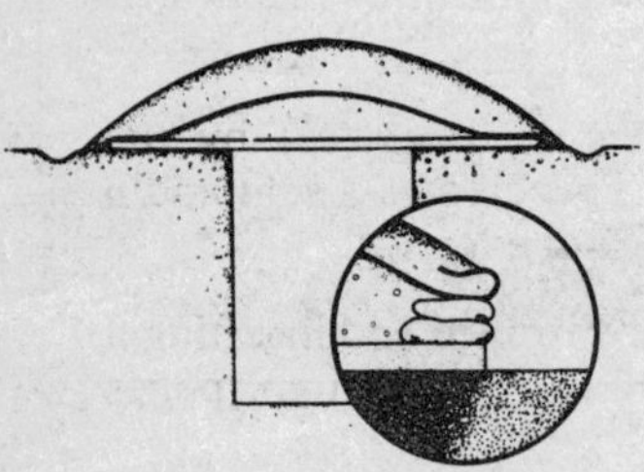

(x)

rests on this, the other on the ground. This will create the necessary slope. Lay your *waterproof* material *directly on the doors*. Mound earth over the door, rising to some 3 feet (1 metre) in the centre (x). Work from the edges inwards. Also, when digging the trench, slope the floor towards the entry end, where a small, covered drainage sump can be dug.

12) Now erect open-sided canopies at both ends of the shelter. These will stop rain and fallout from reaching your entrance and ventilation exit hole. (Detailed instructions for making a canopy are given on pages 118–19.) The canopies must be able to withstand high winds so stake and peg them firmly. Keep them low. The canopy at the entrance must be able to slide up and down to allow entry and exit without being damaged. This means that you must have string ties to fasten it from inside (xiv).

These are your minimum requirements, and must be completed before you consider any further stages in constructing your expedient shelter. If, however, war has not broken out when you have reached this point, you may make further improvements, such as:

13a) Enlarging your shelter, if you have enough time and materials, by digging another one at least 6 feet (1·8 metres) in line with your main trench. This need not be so big and can be used as a toilet compartment and for storage. Make the trench in stages as shown. Enlarge your ventilation tunnel to connect to the main shelter only when the work on the new section is complete (xiii).

b) Digging down another 2 feet (1·8 metres) by the entrance to the new trench. This creates a seat and a place to stand up and stretch and exercise.

c) Building a rigid frame for the entrance and inserting a ventilation device (see the Kearny Air Pump, pages 150–4).

(xi) Trench shape and extent of the mound.

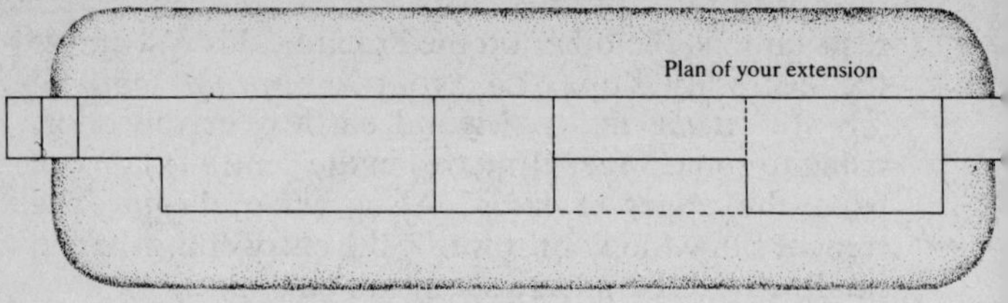

(xii)

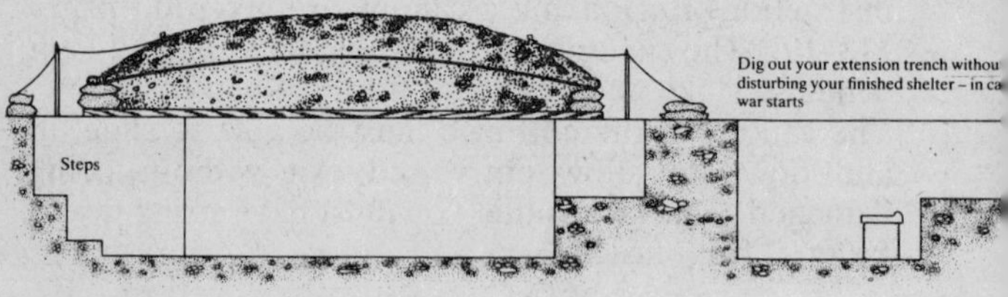

(xiii) Build the roof, mound the earth and connect the two 'rooms'.

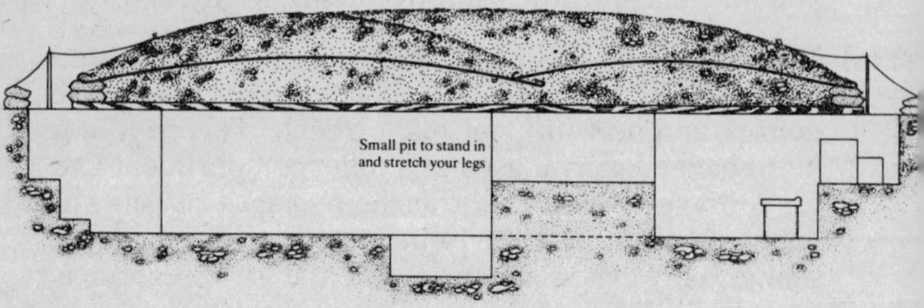

d) Putting slightly raised planking (duck-boards) on the floor to protect you from the damp.

e) Digging a waste-disposal pit about 2 yards (metres) down-wind from the shelter.

f) Making a water-storage pit (see pages 142–3).

14) When your shelter is complete, load in food and bedding (good sleeping bags are best), etc. Fill the dustbin with drinking water, most easily done by means of a hose from your tap. Take in additional water in 1-gallon (4·5-litre) plastic bottles. These make a good barrier against gamma radiation. When you sleep, stack them close around you. You could even use them to make a shelter within a shelter for small children, thus giving them added protection. Remember, children are more susceptible to radiation than adults (xv).

15) Keep small sandbags and water containers inside the entrance to block it almost completely during the first couple of days, when fallout radiation will be intense. Do the same in the ventilation trench. (Remember, in hot weather you will need more air.) If a bomb explodes near by you will see the extremely bright light and may have enough time to block both holes with the sandbags before the blast hits you – provided you are far enough away from the explosion for you and your shelter not to be destroyed by it (see page 85).

(xiv)

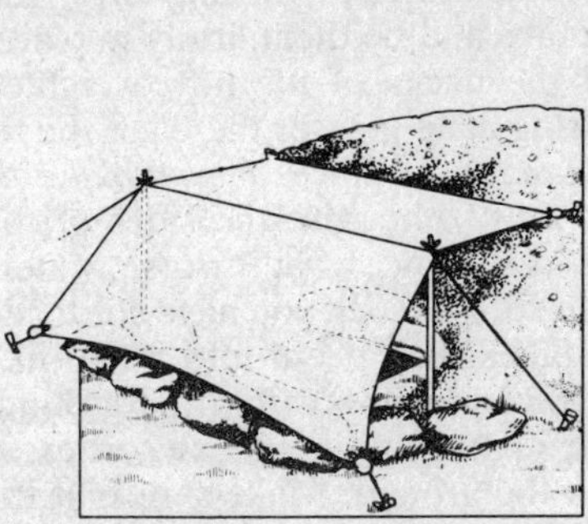

(xv)

How to Make a Canopy

To keep out rain or the sand-like fallout particles it is necessary to build a canopy over each shelter opening (Figure 24). On either side of the opening, drive two stakes, each 4 feet (1·2 metres) long, firmly into the ground. The distance between them should be about 7 feet (2 metres). If, because the ground is soft or the soil shallow, it is not possible to fix these stakes firmly, they should be secured by guy cords stretched from the top of each stake to pegs which, being shorter, *can* be driven into the ground until they are firmly in place. Now lash a cord or a straight smooth stick between the stakes, 27 inches (70 centimetres) above the ground.

Ideal canopy material would be 6-foot (1·8 metre) square groundsheets with eyelets to tie them. If you cannot obtain groundsheets, select a piece of plastic 6½ feet (2 metres) square, which will be the canopy material. Starting 4 inches (10 centimetres) from one corner, cut away a strip 3 inches (8 centimetres) deep and 34 inches (87 centimetres) long, leaving 2 inches (6 centimetres). Then cut away another strip of exactly the same dimensions. Repeat on the edge directly opposite. From each of the other two edges, again starting 4 inches (10 centimetres) from the corner, cut away a strip 3 inches (8 centimetres) deep and 5 foot 10 inches (1·7 metres) long. You now have a piece of material some 6 feet (1·84 metres) square with six tabs, one at each corner, and one in the middle of two of the sides. Select six little stones, something under ¾ inch (2 centimetres) in diameter, roll each of them in one of the tabs and tie them firmly in place, lashing your string round the necks of the now weighted tabs. Leave long ends of string dangling, for these are the tie points which will fix the canopy in place. *Never make tie points without first cutting tabs*, otherwise the sides of the canopy will sag, catching the wind and, what is worse, water.

Lay the canopy across the cord or stick you have stretched between the two upright stakes. Pull it out into a tent-like shape, its sides 7 inches (18 centimetres) from the ground. Lash the string on all the tie points, except on one corner, to pegs firmly hammered into the ground. Make sure that the plastic film or rainproof fabric is stretched and firm, without drooping or sagging. At the corner you have left untied, hammer in a sixth peg: the final tie point is made fast to this by the last person to descend into the shelter. If the cord is made adjustable, this becomes the way in and out; if everything is tied down, entry and exit is awkward and the canopy can easily be damaged.

It is important to make twice as many canopies as you need because if you are only a few miles away from a nuclear explosion, your canopies will be burned or melted by the heat rays, or blown away by the winds following the blast wave. If that happens, as soon as the winds abate you will have to rush outside and replace the canopies before the fallout starts coming down. If the bomb is very close you may only have a few minutes to do this. The moment you see fallout particles, get back inside, even if the canopy is not fixed properly. The radiation is at its most intense in the first few hours and you will stand no chance in it.

The covered trench is an excellent expedient radiation shelter: a well-made trench shelter, with a 6-foot (2-metre) long entrance tunnel and ventilation trench, provides you with a

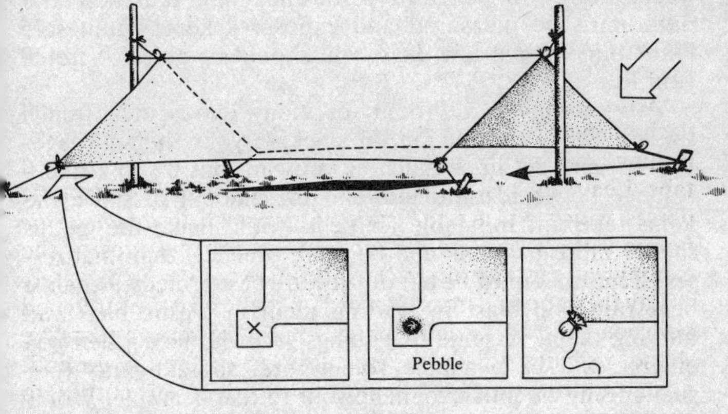

Figure 24. How to make a canopy.

protective factor (PF) of up to 250. This means that the occupants receive 1/250th of the radiation that is present outside. PF 250 is well above the recommended standard set for home fallout shelters by the American Office of Civil Defense.

If the entrance and ventilation trench is packed tight with sandbags this shelter can stand up to 7 psi of blast and protect you from outside winds of 400 mph (640 kph). Such a shock wave and wind would demolish houses. (It would also blow away your canopies, but you would have time to replace them before fallout began to descend.) In other words, in this shelter you could survive a 1MT bomb going off 2½ to 3½ miles (4 to 6 kilometres) away or a 10MT bomb 5 to 7 miles (8 to 11 kilometres) away, depending on whether the bomb is a surface burst or an air burst.

This type of shelter is small and uncomfortable, even if you manage the suggested improvements. Yet, if the choice lies between sickness and death and a few days of discomfort pent up in a hole, it is worth putting up with. As the days pass the radiation decreases dramatically and it becomes possible to spend increasing periods of time in the open. For example, if the fallout-radiation dose rate one hour after the explosion is 1,000R, seven hours later it will stand at 100R, two days after that it will stand at 10R per hour and two weeks later it will be almost zero. The fallout radiation dose rates must be measured and exposures kept within safe limits but, after a few days, you should be able to stretch your legs at least.

You will not have room for many extras in a trench shelter. Study the section on stocking your shelter (pages 154–60) and get in as much as you can, but try to strike a balance between usefulness and the amount of space the items take up. Inflatable air beds would make life in this shelter more bearable and be more practical than mattresses. Items that must be left outside are best protected against heat rays and blast by putting them in plastic bags and burying them. Assume that things you will need when you emerge will be available somewhere, so take into your shelter only essentials to make your retreat bearable. Worry about later later.

Building a Trench Shelter Using a Car

A car-over-trench shelter, similar in many respects to a door-covered trench shelter, would be the best expedient if you had evacuated to a remote district and had no better alternative. It should only be made on very firm ground. It is even more cramped than the door-over type, but it provides excellent protection against radiation.

Study Figures 25 and 26 and you will see how to build it. *Make sure that, while someone is digging the trench, the car is used to collect sufficient water in plastic containers or bags to last two weeks or more.* Once the car becomes the roof, it is immobilised and you are stuck there unless you have more than one vehicle.

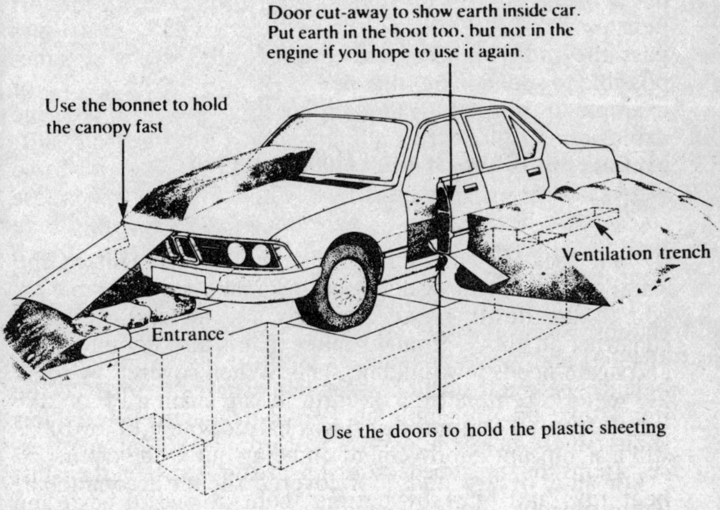

Figure 25. A car-over-trench shelter.

A longer trench could be made by using two cars or a lorry. Once you understand the principle you can work out your own variations with the vehicles at your disposal. The same tools and materials are needed as for the door-covered trench shelter – except for the doors (see pages 109–10).

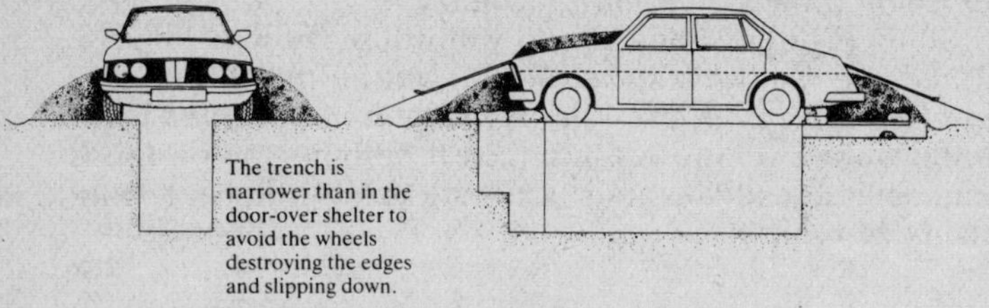

Figure 26. Cross-sections of a car-over-trench shelter.

Making an Above-Ground Door-Covered Shelter

If your location, the state of the soil, the height of the water-table or the prevalence of rock makes it impossible for you to dig down 4½ feet (nearly 1½ metres), you can construct an above-ground shelter that is also door-covered and again needs few building skills. When covered by some 2½ feet (75 centimetres) of earth, it can claim a PF of 200; with 2 feet (60 centimetres) this is halved, but a PF of 100 is still a significant improvement on being out in the open.

For an above-ground door-covered shelter accommodating four people, you will need:

Six doors – if there are to be more than four occupants, add another door for each one. You can use boards or plywood instead if they are *at least* ¾ inch (1½ centimetres) thick.

A great deal of fabric or plastic, since the walls are to be made of earth rolls. There should be sixteen pieces, each the size of a double-bed sheet (and three more for each additional person).

Rainproofing materials, in total about 15 square yards (12 square metres), for the first four persons, of the same kind as those used in the underground shelter – shower curtains, plastic table cloths, etc. – and an extra 2½ square yards (1½ square metres) for each additional occupant.

Similar tools to those for the underground shelter (see page 109) and in addition, a saw and a hatchet, a hammer and at least fifteen small nails, and large buckets or other containers for carrying soil. More cloth or plastic would be useful – two more double-bed size sheets per head than is the requirement – as would further waterproof materials, about 2 square yards (1¾ square metres) for each person. Cloth or plastic containers to make into sandbags are also desirable and can be used in great quantities.

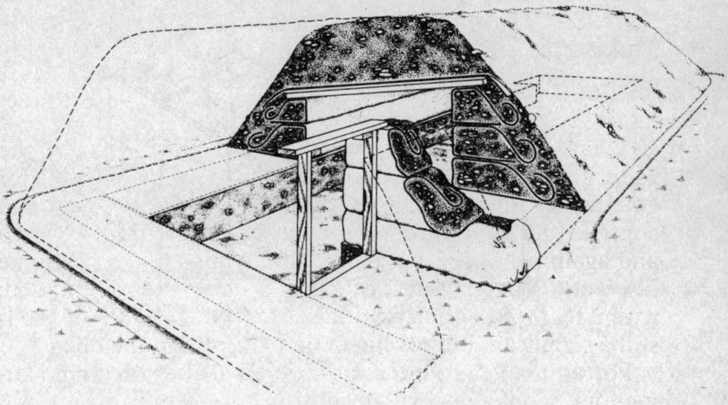

Figure 27. Cut-away showing the construction of an above-ground shelter.

Lay down the doors on the ground to measure the exact length the shelter will be. The two widest should be at the ends, to roof the points of entry. Stake out the dimensions of the shelter in the place where it is to be built – the length you have already determined; it should be 3 feet (1 metre) wide. Since the shelter is to be mostly above ground, the plan you have marked out on the ground is not this time the outline of a trench. Instead, you must build up the walls of the shelter, using earth rolls as your means. The rolls, however, need to be shaped against something firm, and in order to keep the walls straight you yourself will want some indication of the shelter's finished outlines. It is necessary, therefore, to make a form that will represent the dimensions of the finished structure. Fortunately the materials for this are to hand – the six doors, which will not be needed until the moment comes to use them for the roof.

Stand four of the doors on their edges along the lines of the walls, like two parallel fences, and keep them upright by bracing them against each other. Use wooden struts or battens 3 feet (1 metre) long as forms, nailing them to the top and bottom of each door to create a firm, if temporary, structure (Figure 28).

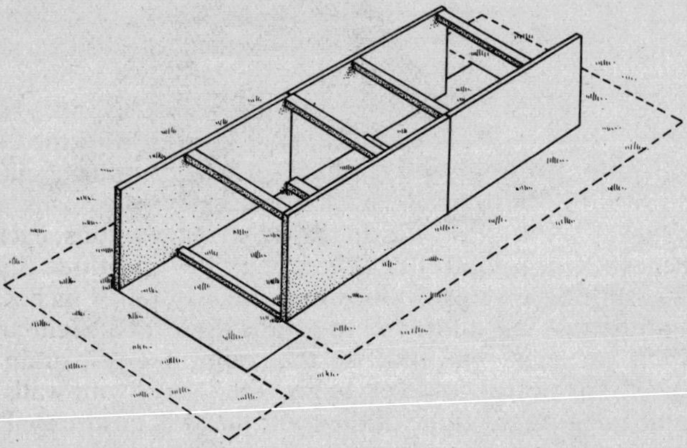

Figure 28. The form determining the shape and size of an above-ground shelter.

Now make the first earth roll: lay some 2 feet (60 centimetres) of the sheet you are using for this on the ground outside the shelter, right up against the wooden vertical of the form. Make sure this is quite flat, then drape the rest of the sheet out of the way over the door.If you are using more than one sheet, make sure there is a good overlap of the adjacent edges – 1 foot (30 centimetres) at least. Shovel earth on the section of sheeting that is flat on the ground, making sure that it builds up against the vertical door of the form. Let the pile of earth extend outwards beyond the edge of the sheeting, perhaps by as much as 1 foot (30 centimetres). Flatten the top of this heap, which should be some 6 to 8 inches (15 to 20 centimetres) deep, and then cut a narrow, shallow trench along the length of the roll and about 20 inches (50 centimetres) out from the uprights of the form (Figure 29). Now carefully lay that part of the sheet which has been hanging over the door down on the piled earth, making sure that it fits snugly into the little trench, and that it has no folds or wrinkles. Into that shallow trench, now lined with the sheet, shovel more earth (Figure 29). Fold the free end of the sheet back over this new pile of soil. Finally, add more earth in order to level off the top, so that the whole roll is flat and the same height, from the point where the sheet contains it, hard against the door, to the outer edge. Shape this outer edge so that it has a sharp slope from top to bottom to make drainage easier.

Now make a similar earth roll on the other side: *don't build up one wall before the other* – the weight of the earth will push the form out of shape. Thus, continue building earth rolls alternately on each side. But *make one wall higher than the other*; you do this by laying two rolls, each 10 inches (25 centimetre) deep, on one side, and three 8 inch (20 centimetres) rolls on the other. This drop of 4 inches (10 centimetres) will allow you to set the doors at a slight angle when you make the roof, so that rainwater will drain off easily. Take care, however, to give the tops of your walls the same angle as the slope of the roof; that will ensure that the doors will lie snugly against them, distributing their weight evenly and providing the greatest possible strength and security.

You will need two entrances, so leave space for these at the very ends of the walls. They must be placed diagonally opposite one another, since the greater the distance between them the greater is their usefulness as ventilation openings that minimise the penetration of fallout. The entrances should be half as wide as the inside room, but the spaces you leave should include room for a protective wall of sandbags, set at right-angles to the side-walls of the shelter. The end walls, to be constructed of earth rolls, will make the other side of the narrow entrances (Figure 27).

To line up these new structures properly, and to create a solid base against which to lay the sandbags and mould the earth rolls, you will need to relocate the forms. Dismantle the forms making certain that removing the nails does not damage the wood. (Set the doors aside until the roofing is to be done.) When you make up the forms again, remember that the braced parallels should now be only wide enough to fit the width of the entrance way. First build the little sandbag wall of an entrance, before tackling the end wall, sloping it outwards from top to bottom to provide drainage, in the same way as the main walls.

Figure 29. Making the first earth wall.

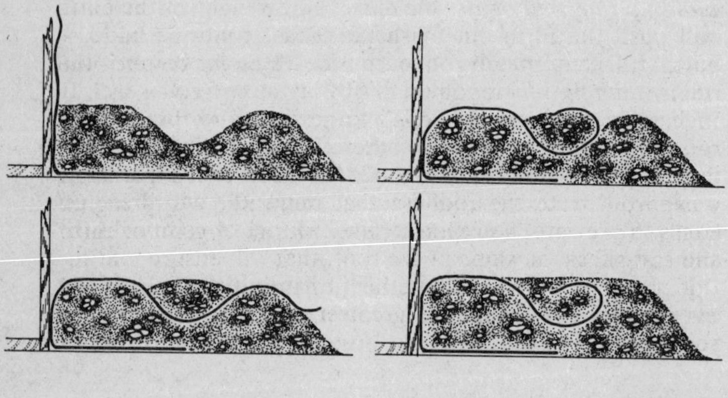

When the sandbags are laid, measure out the end walls. These will be, for a four-person shelter, as long as the shelter floor, both side walls and the little sandbag porch-wall all added together. Begin laying down earth rolls, but when you come to the topmost, allow for the slope of the roof and its differential between one side and the other of some 4 inches (10 centimetres).

If you have the wood and the tools, make a complete frame for each entrance, exactly as high as the earth walls on either side. But, once again, allow for the slope of the roof, tilting the top member of the frame to let the roof fit tightly against it. If there are not enough materials for making an entire frame, embed the ends of a board or a pole, some 2 inches (5 centimetres) by 4 inches (10 centimetres), in the tops of the walls on either side of the entrance. There must be some support here for the doors, which are to make up the roof.

If there is plenty of waterproof material available, line the tops of all the walls with some of it. This prevents water from the soil soaking into the wood of the doors.

Now dig out the floor of the shelter, making a shallow trench some 14 inches (35 centimetres) deep and, of course, the same length and breadth as the shelter chamber. Since the higher wall will be 2 feet (60 centimetres) and the lower 20 inches (50 centimetres) in height, the minimum clearance will be less than 3 feet (85 centimetres). It is possible, of course, that soil conditions make the digging out of even 14 inches (35 centimetres) impossible. If that is so, an extra earth roll on the side and end walls will have to be added – but it should not be forgotten that the lower the better is the rule when constructing shelters.

The time has come to finish the structure by placing the roof. Set the doors carefully in position, making sure that they fit flush to their supports. Cover them, if possible, with waterproof material, folding it well under the doors' higher edges to prevent its slipping down under the weight of earth and the effects of water.

If you have enough material, let it trail 20 inches (50 centimetres) or so beyond the lower edge of the roof. Now you can begin shovelling the protective outer covering of earth on the shelter, beginning by mounding it up at the edges and working inwards to the middle. This helps to give the heaped-up earth an interior strength, allowing it to carry a high proportion of its own weight. Pick out any sharp stones or roots that might damage the waterproof plastics or fabrics you have used. Cover the roof with at least 1½ feet (½ metre) of soil, making sure that the corners are all protected by at least this thickness. Avoid the temptation to make the earth roof covering level; let it follow the slope of the doors.

Take whatever other precautions you can against penetration by fallout or rain – see if there is enough waterproof material to stretch a canopy, perhaps 2 or 3 feet (60 to 80 centimetres) long, over each entrance (see pages 118–19 for the ideal design). Inside the entrances, build little dams, about 5 inches (12 centimetres) high, to hold back ground water. Use whatever waterproof material you have left to cover the floor inside the shelter.

How to Make Sandbags and Earth Rolls

Improvised shelters derive a great deal of their strength from the use of sandbags. Filling them is a task that can be delegated, perhaps to a working party of children, while others struggle with the digging and shelter construction.

Sacks or pillow-cases used for this purpose should be only two-thirds filled with earth, and then securely tied. They can be used to strengthen doorways and other openings, to reinforce the edges of the roof, to give solidity to any other points of weakness and to build extra barriers around entrances and ventilation holes. You can't have too many sandbags.

If there are not enough bags available, you can make long, sausage-like earth rolls. Because these are not portable, they must be formed in the places where they are wanted. Two people are needed to make them. The covering can be of any fabric at least as strong as a bed sheet; even plastic film can be used. Whatever material is chosen, the piece should be about 5 feet across (1½ metres), and 2 feet (60 centimetres) longer than the part to be protected.

Lay 2 feet (60 centimetres) of the 5-foot (1½ metres) width flat on the ground next to a trench. Then stand in the trench while your helper begins to shovel earth on and you keep the free end of the material stretched. As the earth begins to pile up, lean forward against it and stretch the fabric well away in front of you, so that it folds back over the earth (Figure 30). When the soil filling is sufficiently substantial, lay the free end of the material down on it, but keep pulling on the edge. This part of the material should be covered, and once a layer of 3 or 4 inches (8 or 10 centimetres) deep is in place, fold the edge you are holding back over it, so that along the length of the roll some 4 inches (10 centimetres) of the fabric are showing, with the edge towards you. When it too has been covered by a layer of earth, this folded-back section will anchor the material in place. If a higher protective barrier is needed, you can flatten the top of the earth roll and build another above it. Slope the top of the highest earth roll towards the outside of the construction, so that rain water may drain off; a small channel, no bigger than a gutter, cut in the ground at the foot of this rain-slope will allow any accumulated water to flow away.

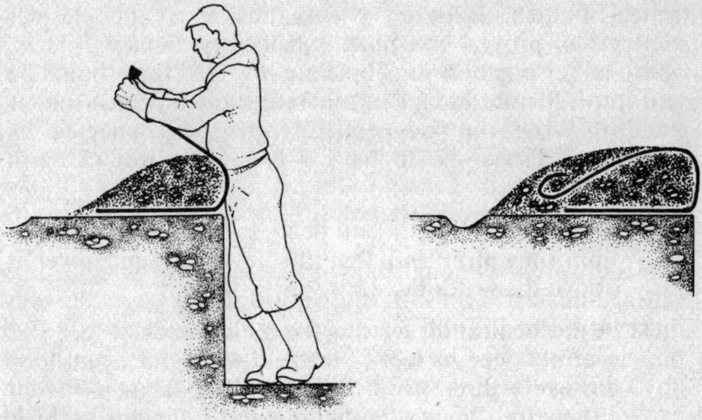

Figure 30. Making an earth roll.

A Communal Trench Radiation Shelter

A larger and more comfortable variation of the trench shelter, which can provide good secondary radiation protection, is made by forming an arch over a 'T' trench. Corrugated iron roofing is ideal for forming the arch. The main trench in this instance can be dug across a field. There could even be rows of these side by side, so that one field could house hundreds of people. This could be an ideal low-cost project for communities, organisations and local councils.

With discipline and mechanical aids, and all the occupants working, many of these shelters could be prepared in less than a week. As mentioned elsewhere, however, the more that is done in advance the better. The site should be selected and tested for water-table height and fresh water pipes could be laid in readiness. Stocks of materials should be bought and stored for use in the emergency. The intending occupants must be selected and informed of what will be required of them.

Researchers in America and Russia have found that when shelters have more than forty occupants, serious management problems arise and physical and psychological health deteriorates. Ventilation problems also worsen with larger trench shelters. Between twenty and thirty people per shelter has proved the most satisfactory number. Thus, where larger numbers of people are involved they should be split into separate groups in separate shelters. Each shelter could then be run independently but be connected by crawlways. These should have 3 feet (1 metre) of earth above them.

1) The site is selected, care being taken that the earth is uniformly firm and that the lower ground level is above the water table.

2) A mechanical digger cuts the main trench, 4 feet (1·2 metres) deep, 7 feet (2 metres) wide and 7 feet long for every three people (Figure 31ii). Thus a 70-foot (21-metre) trench, with full-sized openings at both ends, in cool weather without forced ventilation

would take up to thirty people. In warm weather a ventilation pump would be necessary.

3) Each group works to clear all the earth from the trench and make the sides and floor as smooth as possible. All the earth is removed from the trench to be piled up later on the roof (iii).

4) The edges of the trench are flattened.

5) Metal plates, planks or plywood are laid in position either side of the trench. These are for the corrugated iron arches to stand on. This is important because the iron roof will otherwise cut into the soil, forced by the weight of earth above, or, more seriously, be sharply hammered in by blast from a nearby bomb, injuring the occupants.

6) Whilst the shelter is being prepared a small team

Figure 31. Making a communal trench shelter.

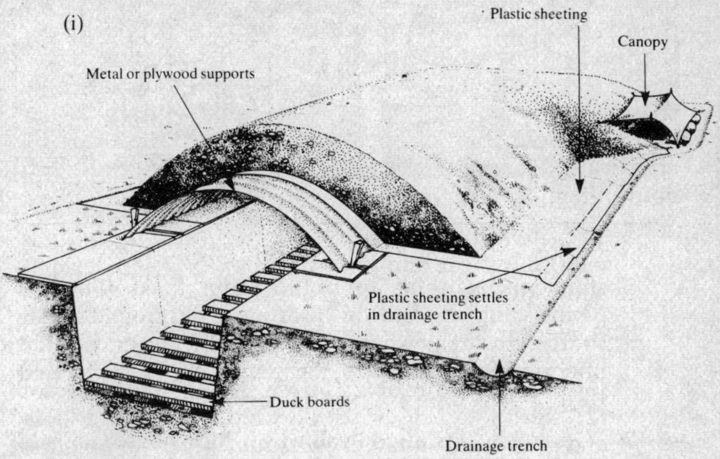

(ii)

(iii)

(v)

(iv)

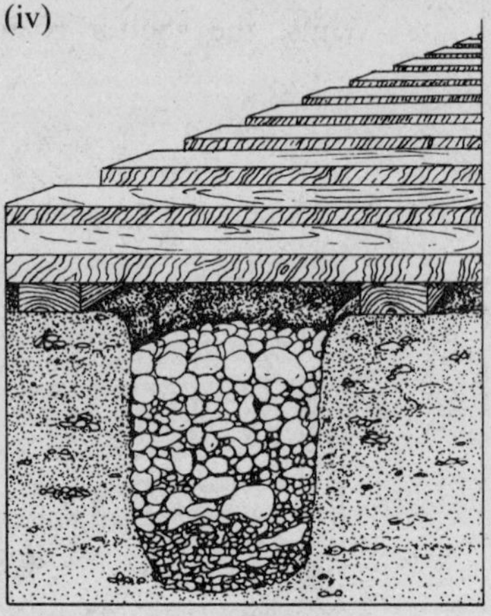

should be working to fix up water tanks. Perhaps piping could be laid on from an underground water source. In areas where water flows from gravity-fed underground reservoirs the mains could be tapped (iv).

7) If possible a slatted walkway (duck-board) is laid

(vi)

(vii)

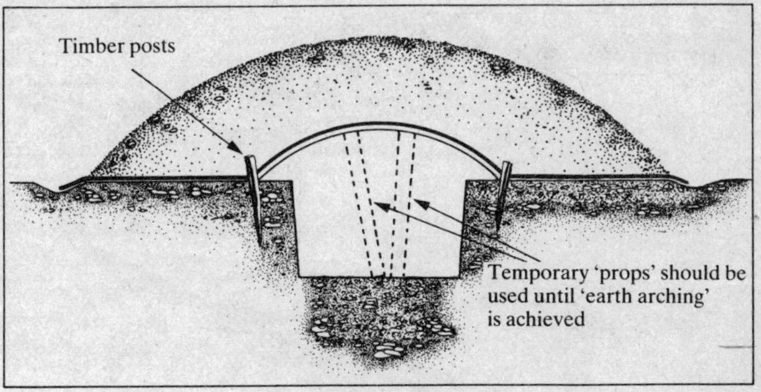

along the bottom of the trench, preferably over a small drainage trench leading to a small covered drainage sump dug at the lower end of the trench (v).

8) The corrugated iron roof arches are positioned, each one overlapping and bolted to the next (vi).

9) Timber posts are hammered in position to stop the corrugated iron from 'spreading' under the weight of the earth before the earth arch is achieved (vii).

10) To prevent rain seeping in plastic or tarpaulin sheeting is laid over the roof and sunk into drainage ditches either side of the roof. The ditches are extended downhill away from the shelter so they act as soakaways in wet conditions (i).

11) Earth is piled on the roof until the 'earth arching' effect is achieved, whereby the weight of most of the earth is directed into the ground so that it does not crush the corrugated roof (vii).

12) Ventilation through the shelter should flow in the direction of the prevailing winds. A series of Kearny Air Pumps (pages 150–4) would draw air through the shelter when necessary. Air exhaust should be through the highest point of the shelter (viii).

13) Build a wall of sandbags around the entrance and exits to prevent drifting fallout from blowing in.

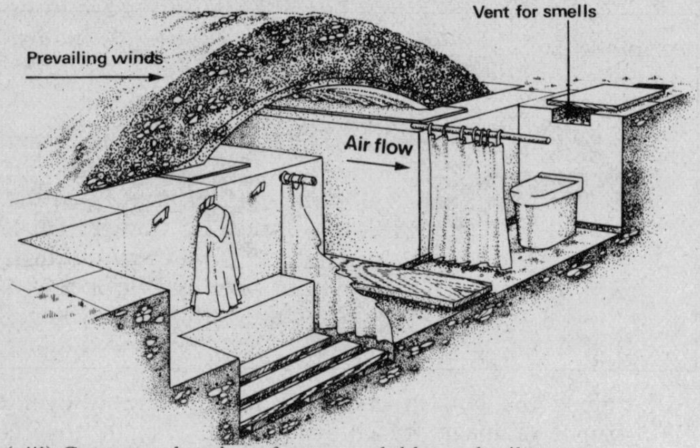

(viii) Cut-away drawing of entrance lobby and toilet area.

Building a Communal Radiation and Blast Shelter

Unlike many other countries, the United Kingdom has few public shelters available. The Government encourages a 'stay at home and improvise' approach. This means that individuals must take it upon themselves to provide their own protection. A shelter project involving several family units is the most economical way of achieving good protection.

Establish a small organising committee to complete the following tasks now:

1) Survey various possible sites. Your chosen site should be, primarily, out of range of any known targets (see page 90). Next determine the geological features. For example, how solid is the ground? How high is the water table?

2) Make arrangements to purchase the site, or if one of you already owns it, check any planning regulations relating to it at the local town hall. There is no need to reveal to officials the nature of your project. You do not need planning permission if your shelter is to be entirely underground. Building reguations require that your shelter should be waterproof and structurally sound.

3) Decide on the size of the shelter you need. Remember the rule for minimum essential floor space (page 65): multiply the number of occupants by ten to find the square footage and add more space for storage. Thus, for twelve occupants you need a 7-foot (2-metre) high living space, 7 feet (2 metres) wide by 17½ feet (5·4 metres) long minimum plus storage space. This would still be cramped so, if possible, allow even more space.

4) Design your shelter. Employ the services of an architect, draughtsman or professional builder, with expert knowledge of the subject, to prepare accurate drawings. Consider buying a modular shelter system; the tubular type, especially, can be added to.

   The ideal, purpose-built, communal blast and fall-out shelter should:

a) Be below ground level, so that at least 3 feet (1 metre) of earth on the roof brings it flush to the surface.
b) Have a roof of reinforced concrete. The concrete should be evenly mixed. If the roof can be domed, so much the better. A dome can withstand enormous blast pressure.
c) Have walls of reinforced concrete.

d) Have a covered ramp or steps to the entrance. This should be protected by a heavy trap door.
e) Have a blast-proof, rubber-sealed door, set at right angles to the entrance area.
f) Have a decontamination chamber.
g) Have an adequate ventilation system that can be powered either by an electric motor or manually, complete with filters to clean air of radioactive dust. All ducts to the exterior must have blast protection valves fitted to protect sensitive apparatus and people.

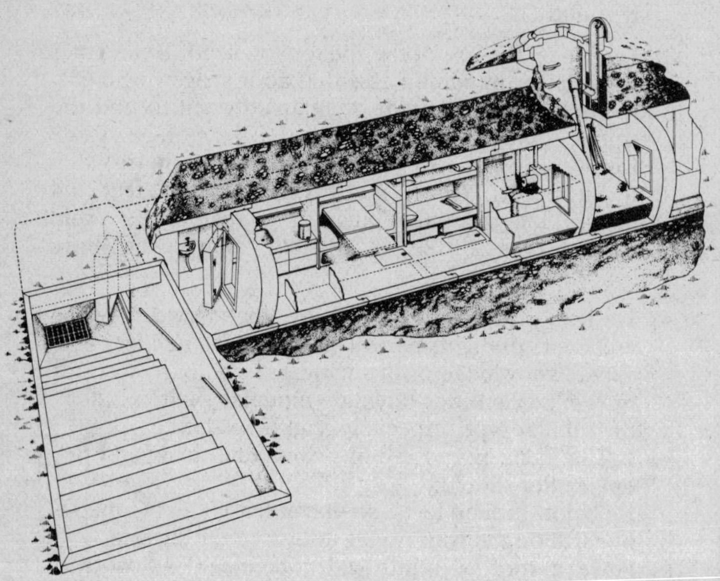

Figure 32. Cut-away drawing of a concrete tube shelter manufactured in the UK.

h) Have a separate room, with its own air intake and exhaust openings, for a shock-mounted generator and engine to run the lights and ventilation system.
i) Have a separate washroom and toilet with sewage disposal by pump or drainage. A separate chamber for water containers could be built. The more water you can store the better.
j) Have a separate emergency exit. This, too, must be protected against blast.

5) Your committee must organise the finance for the shelter. This will usually be paid for, in one way or another, by the members of the scheme. If you build it yourselves you will save an enormous amount of money but it will take longer than having it built.

6) If all or part of the project is contracted out, only reputable firms and intelligent labour must be em-

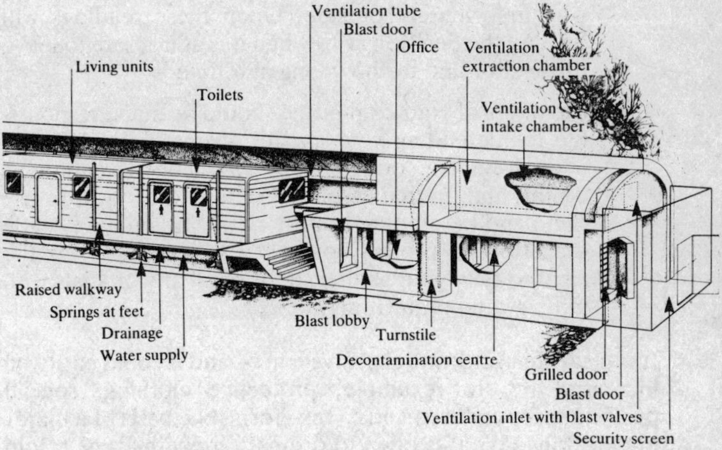

Figure 33. Converting unused tunnels or other underground structures is an economical way for communities to provide themselves with shelter.

ployed. Remember that your shelter is only as strong as its weakest link. If someone fits the blast valves back to front, for example, all your efforts could be for nothing.

7) Once built, your shelter must be stocked. As well as the basic necessities – furniture, bedding, food, cooking and eating utensils (see pages 154–60 for a full list) – you should try to include:

a) A comprehensive first-aid kit, including antiseptics, common analgesics, antibiotics and a selection of useful medicines, together with all appropriate instructions.
b) Standby facilities in case of some crucial failure, such as an alternative power supply using human muscular effort; candles and torches, tools for digging, oxygen bottles, etc.
c) Means of communication protected against EMP effects, notably telephone and a radio receiver.
d) Meters to determine the precise levels of atmospheric contamination and of the radiation received by those who first venture outside. Upon these readings will depend the decision as to when it is at last safe to leave the shelter and for how long at a time.

8) Members of your committee should be made responsible for defending your shelter against possible take-over attempts. You might decide you need weapons to do this and, in that case, you should know how to use them and be prepared to use them. If you have made the effort to protect yourselves no one else has the right to take your shelter, least of all any officials who may try and requisition it.

It is clear that so comprehensive a list – and it could easily be increased by, for example, protective clothing, special provisions for children and so on – forms the basis of a major undertaking. What is open to ordinary individuals is to join together and see if they can use the facilities and materials available to them. It is, for example, possible at no great cost, though at some considerable effort, to reinforce the basement of an ordinary apartment house and turn it into at least a fallout shelter in an area 20 or more miles (30 kilometres) from a probable target.

Selecting a Contractor to Build Your Shelter

Anyone who is thinking of having a nuclear shelter installed at home, whether fallout and blast-proof or proof only against fallout, will find a number of designs on offer ranging from the excellent to the stupid. As well as studying these designs, and viewing installed shelters where possible, he or she should take some account of the personnel employed by the contractor. Is their expertise limited to that of the practical builder, or do they have the architectural, structural and engineering knowledge needed for the design and construction of nuclear shelters? Do they offer a detailed factual account of what they want to do and how they intend setting about it? Will their construction provide:

- A shielded entrance? With a blast door and decontamination chamber?
- Adequate space – including enough room for the storage of food and water needed?
- Adequate ventilation – including a dependable, hand-operated blower and filters to clear the air of contamination, with each orifice protected against blast?
- Adequate sanitary facilities?
- A separate blast-proof exit?

All this, of course, is over and above the most basic requirement – that the shelter will actually do what it says and protect the occupants. An indication of the builder's suitability might be where he intends siting the shelter: if building a blast shelter he should recommend a site that is shielded as much as possible by natural features. He should also minimise the problem of falling and blast-hurled rubble from nearby buildings by siting the shelter, wherever practical, between the nearest building and the direction of the nearest possible target. This means that the rubble from the building will probably be blown away from the shelter.

Another rule of thumb in judging the contractor's competence might be his proposed use of materials: the cheapest and among the most effective is simple earth. Concrete is only marginally more efficient for absorbing radiation or protecting against blast. Steel may be elegant, but it is very expensive; the same is true of lead, evocative though that is of laboratory shielding from dangerous rays.

If you are considering a lightweight shelter buried under earth you must be aware of its main disadvantage. This is the problem of upward pressure from a rising water table as the shelter tries to float. This pressure can crack the shelter so that it is no longer waterproof. (All good shelters should, of course, be waterproof.) If it doesn't crack the shelter, after heavy rains, it could push the shelter to the surface where it will rise like a giant mushroom. You must be convinced that the contractor has solved these problems.

The best contractor will try to combine efficiency with economy. But he will know, as you must remember, that total protection against any nuclear eventuality requires the budget of a Rockefeller. Any contractor not conceding this must be suspect. *The builder of your shelter, to be trusted, must make no extravagant claims, take care over the siting, be happy to use simple materials, and include in his design the facilities ensuring not only safety, but conditions of minimum comfort.*

If you are having a house built and wish to incorporate a shelter in, or close to it, in addition to the above specifications, the following guidelines about radiation shielding should be borne in mind:

> Where a house is built against a slope, the shelter should be on the side that extends into the hill.
>
> An internal shelter should always be in the part of the house best protected by the surrounding materials – wherever possible in a basement or cellar, in a corner if that can be arranged, against a side wall if it can't, with a central position only the third choice. If there are two

levels of basement, it should be built at the lower level.

If the shelter cannot be placed below ground level, it should be made as small as possible and located in the middle of the building.

Exterior features of the house, such as terraces, flower beds or gardens that slope away, can act as natural radiation barriers. Earth piled against the walls will have the same function.

Shelter entrances should, if possible, be positioned well away from windows. If there must be windows in the area, they should have high sills and be small, thereby creating minimum hazard to people rushing for shelter during an attack.

Weak points in the shelter should be protected, so there should be right-angled turns at entrances and all other openings should be protected by baffles.

Your architect should be aware of what is called the time effect, which makes use of the swift deterioration in the virulence of the dangerous gamma rays. The speed of decay makes the first forty-eight hours after a burst – perhaps only the first twenty-four – particularly damaging. It is during this period that the most stringent precautions must be taken. The designer can use this factor to reduce building costs by planning a two-chamber structure. One, the smaller, would be very heavily shielded against radiation, with exceptionally thick walls, impenetrable entrances and no windows. The other, larger chamber could be less heavily protected. When instrument readings or local radio announcements proclaimed that it was safe to do so, the occupants of the inner shelter could expand into the outer chamber, remaining in comparative comfort until it was safe to move outside.

Obtain a copy of *Makeshift Shelters* produced by the Swiss Federal Office of Civil Defence (1983). It is published in the UK by Octagon Press and costs £8.50. It explains in comprehensible terms the technical specifications necessary for erecting shelters in existing buildings such as would, in the opinion of Swiss experts, be suitable in the event of a nuclear attack.

Water and Water Storage

A new 3½-cubic-foot (0·7-cubic-metre) plastic dustbin when filled carries approximately 26 gallons (120 litres). This gives a family of four nearly 1 gallon (4½ litres) each a day for a week or a third of a gallon (1½ litres) each for almost three weeks. Just one dustbinful of water can be rationed to last over three weeks between four people (2 pints per day – 1 litre – per person). A 50-gallon (225-litre) plastic water barrel, available from most garden centres, gives you twice the ration, and has the added advantage of being equipped with a tap at the bottom (Figure 34).

Extra water can be stored close to the shelter in plastic bags buried in the soil, in a pit with a smaller diameter than the bags'. In small trench shelters, this may be the only arrangement possible. The bags should be large and of heavy plastic, of the kind used in large dustbins, and will be more efficient if one is pushed inside another to make a double lining. When you have dug your pit and dropped the lining bags inside, make sure that they do not slide down

Figure 34. (i) Clean dustbins make expedient water containers
(ii) A plastic water barrel.

under the weight of water by fixing them at the rim. You can do this by making a wire hoop a little larger than the mouth of your pit and taping the lip of the bag round it; or by folding the lip of the bag over the edge of the hole and driving half a dozen long nails into the earth, where the soil is firm and compacted. Plywood or boards at least ¾ inch (1½ centimetres) thick should be placed over the filled water hole, earth heaped over it to make a dome, and this covered with waterproof material. More earth mounded above completes the roofing, which will not only keep the water store safe under most assault conditions, but will also prevent contaminated water percolating into it from a fallout-contaminated surface.

An ordinary trench, 3 feet (1 metre) wide, 2½ yards (metres) long and 30 inches (75 centimetres) deep will hold over 200 gallons (900 litres) of water. It can be lined with a large sheet of polythene – large enough to give a sizable overlap at the edges – and roofed in the same way as the smaller pit. The lining in this case can be kept in place by heaping earth over the edges of the plastic sheet. With the earth roof heaped to a height of 30 inches (75 centimetres), a buried reservoir of this sort has successfully withstood blast overpressure of nearly 7 psi – enough to have flattened most substantial buildings, and equivalent to what would be experienced 3 miles (5 kilometres) from a 1MT burst.

The easiest and safest way to take water out of either a buried plastic bag or a plastic-lined pit is by syphoning it. Prepare a length of tube for this well in advance, taping it in position so that it will not press against the tank side and block the water flow, and burying it in a shallow trench to protect it (dig this before you roof either the pit or your shelter). Keep the length of the tube to less than about 7 yards (metres) and remember that the longer it is, the longer you have to suck on it to begin the flow. When you feel the water coming through strongly, bend the tube over double so that it is blocked, lower it into the container to be filled and then let the water out. When you have enough, double the tube again, and keep it folded over with a tight rubber band. Try and hang it on the shelter wall, at some point higher than the level of the water in the tank outside.

Sanitation

In two or three weeks, the time you are likely to be confined in your shelter, the human body produces large amounts of waste material. This has to be disposed of. Privacy and hygiene are important for morale and health. Do everything you can to keep clean. Hygiene is of vital importance in counteracting infection. For people who are weakened by radiation sickness, but who might otherwise make a complete recovery, infection can be fatal. Only the best contractor-built shelters will have comparatively normal toilet arrangements. For the rest, privacy and comfort will be hard to achieve. Nevertheless, by using the outer chamber or entrance way of a shelter, or by judicious hanging of curtains or pieces of sacking, some privacy may be provided.

To improve the basic shelter toilet (a plastic bag), use a large metal container as a stand – a dustbin, 5-gallon (22-litre) paint can, or small oil-drum; if the can you have seems too high to make a convenient toilet, you can always sink it into the floor to the required level. You can also include a vent for the more noxious stinks. Near the top of the container/toilet, cut a hole large enough to take a hose-pipe or long piece of other flexible tubing. Use almost any hard, sharp instrument, even a screwdriver. Secure the pipe firmly with wide insulating tape or wire and run the other end to a point outside the shelter. Anchor it at least 6 inches (15 centimetres) above ground level, since it might otherwise provide a channel for rainwater to run into the shelter. Fit a large plastic bag in the receptacle, leaving the mouth of the vent-pipe clear. Now put on the lid, or tie a piece of plastic film over the top.

Ideally, your toilet should be fitted with a seat so that the very young, the old and those enfeebled by sickness need make no great physical effort in using it. Bring with you, if possible, the lavatory seat from home; otherwise, you might pad the edges of the container, nail together some well-smoothed boards, or cut a hole in the seat of an old chair.

Whenever this improvised toilet is used, disinfectant should be poured in before the lid is firmly shut.

At the first opportunity your toilet should, of course, be emptied: bury the plastic sack of waste in a pit at least 18 inches (45 centimetres) deep and some 33 yards (30 metres) from the shelter. Since the worst of the fallout danger should have passed within two or three days, it should very soon thereafter be possible to go outside for the length of time necessary to do this. For such duties, protective clothing will be invaluable; however, if you don't have a protective suit, wrap plastic round you, and take special care to tie it over your shoes, to help keep dangerous fallout dust from contaminating you and your shelter. On returning discard the plastic and hose or brush down clothing. When not in use protective garments should always be kept in a closed-off ante-chamber, and never be brought into the main shelter.

Obviously, rather than primitive arrangements of this sort, it would be better to use the kind of small chemical toilet used in aircraft or caravans; and perhaps one of these should be standard equipment in every purpose-built shelter. But in the expedient refuges likely to be prepared when a true emergency arises, such luxury will not be possible. You may not be able to make available much more than a pile of plastic bags. These must be sealed after use. But do not make bags containing excrement completely airtight; the gases generated will, especially in warm weather, cause the bags to swell and explode.

These bags can be thrown clear of the shelter. For that purpose, and for any other rubbish that accumulates, a pit should be dug at the same time as the shelter is being built. Make it down-wind and some 2 yards (metres) away.

If you plan to use a waste-disposal pit in this way, use a separate container – bucket or large paint can – for urine. This can be safely and easily emptied outside the shelter. Keep the plastic bags for excrement only, thus ensuring that there will be little spillage when you put them out.

Ventilation

The crudest ventilation in expedient shelters is provided by draughts. Making use of convection, caused by body-heated air rising through an exhaust exit placed at a higher level than the air intake, is a slightly more sophisticated system. Ideally, however, you should pay much more attention to this problem. Your aim must be to gain as much control over the atmosphere in your shelter as possible. You must be able to clean the incoming air of fallout particles and, if necessary, chemical and bacteriological contaminants. No shelter can be efficient and safe, for the length of time likely to be necessary, without a controlled air supply. The optimum is to have an entirely self-contained shelter with built-in ventilation system using the best available equipment designed for the purpose.

Your ideal system, whether homemade or bought off the shelf, should have an inflow pipe, protected against blast and governed by one or more filters, set in an otherwise airtight route to your shelter. It should have some form of power to draw fresh air in and an outflow pipe, also otherwise airtight and protected against blast, for stale air to leave.

It is possible to buy complete ventilation systems to cater for anything from eight to 300 people – that is, from a family shelter to one intended for a medium-sized factory or school. They are imported from Scandinavia or Switzerland and are now easily obtained in this country. The larger models include an electric motor – with a manually-operated alternative for emergencies – dust and gas filters, anti-blast protection and every other essential, even a grille for the air intake. The smallest motorised ventilator, suitable for a shelter holding a dozen people, can be installed at a cost of about £670 (just over $1,200) at 1982 prices; for around half that amount, however, an ordinary family-sized shelter can be fitted with a purely manually-operated ventilator, complete with all the necessary attachments and quite powerful enough to maintain seven people in reasonable comfort. In Switzerland the smallest of the electric-powered fan-filters finds some 10,000 customers every year, an indication of how seriously the Swiss take the idea of defending their families. (Such shelter items as blast doors, emergency exits and dust and blast-proof window grilles are also available in Switzerland and elsewhere – and bought in large numbers. Several companies import this equipment and some UK manufacturers supply home-produced versions.)

The British Home Office gives sound general advice on the requirements of a ventilation system. It should:

- be able to change the air in the shelter at least three times every hour;
- include an air-intake route that is tortuous rather than direct;
- include a dust trap;
- provide alternative motivating power – hand pump, bellows or a battery-driven fan – in case conventional power sources fail;
- be either an intake system, drawing in fresh air, or an extractor, expelling the stale.

The Home Office recommends that for every individual in the shelter there should be available around 65 cubic feet (1·75 cubic metres) of free air space. It warns against smoking, clearly not advisable in an enclosed and sealed environment, and suggests that those who must smoke should do so close to the exhaust pipe during the periods when the ventilation system is operating. It is hard to know which represents the greatest danger, a thwarted smoker or the quantity of carbon monoxide he could create if indulged. The Swiss, too, permit smoking – near the ventilator exhaust, and in relays.

The kind of naked flame necessary for cooking should not be lit at any time when the shelter doors are shut; there is little enough oxygen for the occupants to breathe without drawing any of it off to feed a fire, however small or controlled. The Swiss provide only for cold food in their shelters. If you are building your own shelter, and know little about the problems of providing a flow of breathable air for it, the Home Office wisely suggests that you consult a heating and ventilation engineer; the price of not doing so may be discomfort and even, in extreme cases, asphyxiation – or flight into the fallout zone.

It is possible to build a simple sand filter which, with a powered fan, makes a very efficient ventilation system: sink a wooden or metal container into the earth close to or over the shelter, leaving the top 4 to 6 inches (10 to 15 centimetres) exposed. Place openings in the side, so that air can flow in freely. Attach a pipe at the bottom, perhaps with a bend in the middle to give extra protection. The lower end of the pipe is led and attached to the fan mechanism, and so to its outlet in the shelter. Over the top of the pipe, in the box, place a mesh fine enough to prevent sand from falling through. Then fill the box three-quarters full of coarse sand – even small stones and pebbles will prove of value. But remember, this system will not work unless there is a powered fan available to suck the air through the filter.

Russian civil defence experts recommend a similar device. Their sand filter is a pit, 1·1 yards (metres) deep, with sloping sides. Situated just beside the shelter, it is 3½ yards (3·2 metres) square at the top and only 1·6 yards (metres) square at the bottom. The sides should be lined with waterproof material and strengthened with wood or brick. If this can be sealed to render it airtight, so much the better;

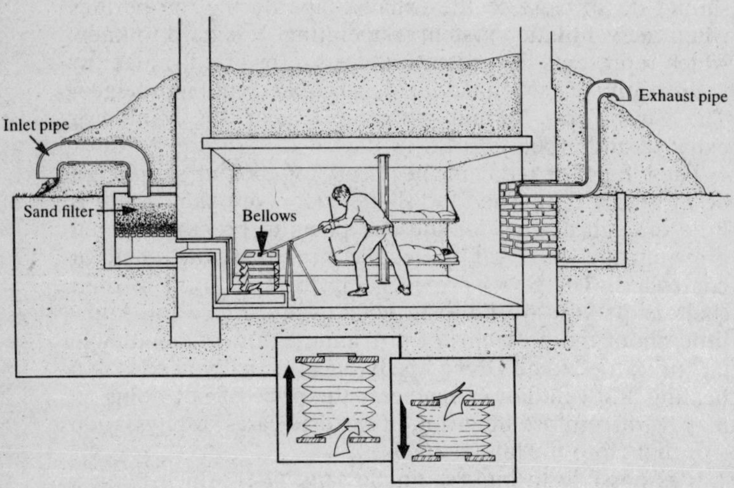

Figure 35. Improvised sand filter (based on a Russian design) installed in a basement, showing simple hand-operated bellows suction. The route from the filter to the bellows must be airtight.

ribs projecting from the sides will prevent air leaks between the walls and the sand when the pit is finally filled. The opening of the shelter's air-intake pipe is at the bottom and above this should be placed a deep grating of wood or metal. On it rests a layer, 4 inches (10 centimetres) deep, of coarse gravel, the particles of which should have a diameter of about 0·8 inches (2½ centimetres). Above that again, should be a layer of finer gravel and, on top of that, the main filtering medium – at least 3 feet (1 metre) of coarse sand or the fine grit of coal slag.

Over the top of the pit should be a shallow wooden roof, to protect it from the weather, with enough room left at the sides for the air to be drawn in. The air-intake pipe runs down the side of the buried shelter; a second pipe leads off at right angles from it, some 8 inches (20 centimetres) from the bottom, to run horizontally into the shelter. At the very bottom of the vertical pipe, some drainage must be provided, perhaps into a small bed of gravel. Inside the shelter, of course, the air inlet connects to a power source – a hand-driven fan, a pair of bellows, a bicycle-driven fan, or, possibly, an electric motor. Naturally, everything must be done to see that the system is airtight, with all the pipes lagged and the joints reinforced.

Wooden blast bafflers should be built to protect the exhaust valves, strong structures rather like small nest-boxes, able to deflect at least some of the blast pressure. Swiss experts have commented that, unless carefully constructed and frequently inspected, the contents of such filters 'solidify into cement'. Consequently it would make sense not to add the sand until an emergency.

If time is short and you are using expedient principles, here are some ideas:

1) Don't make the air intake too small, even if it has no filter. Numerous tests have shown that the hazards from the small amount of fallout particles carried into well-built expedient shelters by unfiltered air are minor compared to the danger from poor ventilation.

2) Your air intake route should move the air upwards. Thus the force of gravity will keep most of the

particles from entering your retreat. The simplest air pipe to use this principle is one inserted through the roof at one end of your shelter – but with a curved ending, like a swan's neck, that points downward.

3) Incorporate a fallout trap if you can. Pumping air through industrial dust filters is a good way to remove even more, and finer, fallout particles.

The Kearny Air Pump

Improvised fallout shelters will benefit from a ventilation device which circulates the air. The Kearny Air Pump has been designed to be built and installed by any do-it-yourself person, in little time, with basic tools and materials.

The frame is of wood. Across this is a grille of tightly drawn wire, nylon thread, or even string, tied or tacked into position about ¾ inch (2 centimetres) apart. Every fifth string has a plastic flap hemmed around it. The frame is hinged to the horizontal support, as shown in Figure 37. Hinges may be acquired from cupboard doors, etc.; they should be well oiled and should have a good 180-degree 'swing'. The pump is operated by being swung rhythmically by means of a string tied to a central support two-thirds up the frame. As the pump swings forward the flaps close, forcing air into the shelter. As it swings back the flaps open, so that all the fresh air is not expelled again.

The pump should be mounted on quick-removal brackets so that when the natural airflow alters its direction, as it will in a two-entrance shelter when the wind changes direction, the location of the pump can be changed to match it.

To use the Kearny Pump efficiently, design your shelter so that the air has unrestricted passage from intake to outflow. The area of the airflow passage cross-section should never be smaller than half the area of the pump itself. The main problem will usually be that of the outflow duct, which tends to be rather small in most shelters, thus limiting the amount of air flowing out. It is possible to make provision against this when building the shelter by installing two or three outflow ducts.

It is also possible in a small shelter to turn the entrance passage, usually already doubling as an inflow duct, into an exhaust duct as well. To do this divide the passage horizontally into upper and lower sections, extending the divider right up to the top if the shelter is underground and, therefore, reached by a vertical shaft. Poles, sticks or battens fixed in the earth walls form the supports for this half-floor, the first of them fixed in the shelter, directly under the main flap of the pump. The dividing material – plastic, canvas, hardboard or any other airtight substance – is laid on the supports and carried up to above ground level, where it is fixed to the central ridge-pole of the plastic roof built like a tent over the outlet. On each side of this tent, a

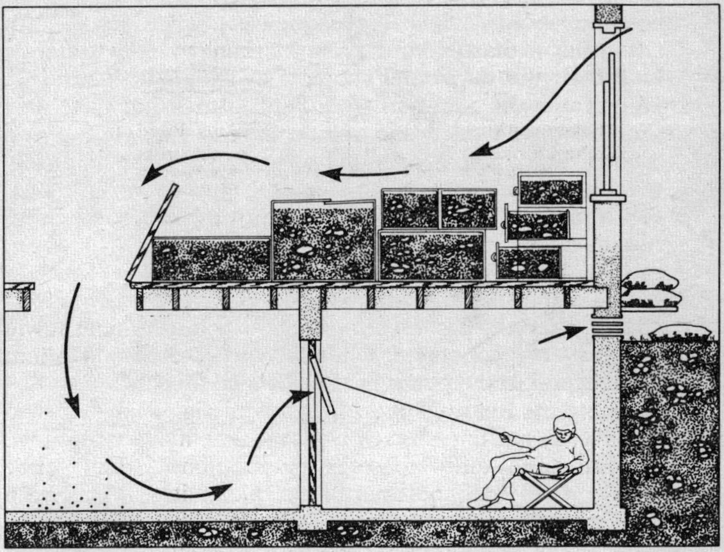

Figure 36. An improvised ventilation system in the home, using the Kearny Air Pump.

low protective wall, of any suitable material, forces the air to rise to the entry-duct just below the roof every time the pump is working down below. Forcing the air to rise these few inches (15 or 20 centimetres) will help to clean it of the heavier radioactive particles suspended in it (Figure 38).

The Kearny Pump, forcing the air into the shelter down one side of the divider, sets up a flow that pushes the exhausted air out. Because air is warmed in use, and warm air rises, it finds its way up the chimney-like exit passage, using the space left on the other side of the divider. This two-way use of a single corridor and chimney ensures a constant movement of the atmosphere inside the shelter, an advantage which in larger chambers can be improved by

Figure 37. The Kearny Air Pump. NOTE: These dimensions may be scaled up or down as required.

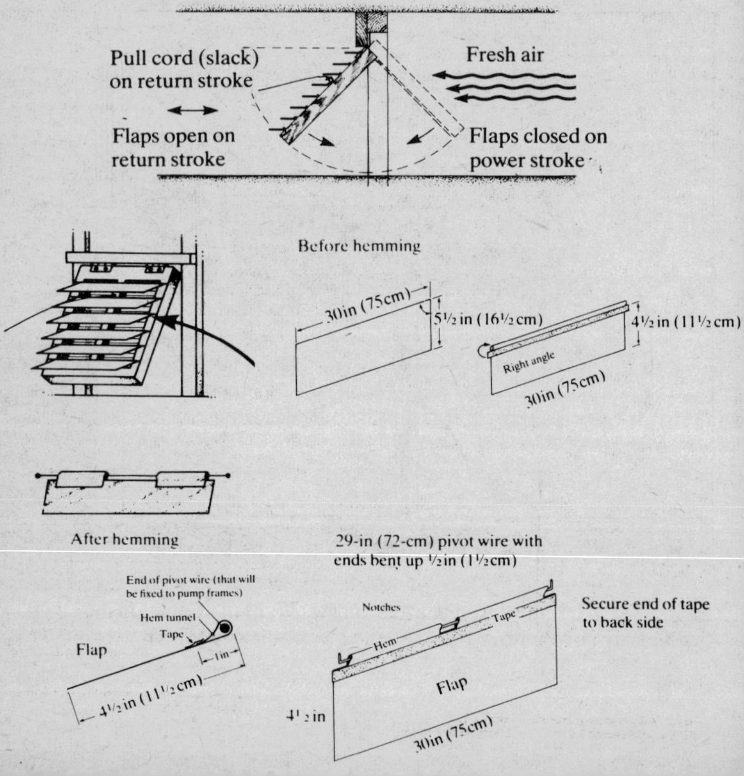

mounting several Kearny Pumps in relays. If the ceiling is not suitable to take their supports, light frames will hold them, a scaffolding of wood or metal rather like that supporting a child's swing. The general rule would be that you should set up one such pump for every twenty-five persons in the shelter.

The cord by which the pump is pulled should be long enough to allow different occupants of the shelter easy access to it: everyone who can should take a turn at keeping it in motion. In narrow, trench-like shelters, everybody should be able to grasp the cord without moving from his or her place – an awkward business in cramped surroundings. Make sure that the end of the cord of a large pump has a

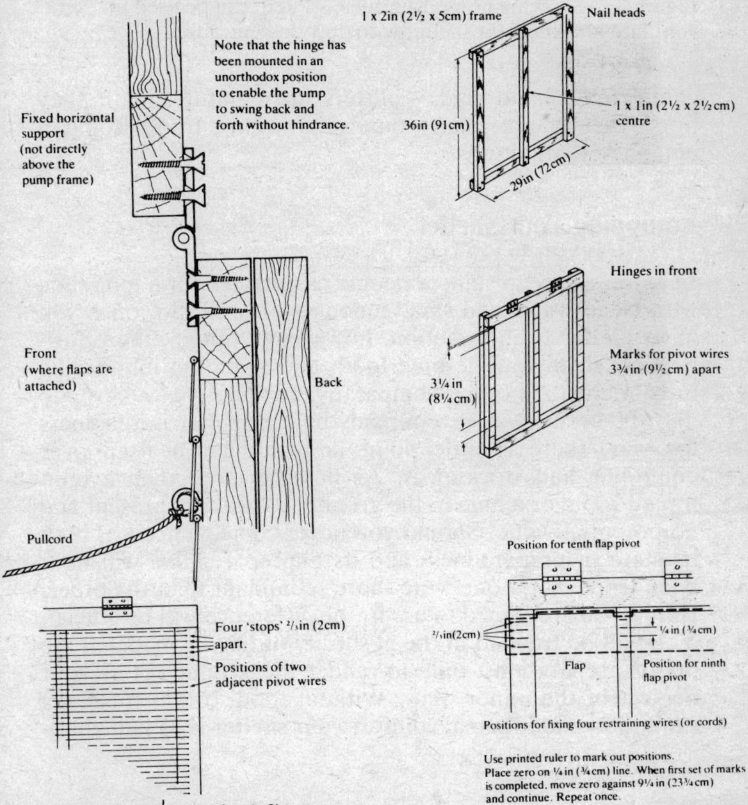

NOTE: All wood for frame is cut from 1 x 2in (2½ x 5cm) except 1 x 1in (2½ x 2½cm) centre brace.

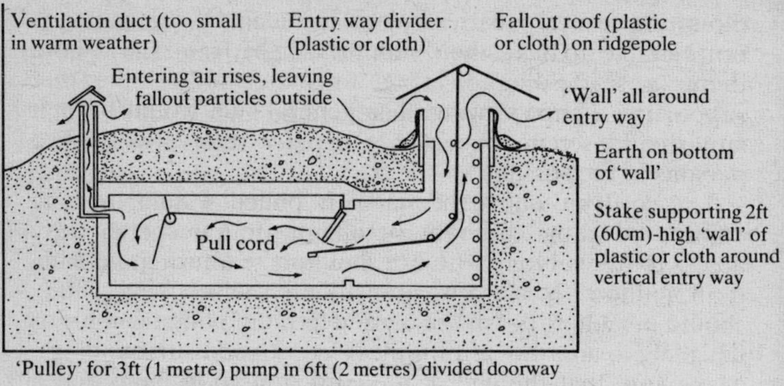

Figure 38. Showing how a Kearny Air Pump can be used to ventilate an expedient shelter with only one entrance.

comfortable hand-hold – blisters are painful and, if they burst, create unpleasant wounds that will be troublesome in emergency conditions.

Equipping Your Shelter

In extreme circumstances people can survive for a long time with clean water and small amounts of food. So, once you have shelter from radiation, however primitive, the priorities are clean water, some food, and radiation monitoring instruments. All else is comparative luxury.

If, however, you have already built a shelter in readiness for war, there is little point in being half-hearted over equipping and stocking it. As nothing more than a reinforced room or a hole in the ground, it has little present and no potential value. Should you never come to need it, both its state of preparedness and its unpreparedness will have been irrelevant – one is no more redundant than the other. But, if you are forced to use it, the difference will be crucial. You will be trapped in the absurdity of having made all the major preparations, only to render them valueless by your neglect of the minor ones. Without food, drink, fresh air, sanitation and minimal comfort your shelter is as uninhabitable as any other part of your home would be in similar circumstances. To stock it well is to complete the final rampart of your personal defence.

The better equipped your shelter is, the higher will be the morale of its occupants and the greater their powers of resistance. It is possible to live out your two weeks – which may easily turn out to be rather longer – scraping a Neanderthal living on a bare earth floor of an underground refuge, but it is likely to leave you and your companions debilitated in a variety of ways.

There are many provisions in addition to food and water that could be stored in your shelter. The following is a luxurious set of supplies, of which radiation detection instruments are the most vital. Many of the items will also be of use in the post-shelter phase. Using this list as a basis you can work out your own priorities:

Radiation detection instruments and, preferably, one dosimeter per person.

Wooden bunks, set one above the other and supplied with pillows and mattresses (air mattresses – with the means to inflate them – might serve here); folding chairs and folding tables; plates, mugs, knives and spoons, all of plastic if possible (forks take too much washing up water).

An adequate set of tools, with such outdoor equipment as an axe, a hatchet, a saw and a spade, as well as the handier devices like a hammer, a screwdriver, pliers and the nails and screws to go with them: a mallet might prove useful, as will sticky insulating tape.

Emergency equipment, such as lengths of strong rope, a jemmy or crowbar, one or more car-jacks for shifting fallen masonry, a whistle and a strong, multi-purpose knife: in the domestic sphere needles, thread and scissors, and perhaps buttons, spare zip-fasteners and some pieces of stout fabric with which to mend large tears.

A strong battery-powered lamp, with spare bulbs and

batteries; candles and matches; a storm lantern with a can of fuel (but be sure that this can be stored safely: a shelter is not a good place to keep inflammables), the same fuel to serve a small, portable camping stove; of course a radio and batteries, preferably two or three. Radios must be wrapped carefully in layers of metal foil and kept stored in a tight-fitting metal box. This will help to preserve them against EMP.

Toilet articles, including toothbrushes, toothpaste, soap, shaving materials, comb and brush, towels and lavatory paper, and also beauty aids as morale boosters; both talcum powder and deodorants have their value; face flannels may help to save water, since a rub with a damp cloth will help to keep you clean; and don't forget a bowl to wash in: it too will save water.

Extra clothes and blankets for comfort and warmth.

Chemicals to purify water, as well as a general disinfectant; a fire extinguisher (but not one using tetrachloride); a wind-up clock, preferably with an alarm, and a calendar; old newspapers, which are always useful, even if only to push inside your jersey to help keep you warm.

Games to keep you and the children amused, such as cards, jigsaws, dominoes, draughts and chess; equipment for occupations that help to pass the time, such as knitting or embroidery; books and notebooks in which to keep a journal, keep the score in the games, or draw; pens and pencils, sticky tape, a rubber, perhaps a ruler.

Protective garments to wear when you have to go out (you can buy one-time disposable, or decontaminatable ones).

Equipment you may need if you must, or after you can, leave the shelter: detailed maps of nearby areas, through which you may have to find your way on foot; rucksacks and similar bags in which to carry basic necessities, should that become essential; perhaps, if there is room, a bicycle; binoculars.

As extensive a medical kit as you can put together; include antibiotics, bandages, safety pins, cotton wool, antiseptic ointment, a thermometer, splints in wood or plastic, as well as remedies for common ailments such as headaches, indigestion and so on, plasters of various different sizes and alcohol to clean wounds. Include medical manuals. All good bookshops contain a variety of first aid and health books.

Planning Your Food Store

The type of food you store will depend on the facilities for preparation in your shelter. Tinned meats and vegetables, for example, may have to be heated to make them palatable, and dried vegetables need to be cooked. Such energy-rich and long-lasting foods as lentils must be soaked in water, and then cooked. Ready-to-eat cereals will need milk and, since after the first day or two liquid milk will all be used up or have turned sour, you will be using dried milk, which needs water. Select your foods with such limitations in mind and allow for any special diets for children, the elderly or the ill.

Lay down the necessary stock as soon as you have constructed your shelter, but keep a careful eye on it. Mark the date of purchase on every item, and inspect all foods regularly. Change any that have reached the end of their 'shelf life', but do not rely only on the calendar. Check that the condition of the tins has not altered: jettison those that show any peculiarity of shape, any bulging. Make sure that your provisions have not been harmed by damp or insects. Look closely at any foodstuffs kept in clear plastic to see if they are becoming discoloured. Discard anything about which you have the slightest reservation.

Any food that is not already in a tin or packet should be kept in a tightly closed metal or plastic container; glass can be hazardous. Remember that *few foods will keep indefinitely*: tinned fruit, tinned vegetables and most fruit juices will begin to go off after a year, and orange and other citrus-fruit products have to be replaced after six months; the useful life of evaporated and fat-free powdered milk is three or four years, if kept in a cool place. A year is the maximum time most cereals can be kept – though in a sealed metal container they might last longer – and ready-to-eat products such as cornflakes will not survive in their original packets for much longer than a month. Only sugar and salt, if kept dry, can be assumed to keep indefinitely. It is important to replace any foods that might be in danger of losing their freshness or going off: the discomfort of even a mild attack of food poisoning is best avoided in the crowded and primitive conditions of most shelters.

You will need enough food to last at least two weeks. Try to plan some sort of diet and arrange for it not to be too monotonous. That it will be restricted is of course unavoidable, but a few sweets and chocolates, a handful of biscuits, a little fresh fruit, fruit juices and instant coffee can all help to give at least an impression of variety. Hold back 'goodies' so as to produce them occasionally as morale boosters.

The continuing imperatives of civilised behaviour will be at a premium. Food may be physiologically less important than drink, but the psychological effect of regular meals during a period of stress, the reassertion of normality this presents in abnormal conditions, and the symbolic cementing of relations within the shelter group at such mealtimes, may, after a week or ten days, assume a crucial significance.

Few shelters will be large enough to carry stocks of food to last for several months. Make sure, therefore, that you include compact rations too. Fifty-five pounds (25 kilos) of whole-kernel wheat, for example, requires only 1 cubic foot (0·027 cubic metre) of storage space. A partial answer to this long-term problem is to hide away as many stocks of useful foodstuffs and other essentials as you can in secret underground caches. These will prove useful if supplies are disrupted for a long period – as they are bound to be in some areas. Make sure all your supplies are in well-sealed, dustproof containers to avoid deterioration and contamination. Do not use metal containers, which rust, often resulting in leaks or the contents becoming inedible within a few months.

Foods to consider stocking include:

Cereals, especially the highly nutritious mueslis; whichever you choose, the addition of bran to give roughage will prove of great and necessary benefit; if you have cooking facilities, instant porridge oats provide a meal.

Tins of meat, especially those that can be eaten cold – corned beef, ham, etc. – and fish, such as pilchards, sardines, even salmon: of course, if you have cooking facilities, the list becomes limitless.

Tins of vegetables, which can always be eaten cold: but try to achieve some variety – sliced beans day after day can only irritate.

Dried vegetables such as lentils are very nutritious and keep a long time: they need water for soaking and must be cooked – but may prove invaluable in the days immediately after your emergence from the shelter.

Dried fruit such as raisins and sultanas, which provide both variety and energy; and, of course, the range of such fruits is very wide.

Fresh fruit will often keep for many months – as long as it is hard: apples, which may wrinkle but improve in taste, pears and oranges are all recommended.

Nuts of all sorts, which even shelled will keep a long time if dry and in a sealed container.

Hard cheeses: whole cheeses naturally keep best – most of the British cheeses are suitable, so are the Dutch, and mountain cheeses like Emmenthaler and Gruyère; processed cheeses also maintain their quality over a fairly long period.

Crispbreads, salty and sweet biscuits, prepared toast, biscottes – all these will keep for long periods.

Spreads, both sweet, like jams, honey and chocolate, and savoury, such as meat or fish pastes; peanut butter, too, falling somewhere in between and full of calories.

Cold sausages, of which the best-known are the

salamis, but which come in many varieties from Germany, Italy and elsewhere; hung up whole, they can keep for many months.

Pickles: cucumber, onion, mixtures such as piccalilli; they take up little space, keep well, and add zest to a monotonous diet, but beware of anything too salty and thirst-creating.

Chocolate, both for pleasure and energy; fruit drops, to keep thirst at bay; chewing gum for freshness.

Condiments – although you'll not need much salt or pepper for a cold diet at a time of water shortage – and sugar.

Powdered milk will keep for a long time in tins, as will condensed milk; and nowadays the Long-Life varieties of liquid milk keep, unopened, for a period of months.

Mineral waters, such as Evian or Perrier, unopened, keep their guaranteed purity and are worth storing if there is room.

Fruit juices help to maintain both health and spirits.

Dilutable squashes of all kinds are valuable additions, if there is an unrestricted water supply.

Instant drinks – coffee, chocolate, even tea – have a place if you can heat water; even if you can't, there are powders designed to be mixed with cold water or milk.

Instant soups and soup drinks, again if there is hot water.

Don't forget tin openers!

This list is not complete and not everyone will want all the items on it. But it provides balance and variety, reinforcing both health and morale. A diet of water, biscuits and cold baked beans is likely to undermine both within a week. If you have cooking facilities, familiarise yourself with 'hay-box' cookery, to reduce fuel consumption dramatically.

Hot food is a potent weapon in the attempt to maintain

morale. Where petrol and similar liquid fuels seem too dangerously inflammable to be used for cooking, you may prefer a stove burning the safer, if less efficient, blocks of solidified alcohol. Even a butane-fuelled camping stove will be less of a risk than one that burns petrol or paraffin. A stove that is made from a bucket and needs only a few lengths of wire to construct, is another of those emergency solutions devised and tested by C.H. Kearny at the Department of Energy's National Laboratory at Oak Ridge, Tennessee.

WARNING: To minimise the contamination of your air by any fuel-burning stove (including carbon monoxide and carbon dioxide), use a stove only at or near the air-exhaust opening of a shelter.

How to Make a Bucket Stove

With a hammer and chisel, or sharpened screwdriver, make a hole 4½ inches (11¼ centimetres) square in the side of a metal bucket, about 1½ inches (3 centimetres) from the bottom. Place the bucket over some solid support such as a large log, otherwise it will become dented and bent. To regulate the stove you will need a damper which can be made by cutting a piece of light metal, 6 by 8 inches (15 by 20 centimetres), out of a large fruit or vegetable tin. This metal damper must be made to slide over the hole you have cut in the side of the bucket, so regulating the air flow into the stove. Out of two wire coat hangers, straightened and each bent back on itself, you make two simple springs. Using a hammer and pliers, curl a 6-inch (15-centimetre) edge around the long upright of each of these springs. When you hang the springs over the edge of the bucket, the metal damper will be suspended above the large opening in the side. The pieces of the wire bent back on themselves will clasp the inside of the bucket. The completed damper can be pushed up or down, and will remain in whatever position you choose.

Punch four holes, equidistant from each other, around the bucket, about 3½ inches (9 centimetres) from the top.

Straighten two wire coat hangers and run each wire up on the outside of the bucket, over the rim and down the inside. Then bend them in towards the centre of the bucket, curling the tips back towards the side: you now have four springs able to grip a pot and hold it in place in the bucket stove. Take four or five more wire coat hangers and twist them together to make a grate, a contraption some 4 inches (10 centimetres) wide and 5 inches (13 centimetres) long, with little legs to stand on and, on the longer sides, two retaining wire parapets; its total height should not be more than 3½ inches (9 centimetres). You can line the stove with aluminium foil and the bottom with ¾ to 1 inch (2 or 3 centimetres) of dry sand, if these are available; they will prevent undue heat loss.

Use the stove as close as possible to the air outflow of the shelter: in an enclosed space, with still air, it will use up

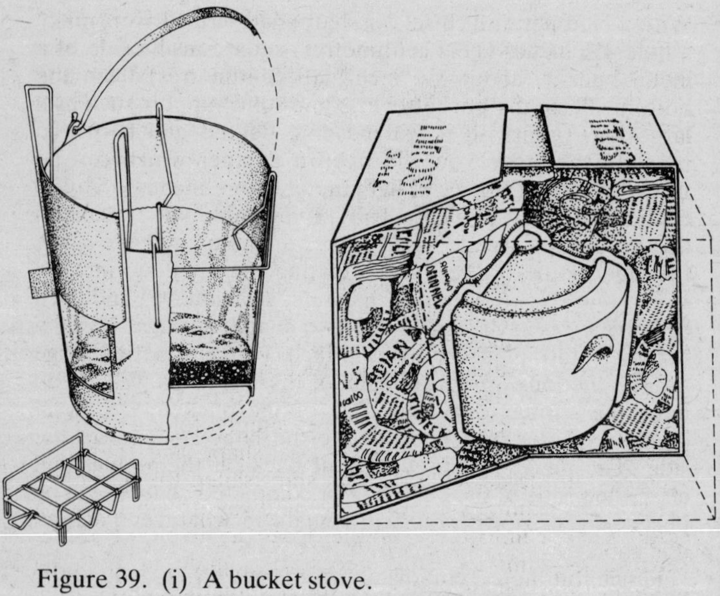

Figure 39. (i) A bucket stove.
(ii) A haybox fireless cooker.

oxygen and create discomfiting fumes. Place wood, or failing that, tightly screwed-up 'sticks' of newspaper on the wire grate. When the fuel is alight regulate the flames so that they reach the bottom of the cooking pot, but do not begin licking up the sides. Close the damper if they begin to do so.

Haybox Cooking

You can use the stove in conjunction with the 'haybox' method for slow cooking, such as making stews or porridge. A pot that has been brought to a high temperature is surrounded with several inches of tightly packed insulating material, for example, compressed hay, thick fabric, or tightly folded newspapers, to maintain its heat. It will continue to cook the contents for another four to six hours – and there are those who claim that the results are more delicious than those of any other method. It is only necessary to boil your food for 5 minutes on your stove, then quickly transfer the lidded cooking pot to a large box into which you have packed the insulating material. Make sure that the pot fits snugly into its insulating 'nest' (Figure 39 ii). Leave it for at least four to six hours, and you can eat.

Making Hammocks and Suspended Chairs

Acute discomfort creates an irresistible desire to escape, even into the invisible but mortal radiation dangers outside, so the provision of somewhere to sit and somewhere to sleep in an expedient shelter should not be considered a luxury.

If you have a suitably strong structure to hang them from, it is possible to use double-bed sheets to make hammocks and suspended chairs. These are simply folded double, pleated at each end to make a boat-shape and then tied securely. In the days when small ships sailed the oceans of the world, hammocks proved the one way in which sailors could sleep comfortably in the space available to them: slinging a hammock (not necessarily made at the last moment from a sheet) might be the best method of ensuring some comfort in the confined space of most nuclear shelters.

On First Emergence

Water

Your first necessity is water. You will have secured an uncontaminated water supply stored just before entering your shelter. This should last during the dangerous period of your confinement. On emerging, however, the water problem will be of paramount importance. It is more essential to drink than to eat, and liquids should not, if at all possible, be rationed. Certainly you should provide a minimum of 2 pints (1 litre) a day per person, and preferably more. Keep containers ready in your shelter – and remember that these need not be of rigid construction: large plastic bags, of the heavier kind used in dustbins, make very effective water-storage units, if placed in smaller-diameter bags or strong pillow cases, and can be easily stored and swiftly filled (a hosepipe kept with them may be useful).

By the time you begin to run out of water, it is likely that enough time will also have passed for the radiation danger to have decreased. If that is so, it will be safe to emerge from your shelter, at least for a little time each day, especially if you have some protective clothing. Bearing in mind that fallout is dust, any water collected where dust cannot reach is likely to be safe to drink. So if your house is intact, the water in any of the tanks, in the pipes and even in the cisterns will be safe.

Any suspect water should be strained through layers of clean cloth or a paper towel (or, failing that, allowed to stand for twenty-four hours until the heavier and more dangerous particles have sunk to the bottom): then, if your facilities allow, you should boil it. One minute of boiling will kill all types of disease-carrying bacteria. But be sure to keep in your shelter chemical purifying agents – liquid chlorine household bleach (make sure that hypochlorite is its only active agent), 2 per cent tincture of iodine or, of course, the special water purification tablets that can be bought at most chemists or camping suppliers. Twelve drops of tincture of iodine are the equivalent of four purifying tablets and will render 1 gallon (4½ litres) of water safe to drink (safe, that is, from pollution and bacteria, not radioactivity) – though if the water is of a suspect cloudiness, you may double these amounts. Once the disinfectant drops have been added, the water should be allowed to stand for at least thirty minutes before it may be drunk.

Filtering Water

In temperate countries such as the British Isles, where rainfall is plentiful, water filtering wells can supply safe water. As with water from deep wells, the distance the water has filtered through the earth ensures that all radiation has been removed. Water filtering wells should be dug on low ground near a relatively clean source of water like a river, lake or stream. Keep the well covered to prevent pollution from above. Let the water in it settle and, when you are ready, draw it from near the surface to avoid stirring up the sediment.

If you suspect that your water supply has been exposed to fallout, you must filter it. Only a very small fraction of radioactive contamination on and in fallout particles dissolves in water. If you remove radioactive particles from otherwise clean water it is drinkable under post-attack conditions. It will not incapacitate you and is unlikely to cause cancer or thyroid gland abnormalities.

If you don't have filtering equipment you can build an effective filter tank from easily available materials, as follows (see Figure 40):

1) Perforate the bottom of a clean 5-gallon (22-litre) can or large bucket, or similar container, with about a

dozen nail holes. Punch the holes from the bottom upwards, within about 2 inches (5 centimetres) of the centre.

2) Place a layer of pebbles or small stones about 1½ inches (4 centimetres) thick on the bottom of the can. If pebbles are not available, twisted wire coat hangers or small sticks may be used.

3) Cover the pebbles with one thickness of terry towelling, sackcloth, or other porous cloth in a roughly circular shape about 3 inches (8 centimetres) larger than the diameter of the can.

4) Take soil containing some clay – almost any soil will do – from at least 4 inches (10 centimetres) below the surface of the ground. (Nearly all fallout particles remain near the surface except those deposited on sand or gravel.) Do not use pure clay (not porous enough) or sand (too porous).

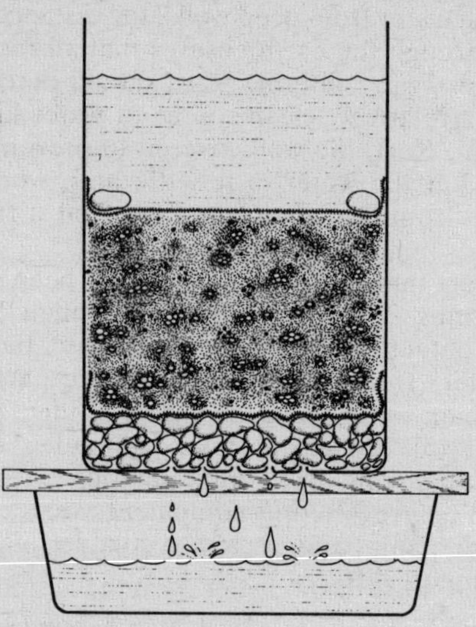

Figure 40. An expedient water filter.

5) Pulverise the soil, then gently press it in layers over the cloth that covers the pebbles, so that the cloth is held snugly against the sides of the can. The soil in the can should be 6 to 7 inches (15 to 18 centimetres) thick.

6) Cover the surface of the soil layer completely with one thickness of fabric as porous as a bath towel. This is to keep the soil from being eroded as water is poured into the filtering can. The cloth will also remove some particles from the water. A dozen small stones placed on the cloth near its edges will secure it adequately.

7) Support the filter can on rods or sticks placed across the top of the container that is to collect the water. Obviously its diameter must be greater than the diameter of the filter can; a clean washing up bowl would be suitable.

The contaminated water is poured into the filter can, and collected in the container underneath. The filtered water should be treated with purification tablets to kill off harmful bacteria.

If the 6 or 7 inches (15 to 18 centimetres) of filtering soil is a sandy clay loam, the filter initially will deliver about 6 quarts (litres) of clear water per hour. After several hours, the rate will be reduced to about 2 quarts (litres) per hour. If the filtration rate is faster than about 1 quart (litre) in 10 minutes, remove the upper fabric and recompress the soil.

When the filtering rate becomes too slow, it can be increased by removing and rinsing the surface fabric, removing about ½ inch (1 centimetre) of soil, and then replacing the fabric. The life of a filter is extended, and its efficiency increased, if muddy water is first allowed to settle for several hours in a separate container. After about 50 quarts (56 litres) have been filtered, rebuild the filter by replacing the used soil with fresh soil. The layers of soil and cloth will have collected radiation particles so handle these with care and bury them when you have finished each filtration session.

Remember that water itself does not become radioactive.

It is the particles that fall into it which create the danger. Thus even open reservoirs will, after a few days, contain water that is safe to drink – certainly after some filtration, given a period of reasonably calm weather in which they can settle, the dangerous elements will be too thinly in suspension to render the water a hazard to health. It is therefore sensible, if you have no radiation monitor, to allow everyone to drink as much as they need, rather than to impose rationing and risk the miseries and dangers of dehydration. The likelihood is very strong that you will be able to replenish your water supplies, should you need to.

Water supplies are so central to human well-being, that no effort can be too great to ensure that they are both adequate and safe. For that reason, *double precautions are advisable* whenever possible. If you make an earth filter, for example, keep it sound: in addition to making the replacements outlined above, test the filter daily with a radiation meter for dangerous accumulations of radioactivity. Your survival, and certainly your health, will depend upon the efficiency with which you maintain a source of clean water.

Food

The rule with all food is to make sure you do not forage for food where it may have been affected by initial radiation, close to ground zero, or that no radioactive particles are attached to it. Use common sense. Wash and peel fruit, for example, and don't eat potatoes in their jackets. The danger of receiving harmful doses of radiation through eating food found in shops and warehouses after emerging is very small – provided the food is still sealed in undamaged containers or you first remove the uppermost 2 inches (5 centimetres) of exposed food. Fallout radiation passes through glass, tin, plastic or other food containers without harming the contents in any way. The only risk is if the container is damaged and fallout particles have stuck to, or mixed with, the contents. Paper containers that have become damp should be avoided. If there is any fallout on food containers, hose or wash it off. You will then be able to get at the contents safely. The same goes for canned and bottled drinks.

Farmers, market gardeners and vegetable gardeners should study the procedures for post-nuclear war husbandry available from their local Emergency Planning Officer. Feeding the survivors will be of prime importance. It may seem a grim prospect but, with a much smaller population, the United Kingdom could quickly become self-sufficient in food after a major nuclear war.

Surviving Attack

Psychological Disturbances

In times of war and unexpected catastrophe, the majority of people react well and sensibly. We are more resilient and adaptable than is generally believed. People rise to the occasion rather than panic. Unbalanced behaviour is the exception. Survival performance in crises is much better when the survivors know what is happening to them and what they need to do to maximise their chances. Spreading practical information in advance to minimise panic and disturbance is therefore essential.

Before the Bomb

Many people believe there will be a tense build-up to war, days or weeks before the outbreak of hostilities, during which people will experience fear and anxiety. Fear and anxiety are normal and often useful reactions in such circumstances because levels of attention to important information and readiness for action are aroused. If there is a build-up period, use it in a constructive way. For example, evacuate or prepare your shelter and gather food stocks and equipment. Listen constantly to the radio and be prepared to bolt into your refuge at a moment's notice. Sleep in it at night.

If you are waiting in your shelter, anticipating an attack on this country, don't rest against the shelter walls. Nearby bombs will generate a shock wave through the earth causing sudden rapid earth movement which may reach you. If your head is against the wall or floor of your shelter, your skull could easily be fractured by the violence of this earth movement. Whilst waiting make sure everyone is cushioned.

During Bombing

The flash, impact and noise of one or more bombs, exploding in nearby regions, will, if you are not in your shelter, cause acute fear. You must, however, instantly start your own survival drill. If a bomb goes off within a few miles and you survive, you may be exposed to large numbers of gruesome casualties and heavy damage. People will be suffering the traumas of extreme distress and shock. By thoroughly learning your survival drill you ensure that a part of your brain will operate automatically for your protection, however bad the circumstances. To reduce surprise and shock, become familiar with accounts of the nature and course of events in a nuclear explosion.

Get to your shelter as soon as possible.

An attack may occur without any public warning. Even in this extreme situation, if you act immediately and are not too close to ground zero, there is much you can do to stay alive.

The moment you realise a bomb has exploded, turn away instantly. *Don't look at it.* If you do you will be temporarily blinded at the one time in your life when you need *all* your senses.

If You are Caught in the Open

For several seconds after the explosion searing heat rays will silently and instantaneously cover many square miles. Remember that heat rays must strike you to harm you. Your only thought at this time must be to throw yourself *immediately* behind any non-inflammable object that will act as a shield. Heat, like light, travels mostly in a straight line, so shield all exposed skin from the direction of the explosion. The heat is intense. Thus even if you are sheltering behind a strong wall at a distance at which you will easily survive the bomb's blast effects, you can receive serious burns on exposed skin from heat reflected off other surfaces. So shelter yourself as best you can from all angles. *Even the smallest feature can offer some protection.* A shallow ditch, low wall, roadside bank, hollow in the ground or a slope going downwards away from the bomb, all reduce the effects of heat and blast pressure.

Remember that whatever protects you *must stand across the path of the bomb.* A ditch or valley that runs in the same direction as the blast wave actually increases its blast effect. (The blast will follow a few seconds after the heat.)

It is useful to understand how the blast wave behaves. When the wave encounters features set across its path, such as hills or cliffs, valleys, ditches, or any really substantial buildings, the check it receives may increase its pressure up to seven times. The wave then passes round or over the obstruction, leaving the far side enjoying rather less of its weight than other places. However, where the separated wave comes together again, pressure increases sharply. Even relatively shallow downward slopes that face away from the explosion provide some shelter. If the angle of the slope is less than 30 degrees, pressure will be decreased by up to 15 per cent; for a steeper angle, that reduction can be as high as 30 per cent.

Tuck your head in close to the object or feature that shields you and make yourself as small as possible. Débris will be hurled about by the blast and blast winds. Protect yourself as best you can. After a minute the force will be spent.

If You are Caught in Your Car

The moment you realise a bomb has exploded, stop the car. *Don't look at the explosion.* Open at least one window so that the shock wave and the overpressure are less likely to implode the glass on top of you. Shout to passengers to get down. Then crouch as low as possible, seeking shelter from the heat and covering as much exposed skin as you can. Again, remember that heat rays must strike you to burn you. Cover the back of your neck with clothed arms.

As soon as the heat has passed take a firm grip on any handles or secure objects and brace yourself. In a few seconds the blast wave will buffet and rock the car violently, possibly turning it over, and shower it with débris. The greatest force lasts only a few seconds. Within a minute of the explosion the first crisis will have passed.

Figure 41. What to do when the bomb falls:
(i) Even the smallest feature can offer some protection.

(ii) Look away.

(iii) Avoid flying glass.

(iv) Make yourself as small as possible.

(v) Throw yourself into the shadows to avoid being burnt.

(vi) In a car, keep well down.

(vii) Throw yourself under something that might protect you from flying glass.

If You are Caught in Your Home, School or Place of Work

The moment you realise a bomb has exploded hurl yourself at the wall *nearest* the explosion, away from any windows. If you rush in the opposite direction you will be shredded by glass shot across the room by the explosion. *Don't look at the explosion.* Avoid curtains or other inflammable items exposed to the light of the bomb. After the heat has passed you have to protect yourself from the blast that may follow in a few seconds. If possible, get under a table, desk or bed. Make yourself as small as possible. Do not move too soon unless you think the bomb has exploded several miles away, in which case you will have time to rush to better shelter in a hallway or basement before the blast hits you. Blast takes approximately one minute to travel 14 miles (20 kilometres) and approximately half a minute to travel 7 miles (11 kilometres). If you have no time, protect and brace yourself.

If you survive the heat and blast more or less intact you must, as soon as conditions allow, search for protection against residual radiation.

NOTE: If you are unlucky enough to be blinded by the light, you must still throw yourself in the direction of any shelter you remember having seen a moment before. Your sight will return in time, and you may be far enough away from ground zero to survive all the other immediate effects of the bomb. *Never stop trying to protect yourself – however bad things seem.*

The above circumstances, in which a bomb explodes without warning, are the most difficult to survive. You have a much greater chance with a longer warning.

Official Warnings: Attack

If the communications system survives the impact of EMP from distant and unseen nuclear explosions, public warnings will be broadcast on radio and television, together with advice on what people should do. Powered sirens will also operate throughout the land, a long wailing rise and fall, familiar to those that remember aerial attack warnings of the last war. It is at this point that a large number of people will regret their own unpreparedness – and the State's lack of preparation – for just such an occurrence.

If the warning sirens give you a few minutes to prepare it is, of course, much easier to shield yourself from the effects of heat and blast than when an attack comes unannounced. Don't try to do more than is practical, however, but just concentrate on protecting yourself, applying the principles described on pages 170–5 as best you can. If you have a shelter, get into it.

Radioactive Fallout

A well-developed system for warning the population of the spread of dangerous fallout is in readiness everywhere. Three loud bangs, or three whistles, or three notes of any sharp and penetrating sound available locally will tell you to retreat immediately to your radiation shelter. This sound, coming after warning sirens and explosions, *is not an all-clear signal.* Remember that radioactive particles in the earliest hours and days after explosions are killers. You must put distance or at least 3 feet (1 metre) of solid matter between yourself and them.

Shelter Management

There are many physical and mental problems that shelter occupants may have to face, particularly if the facilities in their shelter are poor and it has not been properly stocked. Most problems, however, can be overcome by sensible shelter management. Every shelter must have a manager whose task is to bring the group through the ordeal. He or she must have the ability to motivate people plus considerable knowledge of nuclear war survival skills.

The aftermath of nuclear bombings will drastically change most people's lives. This in itself is deeply disturbing. People will perhaps be dazed, perhaps near hysteria. Life in a shelter will be cramped and disagreeable.

If one remembers that people survive years of living in the confined conditions of a prison cell, one can more easily appreciate how a few weeks of shelter life, though unpleasant, would be endurable.

The shelter manager must impose order, both to calm people and to prevent general confusion. He or she must give everyone prescribed tasks – keeping the generator going, maintaining ventilation, cooking, washing up, cleaning, child minding, rationing food and water, checking and maintaining the shelter fabric, monitoring radio broadcasts and so on. These tasks are vital in themselves, but they also keep everyone mentally and physically occupied. They create a feeling of responsibility and mutual support which will be essential for continued survival. Even children should be given certain non-vital but useful responsibilities. In addition, a timetable should be established to bring further order into disrupted lives. Each shelter should have its own agreed codes covering conduct, for example, no loud noise, children to be controlled, meals at set times, acceptance of duty rosters, no hogging of shelter resources, with agreed methods of settling any disputes that arise.

Timetables and duty rosters should be written out and pinned up for all to consult.

In primitive expedient shelters it is especially important to create calm and order in the extreme discomfort, for if someone were to become so disturbed as to leave the shelter too soon, the results could be fatal.

The following is a brief guide to dealing with problems likely to arise during the initial sheltering period.

- Illness or pain: Wounds inflicted by flying débris or radiation sickness may cause a severe loss of morale. Apathy and depression lessen the body's ability to repair the damage.

  Management: The patient must be given the best medical attention possible in the circumstances and maximum attention and moral support from the fit shelter occupants.

- Shock: The sudden massive impact of nuclear explosions may induce shock. The effects of shock involve malfunctioning of the circulatory system and an insufficient blood supply reaching the spinal cord and brain. The symptoms are: a fluctuating pulse, very weak or rapid; pale or blue skin that turns cold or moist; shallow or irregular breathing; sudden chills; thirst; the patient may have stomach pains, and vomit.

  A person can be 'in shock' whether conscious or unconscious. All seriously injured persons should be treated for shock, even though they appear alert. Shock may cause death if not treated properly, even when injuries which brought it on are not serious enough to cause death in themselves. People may go into shock without any physical injuries.

  Management: Keep the patient lying down and warm. *Do not,* however, apply any source of heat to the body.

Do not give alcohol to the patient. Loosen clothing. Keep the head lower than the hips and legs (unless the patient has a head or chest injury or difficulty in breathing, in which case keep the head and shoulders slightly higher than the body and legs). If the patient is conscious, and has no abdominal injuries or nausea, encourage him to drink half a glass of the following solution every 15 minutes: one teaspoonful of salt and half a teaspoonful of baking soda to one quart (1 litre) of water.

'Shell-shock': Near-miss explosions can give rise to acute and persistent anxiety which severely disrupts the mind's ability to cope.

Management: Sedate the patient until there is time and space to treat him or her properly.

- Confinement: A shelter with one person per 10 square feet (0·9 square metre) is very crowded. Such shelters will have few opportunities for people to walk around. This environment is conducive to irritability and depression and argumentativeness.

  Management: To lessen these hardships, each occupant should have his own territory, even if this is only a bunk and small shelf for personal possessions cut off by a curtain. Give sedatives and sleeping pills to sufferers from claustrophobia, to fractious children and over-excited adults. Two or three weeks' mild sedation will do no harm and greatly increase comfort in the shelter for everyone else. Once radiation levels outside have fallen to an acceptable level survivors may leave the shelter for short periods to stretch their legs and perform any necessary outside tasks. This may be possible even after a few days. This activity will greatly boost morale, especially if there is little visible damage in the vicinity. If there is damage, death and destruction outside, well, you have to acclimatise yourself to it anyway.

- Air supply: The air in your shelter is very precious. It is filtered and ventilated at some cost and effort. Your comfort and continued existence depend on its quality and quantity.

Management: Smokers should restrict themselves as much as possible and, if they must, only smoke next to the ventilation exhaust pipe. There should never be more than one person at a time smoking in a small shelter. Likewise, cooking over flames must be kept to a minimum because this uses a lot of oxygen. If you are experiencing difficulties, everyone in the shelter must restrict activity as much as possible. Lying down, resting and sleeping use the least air. If, despite this, you are still short of air you must open up your shelter for as short a time as it takes to change the air completely. You have to weigh up the dangers. A low dose of radiation may kill one of you in twenty years' time, but lack of air will kill all of you in hours or minutes. Remember that the winds may have kept radiation away from your area, in which case there is no need to keep the door closed. Find out with your radiation monitor. Be ready to close the door, however, the instant you see a sudden bright light. It could be a second wave of bombs.

Radiation Detection

Every group of survivors should have at least one radiation dose-rate meter. This instrument measures the intensity of radiation (its dose rate per hour) in an environment or on a person or object. Dose-rate meters will play a major part in saving lives in the aftermath of war. Get hold of a good one and study the instructions that come with it. They are easy to operate and understand.

A radiation dose-rate meter measures the amount of radiation that would be received in one hour if the rate were constant. To determine how much radiation you would accumulate in a short excursion outside a shelter, first take a reading outside your shelter. If your meter is calibrated in

RADS per hour and measures 120, the level is 2 RADS per minute. With such a reading you would accumulate a whole body dose of 16 RADS in an eight-minute exposure. In two hours severe radiation sickness would be the result, sufficient to kill those especially susceptible to radiation injury.

If your instrument is calibrated in R (Roentgens) per hour, proceed in the same way. For external gamma-ray radiation from fallout, the numerical value of a dose given in R is approximately the same as the numerical value given in RADS or REMS.

The above-ground level of beta radiation, received from fallout on the ground, diminishes rapidly at higher levels. The feet and legs of a standing person, therefore, receive more beta radiation than the head. Gamma radiation, however, is only very slightly reduced by going through several feet of air. Since the body is more vulnerable to radiation than the feet, radiation measurements are usually taken with the dose-rate meter held 3 feet (1 metre) above the ground.

Children and crawling infants must not run free outdoors until the radiation dose rate outdoors is very low. They may, of course, go outside if they are carried, and they may run around in buildings once the floors have been swept clean of radioactive dust. No one should lie down on the ground, even if the reading at 3 feet (1 metre) above ground level says it is safe.

For months, possibly, after emerging and beginning work again outside, it will be advisable to sleep most nights in your shelter. This is particularly true for children. Healthy adults and older children will not be incapacitated for work if they receive a maximum dose of 6 units of radiation (RADS, or R, or REMS) per day, even for up to two months. A person living continuously in the open world accumulates a daily dose of 6 RADS when the dose rate is 0·25 RADS (or 0·25 R) per hour. The body can tolerate this much. If you have a reading of 0·50 RADS per hour, you *must* average at least twelve hours a day in good shelter to avoid accumulating more than about 170 RADS a month. For this reason the shelter manager, or management committee, should log the total exposure time of, and the total dose received by, each shelter occupant for at least as long as it takes for the full twenty-four hour outside dose to fall below 6 RADS.

■ How to Use a Radiation Dose-Rate Meter

Make sure the probe is clean and is covered with a thin plastic bag. The instrument should also be covered – preferably with a thin, oversize plastic bag through which the switches can easily be manipulated. If it has a 'window' for taking measurements of beta-plus-gamma radiation, this should be closed while an area is surveyed.

Hold the probe about 3 feet (1 metre) away from the area that you are testing.

Never let the probe touch anything you think might be radioactive: once contaminated, it will never give you trustworthy readings again unless you remove and replace its disposable covering.

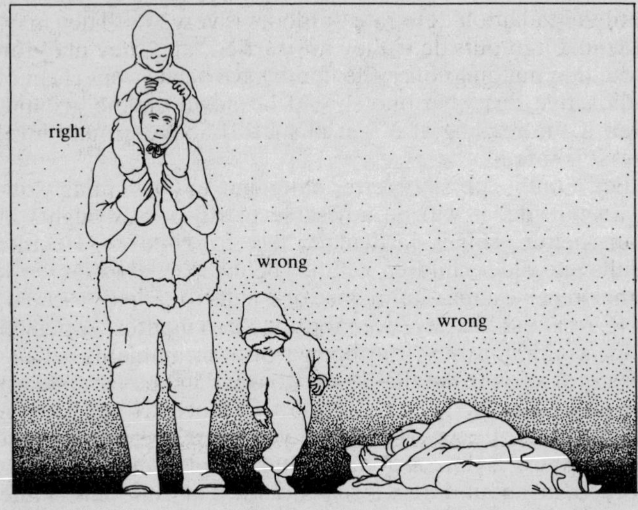

Figure 42. It is important to keep children off the ground where fallout is lying.

After you have tested an object or a building, or even a defined area, such as a field, leave a marker on it, with a note giving the radiation level and the date and time at which it was measured. (In areas contaminated by heavy fallout, the background radiation would become too high to take reliable measurements of particular items such as food, water or clothing.)

Every time you have finished with your radiation meter, remove its transparent plastic protective bag. Next clean first the probe and then its cable with a piece of cloth that has been kept clean in some protected place, such as a sealed box. Then throw the cloth away. Finally, cover the radiation meter with a new, clean protective bag.

How to Use a Dosimeter

It is important for everyone to keep a total count of all RADS received. This is best done by using a dosimeter, but periodic careful calculations with the aid of a radiation dose-rate meter will also give you a good guide.

A simple dosimeter looks like a large pen and is clipped to your clothing. It measures your personal radiation count (in RADS). Most people survive up to 150 RADS of gamma radiation with few or no short-term ill effects. Receive a dose of over 150 RADS within a week and radiation sickness becomes a problem. Using a dosimeter to record your total accumulated dose, you can calculate how long you can remain exposed; and if you are sick from radiation, it will give those nursing you an idea of your chances of recovery. Dosimeters are inexpensive. Get hold of a good model for everyone in your family and make sure each one knows how to use it.

It is vital to keep the level of radiation you receive to a minimum. Keep a count of the number of RADS received on everybody's dosimeter. Radiation does not affect everyone equally. The very young, the elderly, and persons in poor health are most at risk.

You charge your dosimeter by plugging it into a special, battery-powered unit which electrifies a small quartz filament in the meter's barrel. Gamma or strong beta rays passing through the instrument ionise the air around this filament. Interaction between the positive charge of the quartz fibre and the negative ions causes the stored electricity in the quartz to leak away. Because the little fibre takes up a different position when energised, the leakage slowly brings it back to its original attitude. It is the speed and extent of this movement, responsive as it is to the amount of radiation the meter receives, that produce a calibrated measurement of the RADS or Roentgens that have actually reached it – and you.

New instruments, and new versions of the old instruments, are constantly appearing. Micro-chip technology permits levels of miniaturisation and complexities of function that were not even imagined until the mid 1970s. Today it is possible to buy instruments which will ceaselessly monitor the environment for dangerous radiation. They can be pre-set to wail out warnings once radiation reaches dangerous levels. At the press of a button – or, in some models, even without – they will flash out the precise contamination figures.

At the other end of the technological scale the fallout meter, devised by C.H. Kearny, may be put together, as an expedient measure, using no more than the combined skills of an ordinary family. Kearny's detailed plans for constructing this instrument will be found in his book *Nuclear War Survival Skills* (National Technical Information Service, Oakridge Laboratories, USA, 1979).

In the months following a nuclear attack, when radiation levels are comparatively low but still higher than half a RAD per hour, those who have managed to survive a high dose during the dangerous first days of intense radioactive fallout will improve their condition by working out of doors for long periods. What they have, in effect, is a large reserve of recuperative strength, such that small doses of radiation should do them no great harm, with only a slight chance of sickness in future years.

Anyone who has already absorbed, say, 175 RADS will

have little recuperative strength in reserve and must wait until the radiation level has dropped to half a RAD per hour before going outside for long periods. Thus in an area of very heavy fallout several months may pass before it is reasonably safe for such a person to spend long periods in an unprotected environment.

Table III shows the estimated short-term effects from exposure to fallout radiation during a period of less than one week. It reveals the importance of shielding against the intense radiation that lasts for two or three days after an explosion. The body can cope with a higher total of RADS received over a longer period simply because body cells are constantly repairing themselves.

Up to 50 RADS	No visible effects. Your body can keep pace by repairing most damage done.
50 – 200 RADS	Brief periods of nausea initially; 50 per cent may experience this; 5 per cent may require medical attention. No deaths expected.
200 – 450 RADS	Most people will require medical attention for serious radiation sickness; 50 per cent deaths within two to four weeks if dose is more than about 350 RADS and there is no hospital care. If you are alive after five weeks you stand a good chance of recovering, though your resistance to secondary infections, etc. will remain low for a long while.
450 – 600 RADS	Serious radiation sickness requiring medical attention; more than 50 per cent dead within three weeks; still a possibility of survival for some.
Over 600 RADS	Severe radiation sickness; 100 per cent deaths in two weeks.

The Decay of Radioactivity

Radiation levels are not constant. Contamination fades. If all the fallout deposited at a location is from one explosion, then the rate at which it fades can be calculated as follows: for every seven units of time that pass, radiation levels will be ten times less virulent. This is called the *rule of seven.* It means, for example, that if, after one hour, radiation stands at 500 RADS per hour, after seven hours this will have been reduced to 50 RADS per hour. If, after one day it stands at 30 RADS, after seven days it will stand at three. Weathering effects, such as the washing of fallout particles to lower positions, are likely to result in additional lowering of the dose rate. It is obvious, however, that fallout from other, distant explosions, or a renewed attack on targets in the vicinity, or even differing weather conditions, can all modify this calculation. Nevertheless, the rule offers some basic guidance on what conditions you might expect over a period, once you have a reading of the dose rate in RADS or R per hour.

Radiation Sickness

Most of the consequences of radiation exposures are not cumulative. In other words, a low dosage every day for a month or more will not be as damaging as the same total dose received in a short time. People at most risk are those who absorb a large dose in one go, in a few minutes, hours or days.

The symptoms of radiation sickness are well known. After direct exposure to gamma radiation from fallout, in the range of 200-450 REMS, for a period of some two days, the individual will be listless, fatigued, usually too weak to work and constantly assaulted by feelings of nausea and attacks of vomiting. There follows a period which may last up to three weeks, during which these symptoms disappear. Those afflicted ought to make their best use of this time since, sooner or later, the sickness returns with far greater virulence. When it does, livid purple blotches appear on the skin and they will suffer from internal and external bleeding, hair falling out, severe diarrhoea, high temperature and deep lethargy. After several weeks, during which these symptoms continue, some will die (resistance to infection is low during this illness), but most will recover, especially if protected from further radiation and sources of infection – but it will be several months before they regain their old energy.

If the dosage of radiation is not very high – say, 100 REMS – probably only some 15 per cent of those exposed will be affected, and very few of those severely. But if it doubles, almost everyone will have some reaction; and at this dosage, of 200 REMS, a few will die: people vary in their resistance to radioactivity. Half of those exposed will perish when the dosage reaches around 500 REMS. Experts in this field have reduced this circumstance to a formula: $LD^{30}/_{50}$ – the letters stand for 'lethal dose' and the figures for the 50 per cent who would die within 30 days. You may work out for yourself the formula as it applies to dosages of 800-1,000 REMS: $LD^{30}/_{100}$.

With this intensity of radiation, most deaths will occur from fourteen to twenty days after the disaster. This is termed the region of infection death, since most of those who die do so from infections, which they no longer have enough white corpuscles left to fight, and not from radiation sickness.

One of the earliest effects of severe radiation is its interference with the process of division by which most cells reproduce themselves, so that cells reproducing most frequently are the first affected. The lymphocytes and granulocytes that form the white cells of the blood are among the shortest-lived in the body and therefore perish most swiftly. Indeed, they provide an index to the victim's chances of survival; if the lymphocyte count goes down and does not recover after a few days, neither will the patient. If it begins to go up, there is very likely to be a recovery, even though it may take several months. This method of prognosis, however, is useful only in cases where the dosages have been relatively low; above 400 REMS there will be too few white cells left for the count to be accurate.

If the radiation level has been above 600 REMS, we move

into the region of gastro-intestinal death. The cells lining the intestines are also extremely short-lived, with the result that these too are quickly affected. The damage such a radiation level causes to the intestinal lining opens the body to the assaults of the bacteria swarming in those yards of tubing. The consequence is virulent peritonitis.

When radiation levels are higher still, the region of CNS death is reached: CNS stands for 'central nervous system'. Everyone exposed to such dosages will die rapidly, quickly passing through the earlier symptomatic phases, until the organs fail and the nervous system collapses with the resultant seizure of the muscles, this, in turn, leading to an erratic and weakening heartbeat, acute breathing difficulties and the silent fall through coma into death.

The immediate consequences of high levels of radiation are appalling; the long-term effects of lower levels, about which there is a great deal of scientific uncertainty, will incapacitate some survivors. After about five years, some victims will find that they are developing cataracts. After eight years, the symptoms of leukaemia will appear in others. In the next decade, various cancers may attack a proportion of the survivors – cancer of the bone, the thyroid, the lungs. Others will simply die before their time, the causes mysterious, hard to define, the ostensible reasons for such deaths being somehow inadequate and unsatisfactory. Yet, because of the lapse of time, in none of these cases can it be proved that radiation will be to blame. The present evidence is statistical, having been collected from among those regularly X-rayed, those habitually working with X-ray equipment, those exposed to other radiation by their employment, and those in Japan or in test areas who have been the victims of radiation.

Most scientists believe that all radiation exposures increase the risk of cancer. Such cancers usually result late in life. The following is a risk estimate that reflects the average of reputable estimates: if 100 people each received a dose of 100 RADS (or 100 R, or 100 REMS) over a lifetime period, it is probable that there would be one more death resulting from radiation-induced cancer than if these same people had not received this radiation dose.

Some experts take a more pessimistic view: they claim that the slow radioactive fallout from all the nuclear tests of the last few decades is already killing people. But this view is not convincing. Life has evolved surviving considerable natural radiation from cosmic rays and other sources in the earth and air, and fallout radiation now represents less than 1 per cent of the total natural background radiation. It may therefore prove to be less of a long-lived hazard than is popularly believed.

However, young children and pregnant women should receive the greatest possible shielding, since it is known that foetuses in the womb and babies are most susceptible to the damaging powers of radiation. Indeed, it is a general rule that *the young are at greater risk than the old*: cancers develop and spread more slowly in an aged body, so that they are unlikely to make much difference to the lifespan of someone over sixty. For this reason it is preferable to send older people out when the time comes to perform some essential task in an open, radiation-saturated area.

One of the organs of the body susceptible to radiation damage is the thyroid gland. This is because it absorbs and retains iodine, but has no method of distinguishing between iodine that is radioactive and iodine that is not. Radioactive iodine causes the gland to malfunction and become cancerous. Fortunately a daily dose of salts of potassium and iodine, even in quite small amounts, will keep the thyroid saturated with the harmless elements it needs. Potassium iodide, taken in 130-milligramme tablets once a day, an hour before you might be exposed to radioactive isotopes of iodine, has the effect of 'blocking' – saturating – the thyroid with purely beneficial iodine: only 1 per cent of what the gland takes up is likely to be from the dangerously irradiated version. Any excess of iodine, radioactive or not, is then swiftly excreted. The potential side-effects of taking potassium iodide – which range from drastic alterations in thyroid activity, through goitre and fevers, to skin rashes and a runny nose – are extremely unlikely to occur after so small a dosage; although this is certainly one instance in which that hackneyed warning, 'It is dangerous to exceed the recommended dose' should be heeded.

Naturally, if you have been exposed to a dangerous level of radiation, side effects caused by the medicine that might protect you will seem less important. An immediate dose of 400 milligrammes of potassium iodide, and a course of 200 milligrammes taken daily for three weeks, are likely to prevent damage to the thyroid. A prophylactic dose of 169 milligrammes of potassium iodide, supplying your body with a 100 milligrammes of iodine, can also be taken to prevent that dangerous radioactive accumulation in the thyroid; on the other hand, ordinary tincture of iodine has no such effect and, if used for the purpose, may very well poison you instead.

The best way to store potassium iodide is in the granulated or crystalline form. If you keep it in a dark bottle, with a non-metallic, threaded top that can be tightly screwed down, it should last several years. When the time comes to use it, pour about 2 ounces (60 grammes) into a 2-fluid-ounce (½-decilitre) bottle – the bottle should then be about two-thirds full of the granules. Add ordinary pure water until the bottle is about nine-tenths full. Now close the bottle tightly and shake it energetically for two minutes or more. When no more of the potassium iodide granules will dissolve, although clearly some remain in the bottom, you will have the saturated solution you need. Four drops from an ordinary medicine dropper, once a day, are enough for anyone; the only exceptions are babies under one year old, who should be given only two drops. But beware – this medication has a nasty taste, and for most adults and all children you are going to have to disguise the flavour. The most painless method is to take a small pellet of bread, spread it with a little margarine, then drop the solution on it; if the bread is swallowed instantly, the taste will not be noticed. An alternative is to mix the medicine in a drink.

There are other medicaments that have seemed effective as antidotes to aspects of radiation sickness. Mercaptan is a drug that, in one form or another, may be used to counter the effects of the sickness. Etaperasin may be given to minimise vomiting. Enuretics and other agents promoting excretion may be used on occasion, although some of these may themselves be toxic and should be used with care and under supervision. When a contaminating agent has been swallowed, preparations reducing absorption from the gastro-intestinal tract can be used to limit the effects.

Even non-medical methods can have their uses: where a wound or abrasion lies in a contaminated area of skin, the promotion of blood flow can have a vital cleansing effect; and one authority, Dr Tatsuchiro Akizuki, who was less than a mile (1½ kilometres) from the Nagasaki bomb burst's epicentre became ill, but attributes his recovery (he is still alive), and that of many of his patients, to the diet of 'salt with everything, and nothing sweet' which he forced on everyone in his hospital.

Strontium-90 is another danger to health during this initial period of radiation because it mimics calcium and gets into the bones, particularly of young, growing bodies. It is, therefore, important that people avoid milk and dairy produce (an important source of calcium) from animals that have grazed on contaminated fields. Babies must be fed from the breast or with powdered milk until safe milk supplies are re-established.

Surviving Chemical and Biological Weapons

There is a possibility that, to complement explosive weaponry, chemical and/or biological weapons would be used against us – particularly if an enemy invaded this country. Knowledge of what this could entail is therefore important for those intent on survival.

Precautions should be taken if there is the slightest chance of such weapons being used against you: it is an American calculation that some 7 tons of chemical bombs, delivering an agent that paralyses the nerves, can create a lethal area nearly 10 miles (16 kilometres) square. People immediately downwind of such an area would also suffer the effects of contamination. The warmer the weather and the stronger the wind, the swifter the evaporation and dispersal of the toxins; thus in cold weather there would be local concentrations that would be intensely dangerous, while at a time of summer breezes many more people might be affected, but fewer of them would die. Chemical materials used are the nerve gases like Sarin, Soman and the VX range, the psychological agents like Tremorine and Psilocybin and the irritants such as the infamous mustard gas. Even the slightest dose of many of these can kill you in minutes.

Clearly, the best counter to all toxic materials is protective clothing. The kind of comprehensive muffling-up that will keep fallout dust away from the skin will also serve against irritants and other toxic agents. Respirators and tight-fitting goggles, of course, are essential equipment in these circumstances. Otherwise, well-ventilated shelters where the air is filtered will provide protection against almost all chemical weapons.

Such antidotes as exist remain largely in the knowledge and handling of specialists – especially those charged with maintaining the battle fitness of the fighting forces. To wash off gently all contamination is a rule in most cases; when nerve agents are involved, an immediate injection should be given in the thigh of 2 milligrammes of Atrophine (itself a poison to be used only if this diagnosis is confirmed) with 0·14 ounces (4 grammes) of Pralodoxime Mesylate. If there is no improvement this may be followed fifteen minutes later by another injection of 2 milligrammes of Atrophine, and fifteen minutes after that by a third. Artificial respiration may be needed up to ninety minutes or even for two hours.

Mustard gas should if possible be gently washed off *at once*. Otherwise, the blistered skin should be treated as for burns. There will be severe eye irritation and lung congestion, making nursing both necessary and difficult.

The explosive liquid-spray versions of highly toxic agents contaminate everything they touch. Many render foodstuffs dangerously poisonous. This is true of all the nerve agents, and those which blister the skin. Meat, fish, dairy products, fruit and vegetables, even eggs and salt – everything sprayed with any chemical weapon of this sort should be destroyed or buried. When the toxin is sprayed from the air you may, at a time when food is short, take less drastic precautions. Fruit and vegetables should then be thoroughly washed, using a 2 per cent solution of bicarbonate of soda, then peeled and boiled before eating. Rice and cereals, tea and coffee will be safe if you let the air get at them for at least three full days, that is, seventy-two hours. Dry foods of other kinds can be rendered safe in the same way, and may even be eaten after exposure to fresh air for only forty-eight hours. However, the longer the cleansing period, the safer the food will be, especially since there are degrees of sensitivity in people's reactions to these substances.

The other chemical agents, such as CS gas, contaminate foods less drastically, although they may leave behind them a lingering and very unpalatable taste. Any food that has been exposed to them should be thoroughly washed and left in the fresh air for at least twenty-four hours. Dry foods which cannot easily be washed should be left out in the air, away from their containers, for at least three full days. Wherever possible, foods that have been contaminated and then rendered safe again should be made a part of your emergency stores, to be eaten only when alternatives fail. The longer the time that passes before you eat them, the smaller the toxic residue they contain.

The military biologists have been busy too. They threaten us with disasters that overwhelmed our ancestors: the Black Death, for example. The high fever, laboured breathing, swollen glands and dark blotches of the plague may once more assault widespread populations. Bubonic plague can be spread by aerosol and symptoms appear within a week; the pneumonic variety within five days. The former is likely to kill half its victims, the latter almost all of them. Today, we are fortunate in possessing antibiotics; given swiftly and massively, they can bring about a cure. During wartime, however, such treatments may not be easily available. Vaccination against the disease is effective for about six months, but this is a protection hardly likely to be available for everyone during an emergency.

Anthrax, normally an animal disease, can be spread in the same fashion. Once breathed in, it can kill within a day. If it enters the body through the skin, it shows itself within a week. Then high fever, laboured breathing, increasing weakness and death are the phases of its destructive course. Anthrax can be treated with antibiotics and, once recovered, the victims have increased resistance to the disease.

Cholera and typhus, both largely eradicted in Western countries, are also diseases which may be artificially introduced. The former induces severe diarrhoea and vomiting, and so leads to dangerous loss of body fluid. The ensuing weakness may bring about collapse and death. In some epidemics, the survival rate has been as low as 10 per cent. Treatment should include, if possible, a saline drip to replenish the body's losses and doses of Tetracycline to reduce the diarrhoea and permit the retention of body fluids. Vaccines will protect for about six months; thus survival ensures quite long periods of immunity.

Nearly half of those who fall victim to typhus will die without treatment. High fever, aches throughout the body but especially severe in the head, and a dismal rash are the symptoms, antibiotics and cleanliness the treatment. Lice transmit the disease, so that all attempts to control these creatures, especially when people are crowded together in insanitary sanctuaries, will help to contain it. Recovery will confer a period of immunity, as will vaccination; boosters three times a year will be needed, however.

There are many other forms of disease that can be artifically spread. Any deadly micro-organism that can be culture-bred in a laboratory may be disseminated by an enemy. The only defences are protective clothing that prevents sprays reaching the skin or the vulnerable openings of the body; scrupulous cleanliness, even in the most unpromising conditions; the availability of the relevant medicines, especially the antibiotics; vaccination where possible; and the control of insects, rodents and all other forms of vermin.

Protective Clothing

You may, in an emergency, have to leave the safety of the shelter while fallout is still coming down and before the radiation has declined to a safe level. For this purpose it is important to wear garments that protect your skin from fallout particles and dangerous chemicals. It is possible to buy excellent suits for this purpose and any well equipped shelter would have them, together with an airlock decontamination chamber, where such clothing would be taken off and hosed down.

The Russians take the subject of protective clothing very seriously. They can even protect their babies, in an enclosed carrycot which filters radioactive, biological and chemical traces from the air. Known as the KSD-1, the carrycot is part of a range of gas-masks which rely on filters containing a granulated form of carbon and anti-toxic chemicals. There are various models: the GP-5, for example, has a rubber face-mask, with plastic eyeholes that can be stopped from clouding by applying a special pencil; helmet masks, code-named SHM-62, come in five marked sizes; the DP-6M is intended for children under twelve.

Protective clothing issued to Russian civil defence workers comes in two main types: one isolates the skin from the exterior atmosphere and the other filters the exterior atmosphere until it cannot harm the skin. The first is usually made from rubberised fabrics that are fireproof and impermeable to air; the second from ordinary fabrics that have been impregnated with a chemical solution. Because someone wearing, and especially working in, a gas-mask and airtight clothing is likely to sweat and freeze in very low temperatures and to suffer heatstroke in very high ones, the Russians have devised simple rules regulating what should be worn with them:

> When the temperature is below 14°F (–10°C), wear thick underwear, winter clothing and even quilting under your protective suit.
>
> When the temperature is between 14°F and 32°F (–10°C and 0°C), put on thick underwear and winter clothing underneath the protective suit.
>
> When the temperature is between 32°F and 50°F (0°C and 10°C), put on ordinary underwear and summer clothes.
>
> When the temperature is between 50°F and 59°F (10°C and 15°C), wear only light underclothes under the protective suit.

In temperatures above 59°F (15°C), wear a wet cotton overall outside the protective suit and try to keep it wet until the heat abates. Russian experts estimate that even in temperatures of 86°F (30°C), you will be able to continue working for up to an hour provided the overall is not allowed to dry out.

British and American protective clothing is excellent but is not widely available, though it can be obtained through civil defence equipment suppliers. The larger, public shelters should be provided with several suits in different sizes to prevent occupants being entirely cut off from the outside world for long and debilitating periods. Most individuals, however, are unlikely to want, or be able to afford the cost of such protection before an emergency overtakes them, or to find the suits available after it has done so. If you are forced to improvise, remember that what you are trying to achieve is a total dustproof covering for your body. Such protection might well be needed even when the area around your shelter is relatively free of radiation because you may need to move through areas of more severe radiation, for example, to obtain supplies.

The Chinese recommendation is that you first cover your

Figure 43. Examples of protective clothing and face masks which can be bought from civil defence equipment suppliers.

nose and mouth with some suitable article – a towel, a large handkerchief or any other piece of clean cloth. You should tie your sleeves and the bottoms of your trouser legs tightly around wrists and ankles. And you should wear heavy, impermeable boots, reaching to the knees if possible. To cover areas of exposed skin, use rainwear or plastic sheets, or, failing that, ordinary sheets off a bed. When in a contaminated area, you should take the utmost care: touch as little as possible, do not sit or lie down, resist the desire to eat, drink or smoke and, above all, never remove your protective garments until you are well clear of danger. Fallout dust is dangerous, and can be lethal, even when it is so fine that it is all but invisible.

The Russians, too, offer advice on improvising protective clothing: heavy coats, made of Vinyl or rubberised fabric, of leather or even the coarser, denser fabrics can give adequate protection against radioactive dust (though not from its gamma radiation) and, for a short while, even against toxic materials. Rubber boots or galoshes can protect the feet; if footwear cannot be readily removed, it should be covered in several layers of paper or sacking when a contaminated area is left, to protect the cleaner environment. Rubber or leather gloves should be worn, too, or heavy canvas mittens.

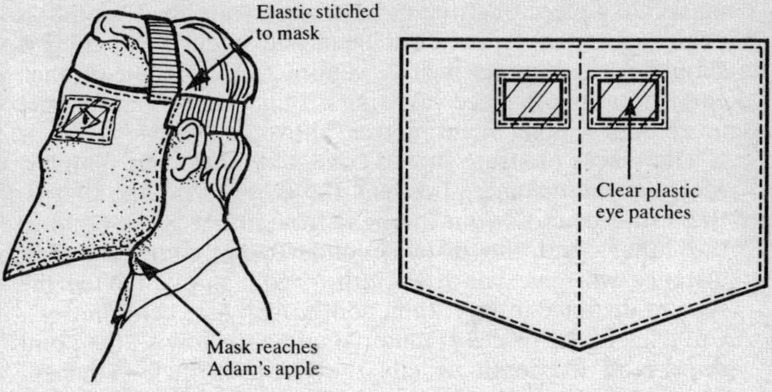

Figure 44. Making a mask to protect against fallout particles. This should be worn under a hood.

And, the Russians suggest, a little elementary tailoring can turn ordinary clothes into adequate protective garments.

The buttoned front of a jacket and the trouser fly are obvious points of vulnerability. The jacket may be strengthened by tying an apron under it, with a collar that fits closely into the neck. A flap sewn under the zip-fastener of the fly will render that, too, rather safer in contaminated conditions; it should be some 1½ inches (4 centimetres) longer than the zip and loose enough for the trousers to be pulled on easily. A hood may also be sewn on the jacket, protecting those parts of the head that are not covered by a respirator mask. A drawstring will help to keep it tightly fastened.

If you do make protective clothing for yourself, you may be tempted to use heavy plastic, or even rubber, since their suitability seems obvious. However, just as these materials allow nothing in, so they allow nothing out: the build-up of perspiration and heat will swiftly lead from discomfort to exhaustion and even collapse. Materials allowing some respiration must be used.

To make a protective mask: the main materials needed are three pieces of towelling or something similar, about 12 by 15 inches (30 by 38 centimetres), a length of elastic and a piece of clear plastic. To find the right measurements for the mask, tie a piece of string tightly round your head, so that it passes over the top of your head and under your chin; it should pass about ¾ inch (2 centimetres) in front of each ear. Tie another piece of string around your skull, a little more than 1 inch (3 centimetres) above your eyes.

The pieces of string should cross very near your temples. Measure the distances between the crossing points; that is, the distance across your forehead from one crossing point to the other, and the distance under your chin. The first distance will give you the width of your mask. Divide the second distance in half, then add ⅝ inch (1½ centimetres). Cut each of the pieces of material into a shallow V, the point down and its depth exactly the extra ⅝ inch (1½ centimetres) that you have allowed. This will make the bottom of the mask(Figure 44).

Stitch together the edges of the three pieces, and stitch

down the centre line. Cut eyeholes and cover them with the plastic, using a single piece which you stitch in place, both around the edges and down the centre line, between the holes. Fold the pieces of cloth down the centre line and stitch the bottom edges together. Make a double line of stitches to give the mask strength. The elastic is stitched to the top corners, one piece on the side, to go above the ears and round the back of the head, the other on the top, which will go over the head. Make sure that these elastic straps are not so tight that they will become uncomfortable if worn for any length of time. You can sew a loose piece of sheeting to the edges of the mask and use it to protect your head and neck against fallout. Put the mask on by fitting it over your chin first.

If there are toxic agents in the atmosphere, it will be useful to know how to impregnate clothes so that they offer you some protection. One mixture is made by heating 2 quarts (litres) of water to around 160°F (70°C), then adding some ½ to ¾ pound (300 grammes) of pulverised household soap to it. When this is completely dissolved, add ¾ pint (½ litre) of oil – either mineral, such as machine oil or caster oil, or vegetable. Stir the mixture for some seven minutes, at the same time reheating the water to its former temperature. Soon you will have a soap-oil emulsion in which you can soak your suit, hood, socks, gloves and protective apron. When the clothes are thoroughly soaked, squeeze out the excess moisture and let them dry in air. Do not iron them.

As an alternative to the oil, you might use ¾ pint (½ litre) of washing-up detergent; a little disinfectant added to the mixture will also be effective. With these ingredients, however, some skin irritation may occur and the underclothes you wear should be chosen with this in mind. Be careful when preparing these mixtures not to expose them to too much heat: do not let the water boil, do not dry the clothes artificially and do not iron them when you have finished. If impregnated clothes become soaked through, they will have to be treated again.

Wear summer clothes under the treated clothes, and an extra pair of socks under the impregnated ones for added protection. Fasten the wrists and the bottoms of the trouser legs, and put on protective footwear and a respirator to complete your preparations.

For some time after a major series of detonations there may be a considerable increase in the ultra-violet light reaching the earth's surface from the sun, causing immediate 'snow blindness', and later, eye cataracts. In these circumstances sunglasses shielding the eyes from ultra-violet rays would be the best protection. Otherwise, cover glasses with black or other opaque material, leaving clear only two horizontal slits 1⁄16 inch (1⁄4 centimetre) wide. Skin should also be covered to prevent severe sunburn. For protection wear an appropriate hat, gloves and clothing. Protective creams would be helpful too, if this hazard developed.

The Aftermath and Regeneration

The Disposal of the Dead

As the appointed Chief Executive of a sub-region put it in a radio programme, 'We'd have to take a volume approach to the problem.' That means using bulldozers, deep trenches, and quick-lime. It is popularly believed that dead bodies lying about are a hazard to public health. People think that not burying or burning them automatically leads to epidemics of infectious disease. But this is not so. Experience gained from major disasters such as earthquakes shows that this just does not happen. Neither was there an epidemic after the Hiroshima and Nagasaki bombs left thousands of dead scattered around, even though there was abundant sewage on the surface, a plague of flies in the hot August weather and no effective medical treatment.

This does not mean that bodies should be ignored, but that their disposal should not necessarily be a top priority. Protecting, feeding and watering the survivors is more important.

The problem posed by the dead breaks down into three areas: finding the bodies, collecting them and disposing of them. Immediately after radiation has subsided sufficiently for movement to be relatively unrestricted, public health parties will probably start on the first of these tasks. In many cases, they will be able to avoid the second and complete the third in a single operation, since emergency graves will have to be dug wherever concentrations of corpses are found. It is unlikely that this work will be attended by much ceremony, either secular or religious, although the administrators will be wise to keep one eye on public morale.

It may be that, as time goes by and individuals begin to die from radiation and other sickness, their families or friends will take on the duty of burying them. And some communities may organise a more localised and personal funeral programme. In the special centres accommodating the homeless, and injured, however, communal graves will be the most effective way of disposing of the dead.

As the weeks and months pass, new problems are likely to appear, notably disease and malnutrition, and some will die from these. Temporary mortuaries and improvised cemeteries will be needed for the bodies.

Public health officers will, wherever possible, keep some record of the people they bury (or burn): probably only the sex, estimated age and location where the body was found; although as the hectic phase of the emergency recedes, records of the dead will obviously become fuller.

Rescue Operations

The dead will have to be buried: at the same time, the buried living will, where possible, have to be dug out. Beneath mounds of rubble in cellars, basements and shelters of all kinds, thousands will be trying to escape. For those who are lucky it will be easy. Others will need help. In areas where radiation levels are not high, or have fallen sufficiently to permit working outside for a few hours a day, rescue operations will be started by the remnants of the civil defence organisation and groups of volunteers.

Rescue teams need detailed, large-scale maps of their areas of responsibility. All major public shelters should be marked on them, together with any underground features that could be used as shelters. In Britain, France, the United States and other Western countries, where individual householders have been left to make their own provisions, the problem of finding who is trapped will be more serious than in the Soviet Union, where large numbers will shelter in constructions built by, or known to, the authorities.

How to Approach the Task of Rescuing People Trapped in a Shelter

IMPORTANT: Do not attempt any rescue operation if radiation levels are high.

1) Locate the shelter accurately.

2) Establish communications with those inside and assess their situation.

3) If necessary, provide the occupants with an immediate air supply.

4) Determine whether major pieces of equipment are going to be essential. If they are – and you have them available – construct the routes along which they will be brought, and the sites on which they will have to be placed to do their work.

   Where débris is less than 3 feet (1 metre) deep, and not especially heavy, a path should be cleared down to the old roadway. If the rubble is deep it may be quicker to smooth a temporary road over the broken surface of brick and stone.

   The route should be wide enough for heavy vehicles and incorporate passing places, at intervals of about 200 yards (metres), to allow for two-way traffic. Surveyors or construction engineers should decide on the best route, reconnoitre it and isolate major obstacles. The route should then be clearly marked for the construction gangs to follow and complete the work.

5) Open up an exit for the trapped people, give those who need it first aid and send serious cases for medical attention.

6) When the work is done, mark the shelter very clearly so that other rescue teams know it has been dealt with, and future occupants realise that it has been opened.

When a shelter has been located, it is important to discover exactly why it has been blocked. Sometimes there is an emergency exit. Then the rescue will be relatively easy. Sometimes a door will have buckled under the impact of blast, or the weight of a collapsing building, and the shelter occupants will not be able to open it; working from outside, however, you should be able to free it. Only when there is no hope of reopening an existing entrance should you begin the time-consuming effort of piercing a shelter wall or ceiling.

If you decide the quickest way in is through a side wall, the best method is to dig a trench beside it and breach an entry from there. If power can be generated, pneumatic drills could be used. The rubble may be so deep, complex and dangerous, however, that this course is not practical, in which case a tunnel will have to be made. Do not build such a tunnel at an angle. Beginning outside the area of deepest rubble, sink a shaft to roughly the level of the shelter floor, and dig a second, horizontal shaft, propped and reinforced with wood, to reach the shelter wall.

Many individuals will be trapped by the débris of fallen buildings, their only shelter the rubble around them. If the radiation level is not too high some of them could be released. Inspect the area carefully and decide on the best line of approach. Where a victim is visible it may be possible to dig him or her out without too much difficulty. In many cases, however, injuries will complicate the problem. When freeing a person who is hurt, complete the final stages of the work as gently as possible, moving the rubble piece by piece and by hand. If possible, begin digging at the victim's head and gradually free the body.

If people are trapped deep within great mounds of loose and dangerous rubble a tunnel must be dug to them. When constructing it, try and use the crevices and openings that already exist in the piles of débris. Use wood to support and reinforce the tunnel, where possible nailing together a ceiling of floorboards and similar timber.

Food Supplies

The main problem for most survivors in the first few months after a nuclear attack will be finding enough food to eat. In 1974, the Home Office produced a list of basic foods in the amounts needed to feed 1,000 people for two weeks. The list included:

370 pounds (170 kilos) of cheese
500 pounds (230 kilos) of butter or margarine
500 pounds (230 kilos) of sugar
124 pounds (56 kilos) of tea
8,800 pounds (4,000 kilos) of potatoes
6,000 loaves of bread of 1 pound (½ kilo) each
880 pounds (400 kilos) of dried milk for adults
3,500 pounds (1,600 kilos) of dried milk for babies
3,300 pounds (1,500 kilos) of bacon
2,000 eggs

In the aftermath of nuclear war the authorities' role in supplying food will be vital. At present they do not hold the stocks to fulfil it. Some basic foodstuffs, such as flour and yeast, exist in stockpiles that are, according to Home Office statements, less than adequate. Rationing only works when there are adequate amounts to ration, together with the means of distribution.

The plans are that regional and sub-regional commissioners will be made responsible for handling foodstuffs, a fragmentation of authority which, while echoing the fragmentation of government itself, makes a national distribution scheme impossible.

The commissioners will appoint commodity officers, experienced in the production, handling, packaging and storage of food. Whatever supplies they manage to organise are intended to reach the hungry through emergency feeding centres, run by local authorities. The Home Office estimates that about one-third of an area's normal population would need feeding, at each mealtime, at such a centre. It recommends that suitable buildings be earmarked in advance for the purpose. In areas where civil defence is vigorously pursued, this has already been done.

At the beginning, the culinary ambitions of emergency feeding centres are not likely to rise much higher than providing hot tea, hot soup, biscuits and bread. Later, vast stews might be attempted; later still, when the demand begins to slacken, as it is hoped it will, increasing variety might be introduced into the menus. The Home Office circulars on the subject accept that fuel may not be readily available, and envisage cooking being done on wood, charcoal, coal, or even ordinary rubbish. The feeling is that fuel is likely to become as great a problem at these centres as the supply of food itself. Similarly, the provision of adequate water supplies, free of contamination, will be difficult.

Meanwhile, an attempt will be made, around the feeding centres, to provide temporary housing. The Department of the Environment will form an emergency works organisation, whose duties will include the swift construction of prefabricated buildings or the rendering safe of the less damaged houses. The military will supply tents and so those permanently 'temporary' cities of the displaced, so familiar in the crisis centres of the Middle and Far East today, will in all likelihood grow up in Britain too.

It is obvious that food cannot be handed out for ever to a constantly hungry population (though some people will be so shattered by their experiences that they will remain direct dependants of the State for as long as the State is able to feed them). Food supplies in general will have to be organised, and a national system of rationing will eventually make sure that everyone receives a fair portion. How long it takes to do this will depend on how quickly central government control is re-established. That may not be as easy as imagined in peacetime. For a considerable period, people in isolated localities and groups living on the edges of devastated areas will have to create their own sources of supply. In other words, in many places, often for the first time, people are going to have to turn to the soil to produce their own food.

Radiation at the higher levels (of several hundred R and

upwards) can destroy crops. Growing plants covered in radiation fallout frequently retain large amounts of dangerous dust. Fortunately, however, most types of new crops can be planted, on land that has not been heavily contaminated, the moment it is safe to work out in the open; the belief that all the soil will in some way be permanently poisoned is without foundation. The new crops will be safe to eat. Thus, if a population is able to survive through one growing season, it will be able thereafter to begin to feed itself.

The earth where crops are to be grown must of course be tested for harmful radioactivity. It may only be necessary to turn over the soil to a depth of a few inches to bury the radiation; but obviously it would be better, before attempting cultivation of questionable soil, to obtain specialised advice. In all developed countries, government specialists will be available to pronounce on these matters. The Russians made plans for this twenty years ago.

When radiation dangers have ebbed, there can be remarkable results of a cataclysm in the natural world; and as a contrast to the hellishness of nuclear assault, we may note the flowers which blossomed in Hiroshima.

The author John Hersey was sent to Hiroshima by the *New Yorker* 'to find out what really happened'. This is what it was like, as far as vegetation was concerned, one month after the dropping of the atomic bomb:

> Over everything – up through the wreckage of the city, in gutters, along the river banks, tangled among tiles and tin roofing, climbing on charred tree trunks – was a blanket of fresh, vivid, optimistic green; the verdancy rose even from the foundations of ruined houses. Weeds already hid the ashes, and wild flowers were in bloom among the city's bones. The bomb had not only left the underground organs of plants intact; it had stimulated them. (John Hersey, *Hiroshima,* Penguin, 1946.)

So much for the wild flowers and weeds. That there is genetic damage possible, or probable, to food plants, and that this may also right itself, seems to be borne out by the testimony of the redoubtable Dr Takashi Nagai of Nagasaki:

> But generally speaking the effect of radioactivity at Nagasaki was not severe enough for the public health to become impaired although crops did fluctuate greatly. The first year following the bomb, nearly all crops dropped sharply; in the sub-surface crops like sweet potatoes, there was almost no yield at all. The following year the harvests were surprisingly abundant, but all kinds of monstrosities appeared. After the third year, things returned to normal and average harvests were again made. So even the dread residual radioactivity disappeared; without having any great effect. (Dr Takashi Nagai, *We of Nagasaki,* Gollancz, 1951.)

Hiroshima and Nagasaki are today the great garden and agricultural seed producing areas for Japan.

Farmers and smallholders should obtain advice now on the rehabilitation and use of land affected by radiation by contacting their Emergency Planning Officer through their local council headquarters. A farmer who has time at the beginning of an emergency to put his livestock under cover, will be a help to his neighbours. Animals, like humans, can receive bad burns from fallout particles that land on the skin. Equally, cattle grazing on contaminated grassland are liable to pick up radioactive material which does not pass through the gut as swiftly as food. Once lodged, radioactive particles damage the tissues and sometimes cause perforations in the wall of the gut itself, resulting in a septicaemia. In the absence of antibiotics and the attentions of an efficient veterinary surgeon, this will probably lead to the animal's death.

In the British Home Office's comprehensive phrase, 'foodstuffs either in store, in process, or in the field' will be safe to eat, *provided that* all dust and dirt is carefully removed before they are prepared in the normal way. The only exception is milk; cows grazing on contaminated pasture will pass on dangerous isotopes in the milk they manufacture from the grass. On the other hand, fish will not be contaminated: the sea, like the land, will not be permanently poisoned after a thermonuclear exchange.

The Home Office conclusion remains emphatically hopeful:

> Food contamination (with the exception of milk) is not a significant problem in the immediate post-attack period . . . nor should food and water ever be denied to a hungry or thirsty population because of possible contamination.

Water Supplies

It is unlikely that much of the piped water supply system will be destroyed by nuclear explosions. Because of their geometry, underground pipes are extremely resistant to bombing or earth tremors. The greatest danger will probably come from contamination, not by fallout, but through damage to the sewage system. Survivors in urban areas who use their domestic water supply may, as the weeks go by, run the risk of dysentery. Until the authorities can give them definite assurances that the water is safe, they should treat it with suspicion. Boiling, using water purifiers and, in extreme cases, distillation will make the water safe to drink.

To distil water, boil it until it turns to steam, leaving all non-gaseous substances behind it. Then run the steam down a long cold tube, or against some surface which will cool and condense it. As it turns back into water collect it in a clean vessel. It should then be safe – although purifying tablets may be added as a double insurance. If you suspect that suspended radioactive materials are still present in the water, filter it (use the improvised earth filter described on pages 165–7).

If your water supply has failed, do not collect rain or snow to drink. They will contain dangerous fallout particles gathered during their descent. And water draining off a roof will collect any particles that gathered there. Shallow pools and ponds are likely to have fallout particles in suspension near the surface. Deeper pools and reservoirs are safer, but take the water carefully from near the surface, after several days have passed to allow dust particles to sink. Avoid disturbing the deeper levels and the bottom.

The safest source of water will be covered wells and reservoirs, protected from the fallout from above and the sewage from below. You may construct a safe source by digging a deep, well-like hole about 5 or 10 yards (metres) from a contaminated pond or stream, as far from any sewage pipes or sewage disposal pits as possible. Water will seep slowly into the pit. As it trickles through the earth it will be filtered in the process. (The soil must not be too porous, that is, too sandy or gravelly.) This is a fairly long-term provision and should, if possible, have been begun before the emergency reached its crisis. Protect the top of your seepage pit both with a lid and with a wide, waterproof rim that will prevent radioactive water sliding down the pit's sheer walls. If you have the means, purify the water you take from it, too, before using it.

The authorities' first concern will be to supply those in greatest need. They intend, therefore, to carry supplies of water only to the feeding stations during the period immediately following an attack. Although it is probable that the water mains will survive intact in most areas, water towers, reservoirs and pumping stations are rather more vulnerable, so even where the distribution system remains unharmed, there may, for a time, be no safe water that can be moved through it. Where there are concentrations of people with no water supply near by, or one not large enough, it may be practical to move the population to where water is available.

Public health experts will be on hand to test supplies for

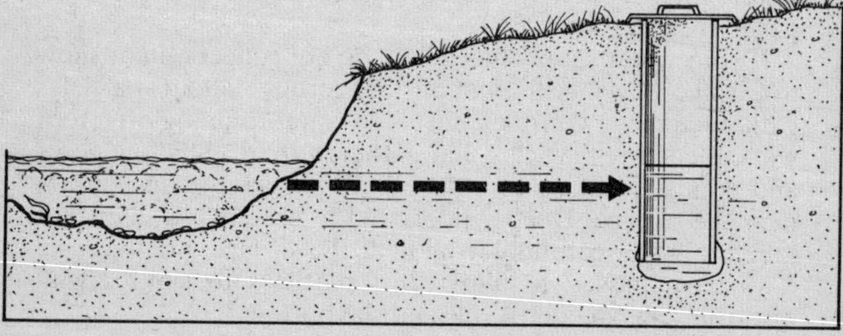

Figure 45. Seepage well showing the rim and cover.

every sort of contamination. However, they will be unable to do more than warn people of the risks they run in drinking contaminated water, since it is almost certain that the chemicals needed to purify it will not be available in sufficient quantities. Thus it will be up to you to take what precautions you can – it would be absurd to survive a nuclear attack and then succumb to a viral epidemic. And remember, people who have suffered radiation sickness, even if only mildly, are for a while more susceptible to disease than they would be otherwise.

A minimum supply of 2½ gallons (12 litres) of water a day per person, for all purposes, including washing and cooking (3½ pints – 2 litres – of this are to drink), has been suggested as a target. This will not be easily achieved in the first few weeks of the survival period. But as time passes it will be easier to find such quantities.

Medical Services

In the aftermath of a large-scale nuclear attack, doctors, nurses, ambulance drivers, first aid volunteers and everyone else connected with aiding the sick and wounded will be faced with a task so enormous that all their resources will not be sufficient for the purpose. First, there will be casualties caused by enemy action: men, women and children hurt by blast and fire, or made sick by radiation, as well as thousands with wounds and broken bones caused by the collapse of buildings. Then, in the weeks and months following, a vast army of those contracting indirectly caused diseases will need attention. Airborne diseases such as influenza, tuberculosis and meningitis can break out in overcrowded conditions. Communal feeding and the difficulty of maintaining high standards of hygiene will lead to outbreaks of food poisoning, dysentery and diarrhoea.

In every civil defence plan, therefore, one of the first conditions is that the hospitals will be cleared of all but the most severe cases as soon as a condition of emergency is established. One reason for doing this is that patients may well be safer in their own homes. The main purpose, however, is to free hospital facilities for the new influx that is anticipated if the hospital is not too seriously damaged. The few former patients who remain can be put in improvised shelters; so can the few personnel needed to look after them, together with essential equipment. The rest of the hospital workers and equipment may then be dispersed, so that at least some skills and materials will survive if the hospital building is destroyed. And to consolidate supplies of drugs and medicines, pharmacies and chemists will have their stocks requisitioned.

As soon as possible after attack, hospital staff will report for duty at previously agreed First Aid Posts set up by the Area Health Director – wherever possible, next to feeding centres. Other such posts will be established in undamaged clinics, health centres, convalescent homes and similar institutions. First Aid Posts will give immediate relief to the wounded and sick; they will also sort out those who can be sent home after treatment and those who ought to be moved on to a Casualty Collecting Centre.

These Centres will be operated by teams of doctors, almost always local general practitioners. The worst cases will be sent for hospital treatment by specialists, in the circumstances usually surgeons. Meanwhile, dispersed hospital staff not needed at First Aid Posts will join travelling teams giving medical help to people in their own homes or billets. These Domiciliary Teams will report to the doctors in charge of the local Casualty Collecting Centre; their role is intended to be largely a supporting one, advising and helping those – often volunteers, members of the family, or even neighbours – who have taken charge of a patient. The teams will supply medicines and dressings, but will also act as scouts and liaison officers for the doctors in charge of each Casualty Collecting Centre. Since these doctors in turn report to the Area Health Director, the final arbiter, the collective opinion of Domiciliary Teams will often be decisive on the vexed question of who is and who is not to be admitted to hospital.

The criteria for admittance will, for practical reasons, be strict. Many hospitals will be destroyed and others will have staff and equipment widely dispersed. At the same time, those still able to function will remain centres of excellence in the medical service, with the only really effective operating theatres and highly qualified surgeons. There will therefore be severe pressure on them from the many thousands seeking help.

Admittance will be based on the optimism of the prognosis – patients with the greatest chance of recovery will also have the greatest chance of admittance. Those in real danger of death will not be accepted. Neither will those suffering from radiation sickness: the only treatment they can be given is rest, care and support. Hospital treatment for radiation sickness, at a time of such desperate demand on space, will be regarded as irrelevant. The basic rule will be that those who, after some medical or surgical intervention, are expected to live another seven days will be allowed in wherever possible. This is because people who survive for that length of time after surgery, at least when a really major operation is not involved, usually make a complete recovery.

There is a great deal of confusion about the treatment of radiation victims in published materials. Many people say that there is no treatment, while others think that the number of deaths in Japan was partly due to the fact that many victims were suffering from malnutrition. It has even been suggested, though not so far as is known on the basis of any scientific evidence, that certain herbs are useful.

But some anecdotal evidence is of interest. Some radiation sickness victims struck down in Hiroshima were successfully treated with suralimentation (overfeeding); eggs and beef juice were forced on them in the intervals between their vomiting, and vitamins and iron pills, and arsenic in therapeutic doses of Fowler's solution.

> Mr Tanimoto's condition was recognised by a nurse as radiation disease, and she gave him injections of Vitamin B_1. She told him the thing was to eat as much as possible, and every few days his mother-in-law brought him vegetables and fish.
>
> As the symptoms revealed themselves, it became clear that many of them resembled the effects of overdoses of X-ray, and the doctors based their therapy

> on that likeness. They gave the victims liver extract, blood transfusions and vitamins, especially B_1. (John Hersey, op. cit.)

Any patient veering towards recovery will be sent home to make room for someone more needy. The Domiciliary Teams and general practitioners will take charge of patients returning home. New patients will be brought to the Casualty Collecting Centres, where Domiciliary Teams, working under the general practitioners in charge, will look after them. Thus it is hoped to establish a pyramidal flow, from home or rest centre to the First Aid Post, to the Casualty Collecting Centre; if necessary, to the nearest hospital; and from there as quickly as possible back home again.

After a large-scale attack there will be areas where, however swiftly that pyramid is set up, no help will be available. Medical teams will be forbidden to enter places where the levels of radioactivity remain lethally high. This is because their value to the community at large is so high that they will not be allowed to put themselves at risk.

As the weeks drag by, the problem of war casualties will begin to clear up. Death or recovery will settle those statistics. Instead, the epidemics will begin. With sewers and buildings in a state of disrepair, and the flow of foodstuffs and other materials in many areas at a virtual standstill, rats and other rodents will range widely in search sustenance. The feeding and rest centres, where the main supplies of food will be concentrated, will become a focus of their forays. As rubbish accumulates – there can be no refuse collection to begin with in cities of rubble – the dirt and parasites spread by the rodents will threaten health. Insects are also likely to proliferate in such conditions. And demoralised people, with inadequate water and facilities, will probably neglect the more rigorous pursuit of hygiene. Infestation will follow; typhus is one fever that is spread by lice.

With vaccines in short supply, the medical services understaffed, some hospitals destroyed and low morale leading to lowered resistance, diseases will weaken, and kill thousands, perhaps millions, of people. It was in the last year of the First World War, and the period immediately following, when the world was at one of its lowest ebbs, that the great influenza epidemic killed nearly 22 million people in eight months. The aftermath of a large nuclear war may well lead to similar outbreaks. Faced with this possibility, the authorities – assuming they remain in effective control – plan to cordon off any area, perhaps a whole city, in which the beginnings of a possible nationwide epidemic are discovered.

Sanitation and Public Health

The collapse of the energy supply system will mean that pumping stations and sewage works will not operate until power is restored. Sewers will become blocked as the flow through them slows. Sewage will seep or over flow into the surrounding earth. At other points, it will run through ancient outlets into open water, becoming an instant hazard to the drinking supply. Drains in many cities will cease functioning, with dangerous results for the occupants of, say, high-rise apartment blocks.

The authorities will provide trench or chemical toilets for people in the Rest Centres. But as soon as radiation levels have fallen sufficiently, groups of individuals who are fit enough should begin to dig trench toilets, in the military style, in parks and other open spaces. Eventually, these will have to be filled in and new ones dug. Special teams must be mobilised whose sole concern is the treatment and disposal of human waste.

Another urgent problem will be the disposal of rubbish. Immediately after the signal is given for people to spend at least part of their days in the open, this problem will become uncomfortably apparent. This is because one of the first tasks people will set themselves is to bring their accumulated rubbish – and their accumulated human wastes, too, in many cases – out of their shelters for disposal. Some local authorities will be able to set up dumping grounds, but in the more damaged towns and cities movement will be very difficult; people will not always be able or willing to make their own way to the dumps. In these circumstances teams must be organised to remove this waste. Once it has been taken to the dumps, it can be buried or, more hygienically, burned.

Other teams will have the task of controlling rats, mosquitoes, flies and other pests. In the prevailing circumstances, these are likely to multiply: certainly, if the open country is full of animal corpses, an overwhelming plague of flies may result. Levels of radiation much higher than those needed to kill most mammals have little effect on flies; they continue to breed. With the cessation of ordinary life, the counter-influences that normally control the insect population, such as birds, will be greatly reduced. In the circumstances, therefore, it may be necessary to use strong pesticides and poisons, for example, arsenic and calcium cyanide, to destroy both insects and rodents.

Another threat to human health might come from surviving cats and dogs. The diseases they can carry, especially rabies (if it ever reaches this country), make it essential that they be destroyed. If possible, this task should be specifically assigned and carried out by shooting, drowning or poisoning.

Energy Supplies

Apart from transportation, there are two major uses made of the energy a nation generates. One industrial, the other domestic. It is only relatively recently that the average home has had its energy needs met by central organisations. A few decades ago, people stored coal or hauled wood, and burnt these in their grates and stoves. They spent their evenings in the glow of oil lamps and candles. In some parts of the world they dug peat and burned that. In India now people burn millions of dried cakes of cow dung every day to cook their meals and refine their medicines. In other words, if the great energy sources are put out of action, it will be possible for people to reconstitute at least part of that way of life which existed on a large scale at the beginning of this century and was still widespread in the countryside after the Second

World War. The mining or pumping of the major fuel sources are major operations and, to restart them after a nuclear strike, may at first be beyond the abilities of the regional authorities. There will be large stocks of various fuels, held in public and private, in many different locations. These will have to be commandeered by whoever takes responsibility for running the community. Survivors who previously worked in industries supplying fuel and generating power will have to be called in; in Britain there are emergency plans to co-opt members of the gas, oil and electricity industries to act as advisers and planners in a post-nuclear world. They will take decisions, not only about where fuel supplies may come from, but also where they should go. No general rationing scheme will be either workable or sensible. Choices, therefore, will have to be made about who will be allowed petrol for vehicles and who will not, who will be permitted heating oil and who will not, who will be allowed to run a generator and who will not.

In any list of priority, the private citizen, the average survivor, would be at the bottom. The shattered supply systems, for both electricity and gas, and the scarcity of oil and petrol, as well as the difficulty of distributing what there was, would leave households and small groups of people without a flame to cook their soup, unless they provided them for themselves.

As soon as movement is possible, start by stockpiling what fuels exist in your neighbourhood. Stockpiling is more effective if undertaken by a group or an entire, well-defined, community. Petrol in abandoned cars, tanks of propane and calor gas, tins of paraffin, any surviving heating fuels must all be searched out, identified and either marked where they lie or taken to a central collecting point. Dry batteries of all sorts should be gathered, as should lamps and torches. Building firms may have generators, as well as the fuel to run them, and even a damaged car may have an engine that could still run and so provide power. If not, vehicles have wet batteries that can be wired together in series, producing valuable electricity. Wet-cell batteries may be discovered in telephone exchanges. Improvised dynamos can be created by harnessing the power of a motor-cycle set in a strong timber frame (cheaper in its consumption of petrol than a jacked-up car). Bicycle-powered dynamos can also be used to recharge batteries. Even the manufacture of such batteries is not difficult.

In addition, organise the collection and distribution of other fuels. Ruined towns and cities will offer an almost limitless supply of timber. And it should be possible, with the connivance or permission of whatever authority remains, to use the various stocks of coal and coke piled beside factories and installations damaged beyond repair.

Once they are collected, you must use such fuels wisely. The Rest and Feeding Centres should be among the first to be supplied. Then you might set up central cooking facilities, as in many rural areas of Europe and Asia, where the village baker rents space in his oven for slow-baking dishes such as casseroles.

The period during which self-help of this sort will be essential may not last as long as pessimists suppose. The buried pipes of the natural gas distribution network may survive largely intact; the terminal at Bacton, on the east coast, where the gas comes ashore, has an independent underground power supply to keep it working through periods of emergency. From there, five different feeder lines channel supplies into the National Grid. The installations out at sea may be more vulnerable, but are likely to be far enough away from the centres of attack to survive. As a result, gas supplies to some parts of the country may be restored in a relatively short time.

In the same way, the electricity power stations are widely dispersed. Many of them will be far enough away from targets not to sustain blast damage. Thus, once the fallout ceases to be dangerous, some of these will swiftly become serviceable. Damage to the National Grid itself, to switch-gear and boosters, is likely to prove more crippling. Nevertheless, there is a great deal of spare capacity built into the system, and many of the crucial switchgear installations are as far from targets as the generating plants. A large number of areas in Britain have two or three potential means of supply, so that even with the failure of one transmission line in each section and of one generator in ten

– admittedly a rather optimistic estimate of the probable damage – full power could be brought to every part of the country. This restoration of power would, of course, depend upon whether suitable arresters had been installed to protect the power lines from the EMP. (According to Home Office figures only £1,000 per annum is spent on the civil defence needs of our energy industries.)

There is another side to the energy equation, however, and that is that much less power will be needed. Millions of homes will have been destroyed – entire cities may have largely vanished. Shops and factories, even undamaged ones, will stand empty and silent. The dead have no needs. The highly industrialised society, voracious in its energy demands, which existed only a few weeks earlier, may well have, to all intents and purposes, disappeared. With such a dramatically shrunken population a much smaller amount of generating capacity will be needed. It is estimated that 20 per cent of pre-war supplies would be more than enough for many months. Any subsequent increase could easily be managed, the energy supply becoming both the object and the means of the nation's regenerative effort. We must not forget that the first electric bulbs began to glow again in the surviving suburbs of Hiroshima within twenty-four hours of the explosion.

Transportation

The two main constraints on the movement of vehicles after a nuclear conflict, will be the amount of fuel available and the conditions of the roads. Fortunately there are large stores of fuel spread across the entire country. This is not a provision for war, but owing to the way we keep traffic flowing in peacetime. Much of this fuel is in tanks and pipelines underground, and most of it in areas which, though they may be contaminated by fallout, are unlikely to suffer the direct effects of explosions. There would probably be enough fuel to keep such vehicles as ambulances, some buses, trucks to distribute food and essential supplies, and cars and motor-cycles for the administrative system fully supplied with petrol or diesel oil for at least a year. Government and armed forces also maintain their own underground fuel stores.

As for the railways, British Rail estimate that, if a massive attack were to be mounted on the country in the course of an average summer, half its passenger carriages and just under a quarter of its goods trucks would be destroyed. So would one-third of its engines. Put another way, this would mean that two-thirds of its engines would be available to pull three-quarters of its trucks and half of its carriages: a reduced potential, but not a crippled service.

The tracks are, of course, widely dispersed; those running into cities that are targets will naturally suffer damage or be destroyed, but the rest of the system is likely to remain intact. In many cases the city centres could be bypassed. For example, there already exists a potential line around London, from Cambridge in the north to Staines in the south. Blast-damaged tracks can be repaired at a rate of up to 30 miles (50 kilometres) per day. Work done far more slowly could still link up in two or three weeks track systems lying around the edges of devastated areas. Centres of operations built during the modernisation programme of the 1960s and 1970s have in many cases been strengthened against emergency. If they fail, mobile control centres, able to communicate with each other by radio, can swiftly be brought into action.

Commercial vehicles and cars are, of course, more flexible means of transport than the railways. Road surfaces can be a long way from perfection without becoming impassable; even the absence of roads is not an absolute bar to movement. Most roads will be far enough from the explosions to escape damage. In destroyed cities, temporary roads can be driven through, or over, the rubble. The fuel for the machinery needed to do this should be high on the list of distribution priorities. Very few such improvised highways will be necessary to provide for the movement of essential supplies and personnel.

In Britain, expert advice on these matters will be given to the regional commissioners by an Inland Transport Administrator supplied by the Department of Transport. Co-ordinators will work with their local authorities under the administrator's supervision. Their main task will be to cobble together an entire system by working with colleagues in neighbouring areas. As soon as possible, those who ran transport organisations, public or private, before the conflict will be encouraged to start them again, in however feeble and attenuated a form. Their work will be fitted into a general scheme. In a few weeks or, at most, three or four months, some recognisable and reliable transport system will emerge.

Communications

Electronic communications face an additional hazard to those of all other installations: the faster than lightning EMP. This can render radio, television and telephone systems useless. It can also take out unprotected power stations and computers. Its range is enormous. For example, at 120 miles (200 kilometres) above North America an explosion, if centred on the state of Nebraska, would affect the electrical devices of the entire United States, almost the whole of Canada in one direction and Mexico in the other, and any ship-borne electronics over thousands of square miles of open sea. A pulse engendered over Britain would disrupt virtually all the radio communications of Western Europe.

Most at risk are radio stations, with their vast array of sensitive machinery and enormous towers and antennae. In the United States, the Defense Civil Preparedness Agency has begun to fit new EMP protective arresters in some of the 600 radio stations which will relay the vital wartime broadcasts. European precautions, however, have not reached a similar level, though the military are tackling the problem for their own purposes. Oddly enough, old-fashioned radio sets, with archaic valves rather than transistors, are less vulnerable. Many Warsaw Pact countries still use valves. In Britain there is provision for an emergency communications network (described on pages 48–50). The public would not have access to it. These lines and radio links will connect sub-regional headquarters with lower levels in their hierarchy, and with each other.

To be effective the entire communications system must be protected against EMP. At present it is not. Civilian survivors are likely to be left isolated. A situation may be envisaged in which authority will be able to speak to authority and Army officer to Army officer, through equipment protected against EMP, while the means of communication to the people at large, and the people's ability to communicate with them and with each other, will cease.

In the aftermath, therefore, local courier services must be set up, perhaps organised by the remnants of the Post Office, or by energetic entrepreneurs. EMP permitting, amateur radio enthusiasts far from the centres of destruction will be incorporated into a network known in Britain as Raynet. When the tatters of the telex and telephone system are being stitched up, an established scheme of priority will ensure that those lines likely to carry official business will be put back into commission first.

Community Planning and Reorganisation

Government plans for post-attack Britain assume fragmentation. Regional commissioners and, even more, their sub-regional colleagues, have powers so extreme that, simply by exercising them, they would begin the process of creating autonomous states. With London devastated, a profound and widespread disenchantment with the very idea of government (since government led the nation into its dire condition), and a tenuous and feeble system of communication constantly on the point of breakdown, the voice of a distant Prime Minister would have little significance. A strong local figure with valid powers, a commissioner, would be accepted by most people as the true inheritor of governmental authority.

If power slipped from the commissioner's hands central government might have difficulty taking it up again. This is because whenever there is a power vacuum someone always comes along to fill it. A local, respected figure, a soldier, politician or industrialist, would assume command, and prepare to defend it. And if that person were honest, with an intelligent understanding of local needs, he or she would be right to do so. Britain would therefore cease, for a while at least, to have a central government.

There would, of course, be remnants of the Army to maintain order. But surviving troops would be attached to the headquarters of the various regions and sub-regions supporting the commissioners. (It is in the regional and sub-regional headquarters, after all, that legitimate civilian rule would reside.) It is hard to estimate just how much power the military would have after a nuclear attack. How mobile would they be, how many of them would be available and where would they be deployed? Under some circumstances they might be standing by to repel invaders. Under others, they might be searching for subversives or terrorists. In any event, they would be unlikely to side with a distant central government when so many local problems loomed and there existed a local authority to which they could turn for orders. If the fundamental cohesion of the country were threatened in this way – by the exercise of what would seem to be legitimate authority – what would *be* legitimate authority? It is unlikely that the military would attempt to reverse the trend. In Britain, the Army has no tradition of interfering with politics.

The fragmentation could go further, and, as time passed, surviving groups would need to piece together the nationwide picture. For example, some sub-regional governments might find it impossible to wield genuine power over the communities they nominally controlled. In the conditions that would prevail, the co-operation of the entire population would be needed to ensure the effectiveness of regional administrations – provided, of course, that those same conditions did not make such co-operation impossible.

With services broken down, people may have to find ways of obtaining supplies for themselves. But they must be seen to be useful. Some bureaucrats, categorising this as looting, will issue orders forbidding it; though at least one official has publicly expressed doubts on the feasibility of doing so. Such orders would be meaningless to the many thousands foraging among the ruins for their sustenance. After all, how do you discriminate between necessary foraging and looting?

As the various commissioners appreciated the weakness of their positions they might increasingly be tempted to reassert their authority by force. They might argue, as justification, that it was for the greater good. The likely result of such a course, however, is that the people would become the enemy of the Government, regarded as a source of disruption and anarchy and the objects, or even the victims, of a coercive campaign to restore law and order. Yet, for their part, many people would still be in a state of shock, terror, profound grief or confusion. Their attitudes might, as a result, be quite unpredictable. They might be apathetic, passively accepting authority; or desperate, turning to authority for reassurance; or sullen, refusing all outside discipline; or even angry, turning against the Government in fury, with an irresistible desire to punish those responsible for their plight. They might express a mixture of all of these, with one emotion predominating in one group and a different one in another, or with all these and similar feelings succeeding one another in the same individuals.

It is clear that, if nuclear war occurs, everything for which the Government has contingency plans must be done: the survivors will have to be looked after or will have to look after themselves. It is, however, part of the unreality which surrounds all administrations that the mere fact of having a plan, approved by committees and packaged in neat paragraphs, creates a belief that the event will be equally amenable to control. But there are no precedents for a nuclear war. Hiroshima and Nagasaki were isolated events, single catastrophes in a relatively unharmed country. That is not the situation strategists envisage. Future explosions will be larger and there will be, not one or two, but hundreds, perhaps thousands, spread across the industrialised world. Dislocation will be extreme. For a period, perhaps for ever, some nations will cease to exist.

It is in this situation that the identifiable community will come into its own. It will be the only reality left and, if the authorities cannot offer practical help, survivors will have to do without them. The area within which people can meet and speak with each other, the area that can be usefully covered on foot, the area in which they feel at home – however little like home it will have come to look – is the area in which they will be able to operate most effectively. People will see what should be attempted, and whether and how to do it. They will also know if they are successful.

Your community, particularly in the weeks immediately following the attack, will have to look to itself for the energies and the strategies of regeneration. When planning to survive you must not imagine that building a shelter and storing the supplies necessary for two or three weeks of isolation are all the preparations that are needed. You must also allow for the physical and mental effort and psychological steadfastness you will be called upon to maintain in the demanding months that follow the catastrophe.

In your effort to survive, you will find yourself developing new standards. There will be a constant measuring of evils, and hard choices will have to be made as a result. Marginal advantages may decide crucial issues, and it may prove hard to rediscover or hang on to what would once have seemed your essential humanity. Yet it must always be remembered that the decision to survive, and to help your dependants, neighbours, friends and fellow citizens survive, is itself an assertion of the most important human values.

Regeneration of Your Community in the Aftermath

The following will give you the basis of a scheme to help you rebuild your community if it has been shattered by nearby explosions. By carrying out the objectives you will give cohesion and unity to the survivors in your area.

1) When the radiation has died down sufficiently to allow excursions outside, marshal your resources, both human and material

2) Find, store and guard whatever usable food and essential goods remain intact in the area.

3) Establish a rationing system.

4) Register the skills available in your community.

5) Form teams, under the leadership of whatever experts you have, to perform the following tasks:

a) Search and rescue
b) Dispose of the dead
c) Provide for the sick and injured
d) Care for the elderly and the very young
e) Establish a health centre where whatever skills and medicines you have can be based
f) Establish a communal feeding centre
g) Organise foraging parties to supplement your supplies
h) Ensure a safe water supply
i) Locate and collect fuel for power and transport
j) Provide power for light, heat and other uses
k) Collect and dispose of refuse
l) Dispose of sewage
m) Register survivors' names and those of people known to have died (not an urgent task but one that could be given for reasons of morale to people who could not participate in more physically demanding work)
n) Establish a communications network within the community and to surrounding areas, including to any functioning authorities
o) Maintain public order within the community and guard against disorder from outside
p) Establish a trading network with surrounding communities
q) Establish vegetable gardens and chicken runs, as many as possible; open up discussions with the nearest farmers and, if it will help, participate in their work, trading your group's labour for a future share in the produce.

As much planning and preparation in advance of an attack as is reasonable would help make all the above aims easier to achieve.

Afterword

As the fighting began on the Falkland Islands Margaret Thatcher asked a BBC radio reporter the rhetorical question, 'What would the rest of the world think of us if we failed to protect our own people?' (She had already forgotten that the Argentinians were able to invade in the first place simply because we were not protecting the Falkland Islanders.) By asking the question she was, of course, acknowledging the internationally accepted duty of a government to protect its people. But, as the Falklands war demonstrated, protection always needs organising before a disaster, not afterwards.

British civil defence, however, is not organised to 'protect our own people'. It is designed to protect only the established authorities. This is a mistaken policy that frustrates many of the workers in civil defence who would sincerely like to protect as many people as possible. It is also a policy that appalls those in 'the rest of the world' who uphold a humanitarian view of the duties of government.

Of course the duties of government also include the obligation to promote peace courageously and imaginatively in peacetime. Instead of aggressively siting cruise missiles on our soil, therefore, we could better express our determination to protect ourselves by creating effective civil defence. And, on the political stage, instead of doing battle in the illusory world of ideologies, we could seek, test and promote practical solutions to the problem of maintaining peace.

And there are solutions. For example, one that could be tried involves a return to the principle of voluntarily swapping hostages. In ancient times rival kingdoms, to maintain peace, exchanged their most loved sons and daughters, often princes and princesses, who lived well in the foreign courts but whose lives were forfeit if non-aggression treaties were broken. Today, with all the modern conveniences of easy travel and communication, there is nothing stopping, say, the Russians having a huge administrative enclave, serving some vital purpose, living in America on a rota basis. At the same time American hostages, in similar numbers, would live in the USSR. Large numbers of high officials and their families would then always be at risk should hostilities develop. It is hard to imagine a better guarantee of peace, one that would also encourage a greater understanding between these two nations and thus offer real hope for progress in disarmament.

But although we know co-operation like this could reduce the risk of war, we let rivalries, dogma, ideological disagreements or the ever-tightening constraints of a shrinking world economy act as justifications for brutal excesses. We even know how the behavioural mechanism works by which people are conditioned and coerced into committing atrocities. But we still allow ourselves to dominate or be dominated in quite inappropriate circumstances.

It is not true that, simply because a weapon has been brought into existence, it must be used. Our leaders may pretend that nuclear bombs, having been created, cannot be put aside, but in our hearts we know this is not the case. Disarmament *is* possible. Because it is possible, however, doesn't make it happen. Many things are possible that don't happen. It is prudent, therefore, as well as working for peace and disarmament, to protect ourselves from the folly of those blighted souls who are trapped in the institutions of power, and deaf to the call of a greater destiny, and who threaten us all.

Every nuclear shelter, and every individual prepared for nuclear attack, represents an effort to create a barrier against which the great lunacies of the world can break – if not harmlessly, at least without carrying entire populations away. To make that attempt might seem a duty, both immediate, to those for whom we have responsibility, and general, to whatever we value in our culture. It is also an assertion of the human will to survive. As such, it is an action which changes individuals from passive and fatalistic spectators of an insane political drama into men and women doing what they can, in a dangerous world, to take some control of their own destinies.

Index

Psychology/Life Sciences

Crime and Personality £1.25 ☐

H J Eysenck

A revised edition of the controversial and classic study of intelligence, genetics and criminality.

Human Beings £2.50 ☐

Liam Hudson

Liam Hudson's study of human psychology is readable, accessible and sensible. This is a book about ourselves—our dreams, our fears, our triumphs, disasters and experiments.

The Myth of Mental Illness £2.25 ☐

Thomas S Szasz

'I submit that the traditional definition of psychiatry, which is still in vogue, places it alongside such things as alchemy and astrology and commits it to the category of pseudo-science.' ***Thomas Szasz.*** The book that rocked the psychiatric establishment.

The Manufacture of Madness £1.75 ☐

Thomas S Szasz

'In the past, man created witches; now he creates mental patients.' A comprehensive study of Inquisition and the psychiatric establishment. A highly controversial and persuasive work.

Confessions of a Knife £1.95 ☐

Richard Selzer

Richard Selzer attempts to find meaning in the ritual of surgery, a ritual 'at once murderous, painful, healing, and full of love'. In the careening, passionate language of a poet he speaks of mortality and medicine, of flesh and fever, and reveals something of the surgeon's thoughts and fears as he delves into the secret linings of our bodies.

The Unmasking of Medicine £2.50 ☐

Ian Kennedy

Based on his highly controversial 1980 Reith Lectures, this book is a searching examination of the state of health care today; a disturbing but timely exposé of questionable medical ethics and misguided Government policy.

PAL11182

Physics/Astronomy

In the Centre of Immensities £1.50 ☐
Bernard Lovell
A fascinating history of the quest to understand the cosmos through astronomy, an explanation of modern theories on the origins of the universe and life on earth, and a study of the use and abuse of our knowledge, both on Earth and in space.

Whispers from Space £1.50 ☐
John Macvey
Messages are being picked up on our giant radio telescopes. What does this cosmic babble and chatter reveal—and who is sending out those signals?

Earth's Voyage Through Time £1.75 ☐
David Dineley
A revolution has taken place in geology. The first readable account of what we know of Earth's past, present and future life. Illustrated.

Philosophy/Religion

The Sound of the One Hand £1.50 ☐

Yoel Hoffman

Never before has it been possible for an English-speaking reader to experience the profound exchange which occurs between a Zen master and his student. Here, for the first time, is the series of questions or 'Koans', together with their answers, through which the Zen master initiates the novice into the wisdom of Zen.

The Aquarian Conspiracy £2.95 ☐

Marilyn Ferguson

Slowly, almost unnoticed, a revolution is taking place. A leaderless but powerful network is working to bring about radical change in our culture. Its members have broken with certain key elements of Western thought, and they may even have broken continuity with history and are working to create a different kind of society based on a vastly enlarged concept of human potential.

A Smile in the Mind's Eye £1.95 ☐

Lawrence Durrell

Lawrence Durrell has had a lifelong interest in and sympathy for the philosophy of Taoism. In this entertaining, charming and informative short memoir he gives us a totally absorbing account of an inner journey to growth and spiritual enlightenment.

New Age

The Clandestine Farm £1.50 ☐

Anthony Wigens

Tony Wigens, inspired by Cobbett, Jeffreys and White, built a clandestine farm on verges and in corners of fields and woods. He also delved into common law and the lore of the land.

Person/Planet £2.50 ☐

Theodore Roszak

A uniquely penetrating and deeply committed analysis of human and environmental problems encountered in the 1970s and to be challenged in the 1980s.

The Quest for Gaia £2.50 ☐

Kit Pedler

An impassioned plea for an end to the alienation and materialism of modern industrial society and a return to the organic unity and wholeness of a life lived in harmony with ourselves, our planet and our fellows.

The Dyadic Cyclone £1.50 ☐

John C Lilly and Antonietta Lilly

A deeper journey into the interior of the mind. John and Antonietta Lilly describe their dyadic relationship and Lilly includes his theories on the intelligence of dolphins in this revolutionary work.

PAL9082

Archaeology

The Piltdown Men £1.95 ☐
Ronald Millar
The case study of the most notorious hoax in the history of archaeology. Illustrated.

A Guide to the Megaliths of Europe £2.95 ☐
Alastair Service and Jean Bradbery
The first comprehensive and fully illustrated guide to the great megalithic structures of Western Europe.

Lucy: The Beginnings of Humankind £2.95 ☐
Donald C Johanson & Maitland A Edey
Lucy is 3.4 million years old and is the oldest, most complete, best-preserved skeleton of any erect-walking human ancestor ever found. This single discovery has taught us more about early man than any other discovery so far. Illustrated.

The Cult of the Immortal £2.95 ☐
Ange-Pierre Leca
A thorough and stimulating study of mummies and the ancient Egyptian way of death. Leca outlines the reasons why they were made and the deductions which modern science can draw from them; he describes the ancient methods of mummification, the various types and the associated rites. Illustrated.